Political Reform in Japan

Political Reform in Japan argues that the quality of political leadership is the crucial determinant of whether politicians pass or reject policies such as electoral system and campaign finance reforms that could harm their future electoral chances. Alisa Gaunder reveals that while scandal is necessary to open windows of opportunity for reform, scandal itself does not produce reform. A leader with a certain set of resources and personal attributes is also needed, both to persuade self-interested politicians to support reform and to keep this support mobilized.

By comparing successful reform drives led by Miki Takeo, Ozawa Ichiro and Koizumi Junichiro with unsuccessful reform efforts pursued by Kaifu Toshiki, Miyazawa Kiichi and Kōno Yōhei, the book illustrates the decisive role that leaders who display vision, commitment and a willingness to take risks can have on the course of politics. Gaunder forces a reconsideration of the conventional wisdom on Japanese politics that consensus decision-making norms and factional power-balancing produce little in the way of political leadership.

Using supporting interview material obtained from discussions with prominent Japanese politicians, including former prime ministers, party heads and cabinet ministers, *Political Reform in Japan* will be highly relevant to policy makers and those studying comparative policies, Asian studies and leadership studies.

Alisa Gaunder is the Henry Luce Assistant Professor of East Asian Politics at Southwestern University in Georgetown, Texas.

Routledge Contemporary Japan Series

Political Reform in Japan

Leadership looming large

Alisa Gaunder

Routledge
Taylor & Francis Group

LONDON AND NEW YORK

First published 2007
by Routledge
2 Park Square, Milton Park, Abingdon, Oxon OX14 5RN

Simultaneously published in the USA and Canada
by Routledge
270 Madison Ave, New York, NY 10016

Routledge is an imprint of the Taylor & Francis Group, an informa business

© 2007 Alisa Gaunder

Typeset in Sabon by
Book Now Ltd, London
Printed and bound in Great Britain by
Biddles Ltd, King's Lynn, Norfolk

British Library Cataloguing in Publication Data
A catalogue record for this book is available from the British Library

Library of Congress Cataloging in Publication Data
Gaunder, Alisa, 1970–
Political reform in Japan: leadership looming large / by Alisa Gaunder.
    p. cm. – (Routledge contemporary Japan series; 12)
Includes bibliographical references and index.
1. Japan–Politics and government–1945– 2. Political leadership–Japan.
3. Political corruption–Japan. I. Title.

JQ1631.G38 2007
320.952–dc22   2006026122

ISBN10: 0–415–41590–X (hbk)
ISBN10: 0–203–96449–7 (ebk)

ISBN13: 978–0–415–41590–3 (hbk)
ISBN13: 978–0–203–96449–1 (ebk)

In memory of Eleanor Gaunder and Judy Gruber

Contents

List of illustrations

Figures

Tables

Acknowledgements

I have many people to thank for their support of this project. This book began as a doctoral dissertation at the University of California, Berkeley. I will never forget the day I formulated the research question, having no idea at the time the long research journey I was embarking on. I was at an informal prospectus writing group meeting with Professor Nobuhiro Hiwatari, Rob Weiner, and Jon Marshall. It was my week to pick the readings, and I chose several articles on political reform. I had been intrigued by scandal and reform since working as an intern for Representative Matsuda Iwao on a Fulbright Fellowship in Tokyo during the turbulent time of 1992–93 which marked the split of the LDP and led to the passage of reform shortly after my departure. The discussions that followed led to the puzzle that drives this research – when and why politicians pass laws that negatively affect them. This group eventually added Mari Miura to its membership and adopted the name "BSG" (the Berkeley Study Group). It was when we all found ourselves conducting research in Tokyo at the same time that my random thoughts and observations grew into researchable questions. I am grateful for the unwavering support and critical intellectual stimulation that each member of this group has provided. They were my Tokyo family for two years and have supported this project from beginning to end.

Many additional people have supported this project as it developed from drafts to a dissertation to a book manuscript. First, I would like to thank Steve Vogel, Ken Jowitt, Bruce Cain, and James Lincoln, the members of my dissertation committee at the University of California, Berkeley. Their support, encouragement, and critiques were critical in the development of this project. As my dissertation chair, Steve read numerous drafts of each chapter, some much more polished than others, and always gave excellent feedback. He provided interview connections in Tokyo and has given much guidance in navigating the publishing process. His support has been invaluable over the years. I would also like to thank Kenji Hayao and the two anonymous reviewers who read this manuscript in full and provided excellent suggestions for revision. Finally, I would like to extend my deepest gratitude to my dissertation writing "buddy" and close friend Sarah Wiliarty. She has been incredibly generous with her time, reading just about anything I wrote on this topic and all the versions and revisions that followed. Her confidence in my work has been a constant source of strength.

Many other people have read portions of this project and provided feedback, including Teena Gabrielson, Tomek Grabowski, Nobuhiro Hiwatari, John Leslie, Abe Newman, and Sara Watson. I would like to extend a special thank you to David Leheny for reading the introduction and helping me figure out how to turn a dissertation into a book. Steve Vogel and T.J. Pempel provided excellent feedback on my book prospectus and helped me develop a strategy for marketing the book to publishers. At Southwestern University, Shana Bernstein, Mary Grace Neville, and Katy Ross kept me true to deadlines, and the members of the Political Science Department, Tim O'Neill, Eric Selbin, Bob Snyder, and Teena Gabrielson, provided moral support. At Routledge, Stephanie Rogers and Helen Baker have shepherded me through the editorial process as a first-time author, always promptly responding to my queries and making the distance between London and Austin seem minimal.

Several institutions have aided in the completion of this project. I would like to thank three organizations at the University of California Berkeley for funding support – the Center for Japanese Studies, the Department of Political Science, and the Institute of Governmental Studies. Grants from Southwestern University's Cullen Faculty Development Fund have also funded more recent research trips to Japan.

I owe a debt of gratitude to many people in Tokyo for their assistance during my various research trips. The offices of Matsuda Iwao and Yamamoto Takashi, as well as the staff at the International Bureau of the Liberal Democratic Party provided me with access to the Diet and several critical introductions. Kohno Masaru, Miura Mari, and Hiwatari Nobuhiro provided entrée to the academic community. The Institute of Social Science at Tokyo University extended an institutional affiliation to me twice during this project. Nakano Yukiko and Asaumi Wakaba provided excellent translation assistance. Finally, I could not have finished this project without the research assistance of Nishimoto Hikari, who was literally running over to the Diet library in Tokyo to verify citation information days before the completion of this manuscript. Her competence and conscientiousness continue to impress me. I am very grateful for the assistance from all those mentioned above. Any errors that remain, however, are my own.

On personal note, I would like to thank the friends and family members whose support has allowed me to keep my sanity and sense of humor throughout this process. Many of these friends have been mentioned earlier because they wear the dual hat of colleague and friend. Sarah Wiliarty, Sara Watson, Mari Miura, Jonathan Marshall, Robert Weiner, Tasha Fairfield, Abe Newman, David Bach, John Leslie, Anna Schmidt, Ken Greene, Jack Porter, Calvin Chen, Ken Haig, Dwight Dyer, Ethan Scheiner, Margaret Alkon, and Kevin Wiliarty are all friends from graduate school who have supported me along the way. Dana Flynn Schneider is my closest friend from childhood and has always been in my corner. As academics, my parents, Robert and Eleanor, provided both inspiration and motivation. The self-confidence I have built over the years comes directly from their love, support, and praise. My sister, Laura, has been my biggest cheerleader, never doubting me or this project. My husband, Robert McAlister, has brought even more love and laughter into my life. He has encouraged research travel to Tokyo and made the distance bearable with his frequent calls and emails. His sense of humor and sense of play make each day even more joyous than the one before.

Two people extremely important to me passed away before this project was complete – my mother, Eleanor Gaunder, and my graduate school mentor, Judy Gruber. A professor of English and a true lover of learning, my Mom was always interested in what I was working on and read much of my work, acting as editor in many cases. Her ability to balance work and family – and excel at both – was an inspiration. Judy Gruber took a special interest in me in graduate school even though our areas of specialty were different. She was extremely generous with her time and support and a phenomenal teacher-scholar. Her encouragement helped me get where I am today. I learned so much from these strong, caring women. It is in their memory that I dedicate this book.

1 The puzzle of political reform

Why would any politician support reforms that could increase the uncertainty of re-election? More specifically, why would any politician change the electoral rules they were successfully elected under or make it more difficult to raise funds for re-election? The answer to this puzzle is not readily apparent. The public often supports reform, but politicians usually do not. What is surprising is that politicians sometimes also favor new regulations that could make their political lives more difficult. The passage of political reform is rare; yet, when exploring the history of parliamentary politics in postwar Japan we can find several advocates of political reform.[1] Take, for example, the case of a current member of the Upper House of the Japanese Diet, Matsuda Iwao.[2]

Matsuda Iwao's political career has been a turbulent one. He has been the member of three political parties; he lost his seat in the Lower House in 1996 after serving three terms; after two years out of office he ran as an independent for the Upper House; and finally he rejoined the powerful Liberal Democratic Party (LDP) despite the fact he had left the party in protest of its anti-reform stance in 1993.

Matsuda was elected to the Lower House of the Diet, the more powerful house of the Japanese parliament, in 1986. At this time, as is the case with most politicians in the dominant Liberal Democratic Party of Japan, he affiliated with one of the party's factions. When he became a member of the largest faction, the Takeshita faction, the faction leader Takeshita Noboru promised him that the costs of being a politician would decrease over time. But when I talked with Matsuda in 1999, he revealed that contrary to these expectations, the costs were still quite high. Matsuda pointed to two reasons for the lingering difficulty in raising funds. First, in 1999 Japan was in the middle of a prolonged recession that had made raising political funds much more difficult. Companies were cutting back on extra expenditures including contributions to politicians. Second, between his first election to the Lower House in 1986 and when I talked with him in 1999, the Diet had implemented a comprehensive political reform package (personal interview with Matsuda Iwao, 21 May 1999).[3] Among other things, this law lowered the upper limit on contributions from individuals and companies, established stricter

disclosure regulations for contributions, and created national party subsidies. Despite the fact that these laws contributed to Matsuda's fundraising
difficulties, he along with other politicians who were equally affected by the
new regulations ardently supported these reforms. The question remains,
why did Matsuda and other politicians support such reforms?

In Matsuda's case, he strongly believed in reform so he followed Ozawa
Ichirō, a disaffected leader inside the LDP who was a strong advocate of
reform. Until 1993 when he lost the battle to become the new head of the
LDP's Takeshita faction, Ozawa was an influential leader inside this faction.
When Matsuda joined the faction, Ozawa was in charge of distributing faction funds to new candidates. Many newly elected politicians felt indebted to
Ozawa due to his decision to support them during the election. Ozawa built
a support base within the LDP using these ties.[4] He formed a study group on
political reform and began to push the party to earnestly pursue the creation
of a single-member district electoral system and implement political funding
reform. In 1993, when the Miyazawa administration would not support a
proposal that had a realistic chance of passing the Diet, Ozawa left the party
and took over forty party members with him. Matsuda was among these
politicians. In a second interview with Matsuda in 2001, he reflected on
Ozawa's role in the reform process:

> Ozawa was the one who was responsible for saying that reform is
> something that we have to do. I do not believe that Ozawa is completely
> responsible for the passage of reform. Everyone still had to vote for it.
> Ozawa, however, created the opportunity. He had the courage and
> confidence to try to make this happen.
>
> (personal interview, 20 February 2001)

Ozawa made sure that reform stayed on the policy agenda long after the
Sagawa Kyūbin scandal originally made the issue salient in 1992.[5] He persuaded a large number of politicians both within and outside the LDP to
support a political reform package that had both permanent and adjustment
costs for politicians. He then mobilized this support by convincing a large
number of politicians to leave the LDP with him in protest of the party's
unwillingness to support realistic reform. He also mobilized all the other
opposition parties, excluding the Communist party, to join an anti-LDP
coalition. This coalition took control of the government in 1993 and enacted
political reform in January 1994.

Clearly, leadership plays an important role in the passage of reform. The
overarching theme of this book is that leadership matters. Leaders, like
Ozawa, play a critical role in shifting individual politicians' narrow self-
interest away from support for the status quo to a broader interest served by
enacting reform. That is, leaders play an important role in showing politicians how supporting initiatives like political reform can actually benefit
them in the long-run by doing such things as bolstering the overall legitimacy

of the system. Creating a shift from short-term concerns to broader long-term concerns requires both persuasion, in terms of getting politicians to realize the larger interest served in reforming, and mobilization in order to get a majority of politicians to actively support reform. Leaders play a key role in this persuasion and mobilization.

The conclusion that leadership matters forces a reconsideration of core debates in political science in general and Japanese politics in particular. Many scholarly accounts of the policy-making process focus on the constraints, in the form of the international environment, domestic institutions or individual rationality, that stand in the way of politicians passing laws that could negatively affect their own behavior.[6] This book demonstrates that effective leadership can overcome these constraints. The conclusion that leadership matters also challenges the conventional wisdom about Japanese politics. Japan is viewed as a country where leadership is secondary. The exploration of when and why reform was implemented throughout the postwar period in Japan, however, demonstrates that quite the opposite is the case. Leadership is the difference between the successful and unsuccessful cases of reform explored in the chapters to follow. As we will see, a scandal serves to open a window of opportunity for reform. A scandal, however, is not sufficient to produce reform. A leader with a certain set of resources and personal attributes is also needed to persuade self-interested politicians to support reform and then mobilize this support.

Conventional explanations for reform

Political science provides more answers for why reform is not passed than for why it is.[7] These explanations focus on the constraints that stand in the way of the passage of reform. These constraints come in a variety of forms depending on the level of analysis. Some political scientists emphasize the constraints at the international level, others point to the constraints present at the domestic institutional level, and still others see the major constraints as resting at the individual level.

International level approaches focus on the pressures of the external environment on the domestic policy-making process. For example, in the case of Japan, some analysts emphasized that during the Cold War the international environment put pressure on the ruling conservative politicians to maintain the status quo, an electoral system that favored one dominant party, the LDP. During the Cold War, due to their ideological underpinnings, the opposition parties, such as the Socialists and the Communists, were seen as a threat to the security arrangement between the United States and Japan in particular and the Cold War balance of power in general. Changing the electoral system to a single-member district system that favored party alternation was unpopular in many corners because such an electoral reform would threaten the dominance of the conservative LDP and allow for the possibility of more radical elements to gain power. The end of the Cold War, however, opened up the ideological space by making the previous cleavage less salient. This development created an environment that made changing the electoral system less threatening (Narita 1997: 40–42).

In contrast to international level explanations, institutional explanations focus on organizational rules and norms that constrain the options available to policy makers. With institutional explanations, features of the political institutional structure inhibit the passage of reform.[8] For example, in Japan, much rigidity exists in the policy-making process. In particular, there are many opportunities for new bills to be killed in the internal LDP policy-making process. The LDP has a committee structure that parallels that of the Diet in its Policy Affairs Research Council. Bills are debated here to determine party policy. Opponents to reform can use the cumbersome policy-making process within the LDP to slow down the proposal of new legislation or block it completely. In this way pro-reformers are constrained by the party's decision-making apparatus. Diet rules and procedures pose more institutional constraints. One norm that has developed over time holds that in order for a bill to pass committee it must be passed unanimously. The opposition parties often have used this informal rule as a bargaining tool to gain concessions on legislation or to block government bills. If parliamentarians do not reach an agreement on a bill before the end of the session, the legislation is shelved and must begin the process anew during the next session (Sakamoto 1999: 158, fn. 29). Other institutional constraints that influence the policy-making process in Japan are factional politics within the LDP, the limited formal powers granted to the prime minister, and the informal norm of seniority in the distribution of positions of power within the LDP. Institutionalists point to these types of constraints as standing in the way of the passage of reform.

A final explanation for why reform rarely is passed focuses on the constraints posed by individual rationality.[9] In this school, the choices of actors are derived from their preferences and are therefore predictable. The actors' choice is by definition determined by the actors' maximizing behavior in which they weigh the costs and benefits they anticipate encountering given a particular decision (Bawn 1993; Brady and Mo 1992; Geddes 1991). The only reason that a politician or party would consider reform was if the benefits outweighed the costs of the increased uncertainty caused by a change in the rules governing elections and political fund-raising. For example, in the US Congress, politicians have long been characterized as supporting particularistic policies that maximize their chances for re-election above all else (Mayhew 1974).

Overcoming any of these constraints is difficult. No matter what the level of analysis, the main way scholars envision that these constraints can be overcome is when an exogenous shock occurs which shakes up the system. An exogenous shock can loosen the institutional constraints by redefining the rules of the game. For example, at the individual level, the change in the environment resulting from an exogenous shock causes individuals to readjust their preferences, and leads to change. These accounts, however, leave little or no room for the possibility that an individual can overcome these constraints and change institutions or individual preferences. We shall see that individual agency proves to be critical in the passage of reform.

The relationship between scandal and reform

Politicians pass political reform following scandals. This statement reflects the most common answer to the puzzle posed at the beginning of this chapter. Scandals are the exogenous shock often seen as loosening the constraints at any or all of the three levels mentioned above. Some observers have gone as far as to suggest that scandal initiates a cycle that results in reform. Stages in this recurring cycle include the discovery of a possible transgression, public disclosure of this information, public reaction to the exposed behavior (Moodie 1988: 244–45), and punishments and reforms (Markovits and Silverstein 1988: 3). This characterization implies that the implementation of punishments and/or reforms is a natural outcome.

At first glance, this explanation seems to accurately capture the empirical evidence. Take, for example, political reform passed in the twentieth century in the United States. Speculation that large corporate contributions to presidential campaigns were buying favors plagued the United States prior to the passage of the Tillman Act, the first comprehensive legislation concerning contribution limits in 1907. In the 1920s the Teapot Dome scandal preceded the passage of the Corrupt Practices Act of 1925, and in the 1970s the passage of amendments to the Federal Election Campaign Act followed the outbreak of the Watergate scandal. Most recently, Congress passed the Bipartisan Campaign Reform Act of 2002 following the Enron scandal (Corrado 2005). The Japanese case presents a similar picture. The Diet passed the first revisions to political funding regulations in the postwar period following a real-estate scandal involving Prime Minister Tanaka. Similarly, the Sagawa Kyūbin scandal occurred before the revisions to the Political Funds Control Law and the Public Office Election Law in 1994. Although both these examples include the major reform packages passed in the twentieth century in the United States and Japan, the examples do not exhaust the complete list of scandals in either country.

Indeed, one of the biggest problems with an explanation that focuses on scandal is that it fails to explain why legislators only pass reform in the aftermath of some scandals. The conditions that favor reform occur far more often than the actual instances of reform. That is, there were many more times when the conditions were ripe for reform than there were times when politicians actually passed reform. Explanations that suggest a cycle of scandal and reform ignore the role that politicians play in the process. Although scandals might heighten the demand for political reform, scandal alone is not sufficient to bring about change.

Windows of opportunity

Scandals do not always initiate a cycle that results in reform. However, scandals do create an environment conducive to reform. The distinction between these two statements is important. The first statement suggests that the event itself causes reform, while in the second statement reform is not a forgone conclusion. As we shall see, there have been many instances when the environment has favored reform, but reform has not been enacted. For example, in Japan at least one national scandal has occurred almost every year in the postwar period (Murobushi 1988; Reed 1996a; K. Yamamoto 1992). Comprehensive reform, however, only has been passed twice. The key to explaining the difference between successful and failed cases of reform is the presence of a leader willing and able to capitalize on the environment created by scandal.

So what kind of environment do scandals produce? Political scandals have the dual effect of increasing the salience of political reform and decreasing support of the government. These two developments push open a window of opportunity for reform.[10] Scandals involving such activities as bribery, conflict of interest, and illegal campaign contributions highlight the weaknesses and loopholes in the current regulatory regime and have the potential for increasing calls for political reform. Misconduct on the part of politicians can also serve to negatively affect the public's support of the government, increasing the sense that all politicians are dishonest, dirty crooks. Following a scandal, the public immediately becomes more concerned with the activities of politicians, and they begin asking difficult questions: What moral and ethical standards should we hold our politicians to? How can we prevent political funding violations? How can we make politicians more accountable for their activities? In most cases, the answer to these difficult questions is reform. If a leader appears with a viable plan when people are more aware of the weaknesses in the regulatory regime, then he or she has a good chance of capitalizing on the increased interest in the topic. The leader, however, must act quickly.[11] The leader only has a window, a certain period of time during which people will be interested in reform. But the opportunity to exploit this window is there.[12]

The image of a window of opportunity for political reform still might seem a bit vague. If you think about it, though, there are some concrete ways to measure both increased salience of reform and decreased government approval. A good measure of increased salience of reform is the amount of media coverage that political reform is receiving. That is, how often does this topic receive coverage in the political and/or editorial section in printed media? After the outbreak of a scandal, the press can play an agenda-setting role by acting as the public's advocate and pushing for reform. The media often ask the difficult questions and provide the answer of reform (Farley 1996). The more calls for political reform that appear in the media, the more difficult the topic is going to be to ignore and the more favorable the conditions are for politicians who support reform to pursue their cause. In response to increased media attention, we might also see increased legislative activity related to reform. This legislative activity also reflects increased salience.

As for declining public approval, we can measure it in several different ways as well. Government support ratings, national election results, and by-election results all gauge the public's attitude toward government. Large losses by the ruling party or pronounced decreases in cabinet and/or ruling party support ratings reflect public disillusionment with the status quo. In Japan, by-election results are often seen as predictors of how the parties will do in the next national election. As a result, much importance is attached to the dominant LDP losing what was formerly a relatively secure seat. In fact, any loss by the LDP, especially if it held the seat prior to the election, is seen as a lack of faith in the ruling regime. "Throwing the rascals out" certainly illustrates the public's desire for change.[13]

So, how can we tell when a window closes?[14] Here, we need to look for indications that the above trends have begun to reverse. That is, we need to look for evidence of the salience of reform decreasing or government approval increasing. It is not so easy to tell with certainty when a window of opportunity closes. Sometimes the reversal of trends is abrupt and the window of opportunity is quickly slammed shut. In other instances, the window gradually closes as the salience of reform dies down or as government support begins to increase.

One way a window can close is when other issues come to the fore and overshadow the scandal and the need for political reform. Politicians often emphasize other issues in an attempt to sweep the scandal under the carpet. In other instances, a new crisis breaks out and takes away from the salience of reform. In the Japanese case, events that have distracted the public's attention from scandal include, for example, the 1970s oil shocks, the Gulf War, and foreign trade pressure. A new issue that overtakes political reform in salience does not have to be this big, though. Another domestic issue could emerge and overtake political reform in importance. Many politicians look for such issues and enthusiastically seize the opportunity to focus on something besides political reform.

Various circumstances can increase government support following a scandal. One possibility is that politicians successfully handle the scandal. Hearings, arrests, or the establishment of investigative committees might be enough to satisfy the public that politicians are taking the transgression seriously. In this case, the pressure to reform is not strong, or even present. A big win at the polls also makes politicians realize that the window is closed. Politicians might have been functioning as if the public had lost faith in them until election day when the election results suggest otherwise, especially if the election results are inconsistent with the most recent government support ratings. Indeed, government support ratings could be specific to a particular prime minister explaining the discrepancy. Once the ruling party/coalition convincingly has won, the pressure to pass reform lessens. Support of the ruling party is certainly more secure. As a result, the window is closed.

A new explanation for the passage of political reform

The notion of a window of opportunity for reform gets us closer to an answer to our puzzle. A leader, however, is needed to exploit the opportunity for reform presented by scandal. Indeed, two things increase the possibility that legislators will pass laws that affect their own behavior – environmental conditions and agency. Environmental conditions include a window of opportunity opened by scandal and closed when public support of the government starts increasing or the salience of reform begins declining. My explanation, like the cyclical explanation, recognizes that scandal is important because it increases the salience of reform. Unlike the conventional explanation, however, my argument claims that scandal alone is not a sufficient condition to bring about reform. Agency is also needed. Agency manifests itself in a leader who advocates reform. Successful reformers are distinguished from other leaders by their willingness to take risks to achieve reform, their vision for reform, and their commitment to reform. These personal characteristics when combined with resources, such as patron–client ties and connections with other parties, place reformers in a position to exploit the window of opportunity and realize reform.

The role of leadership

Let's return to the puzzle posed at the beginning of this chapter: why would any politician support reforms that could increase the uncertainty of re-election? I have suggested that political leaders play an important role in persuading politicians to support reform and then mobilizing this support. In order for reform to be enacted, an advocate of reform needs to be on the scene and prepared to exploit the opportunity presented by an open window. I would like to take a moment here to consider what kinds of leaders tend to take on this role.

Politicians who support reform do so for a variety of different reasons. The motivations of reformers do not directly influence their success or failure to pass reform. These motivations are important, however, in explaining why a leader might choose to take up the banner of reform. In most situations, advocates of reform are in the minority. Convincing or even forcing those opposed to reform to support their cause remains a formidable task for advocates of reform. Potential actors include, career reformers, victims of the current regulatory regime, and opportunists seeking to increase their power by supporting political reform. The motivations of each of these actors are different.

A career reformer is a policy advocate with a specific agenda. Career reformers who support political reform are always trying to clean up dirty politics by increasing the restrictions on the activities of politicians and strengthening the penalties for those who violate these restrictions. Career reformers who support political reform are usually in the periphery of politics, but occasionally an exogenous shock, such as political scandal, can bring them and their cause to the fore.

In the Japanese case, Prime Minister Miki Takeo falls into the category of career reformer. Long before he became prime minister, Miki was a vocal advocate of reform. Above all else his voice was one advocating clean politics. He headed a small anti-mainstream faction within the LDP that supported political funding reform and internal party reform. As we will see in Chapter 2, Miki had a career-long commitment to reform. The LDP selected him as party president and prime minister after Prime Minister Tanaka was forced to resign due to his implication in a real-estate scandal. Miki used this opportunity to push through political funding reform. While prime minister, he also took a hard stance against former Prime Minister Tanaka, doing nothing to stop his indictment for his involvement in the Lockheed scandal. After his tenure as prime minister, Miki continued to push for internal party reform until his death.

Other possible supporters of political reform are those who are harmed by the current regulatory regime. The rules of the game often favor veteran politicians; thus, a constituency for reform is often found in the newly elected or relatively junior politicians. In systems where seniority determines decision-making power, though, junior politicians frequently find it very difficult to change the rules of the game (Narita 1997: 38; Wolfe 1995: 1074). Similarly, one could imagine the opposition parties wanting to change laws governing campaign finance and campaigning practices if the current regulations favor the ruling party/coalition (Narita 1997: 39). If the public seems receptive to reform, one strategy used by opposition parties that want to gain power is to run on a platform supporting such measures. If former opposition parties find themselves in government, they often propose changes to rules in an attempt to secure their power.

Junior politicians have been particularly ardent supporters of reform in Japan. Kōno Yōhei led six fellow junior members out of the LDP in 1976 to form the New Liberal Club. The members of this party were frustrated with the LDP's unwillingness to enact internal party reform. They were also disillusioned by the pervasiveness of money politics within the party. These members left the LDP on the heels of the Lockheed scandal in which former Prime Minister Tanaka was accused of accepting bribes from the US company to broker contracts for Lockheed with a Japanese airline company. As is often the case with junior politicians, however, they did not have the political resources to mobilize support for reform. Several other groups of junior politicians supporting reform emerged in the late 1980s and early 1990s, including *Wakate Kaikaku Ha*, the Utopia Study Group, and the League to Restore Political Trust. These groups along with the New Liberal Club will be considered in Chapter 6.

In addition to career reformers and victims of the current regime, opportunists might sense that the environment is ripe for political reform and support it with the hopes of gaining public support and power. Restricting the amount of money spent on campaigns, making contributions from lobbyists and big business more transparent, increasing the restrictions on contributions, refraining from increasing politicians' salary, and generally making the rules of the game more explicit and the penalties for violating the rules of the game more severe may not be popular with politicians, but these policies are generally well-received by the public. Although the public might be opposed to changing the electoral system, it is usually behind closing loopholes in funding and campaigning regulations and making the formal rules more difficult to circumvent. Political reform is not usually a decisive issue when voters go to the polls, but a precipitating event certainly can increase the issue's salience with the public. Opportunists take advantage of the environment created by the precipitating event and try to increase their power or popularity by supporting reform.

In the cases that follow, Ozawa Ichirō, the subject of Chapter 5, comes the closest to being an opportunist. Ozawa was a child of the political machine. Early in his career, Tanaka Kakuei, the politician credited with taking the political machine to its zenith, took Ozawa under his wing and began grooming him as a future successor. After Tanaka became ill and fell from power, Ozawa became the protégé of Takeshita Noboru and Kanemaru Shin, the two politicians who took over the Tanaka faction. As one of the favored ones, Ozawa was privy to backroom deals with opposition parties and monetary supporters of the LDP. Ozawa even was in charge of distributing party funds to new candidates for the Takeshita faction. While never legally implicated in a scandal, Ozawa clearly was involved in the structural corruption that kept the money coming into the LDP's political machine. Despite his involvement in machine politics, Ozawa advocated political reform. His motivations were complicated. In his book advocating reform, *Blueprint for a New Japan*, it is clear that reform is a means to a larger end for him. Ozawa saw reform as a way to push Japan toward becoming a two-party system with regular party alternation. Such a change would force parties to compete on policy, not personal favors. This change would improve political leadership in Japan, thereby enabling Japan to garner more international respect and thus play a greater role in the international political arena (Ozawa 1994). Implicit in this vision was that Ozawa would stand at the head of this new party competing with the LDP for power in a single-member district system that supported two parties. At least part of Ozawa's motivation for supporting reform was to increase his own personal power.

While the motivations of advocates of reform can vary, one's motivation does not determine one's success or failure in the pursuit of reform.[15] Instead, a leader's resources and personal attributes are important in distinguishing between the successful and unsuccessful attempts to pass political reform.

Resources

Intuitively it is easy to accept that resources play an important role in achieving policy success. Resources are necessary to accomplish goals in all realms of life. You need money if you want to start your own business; you need money, volunteers, and connections if you want to run for political office; and you need a computer, free time, and office space if you want to write a book. Clearly the types of resources you need vary according to what you hope to accomplish. Volunteers are not going to help you if you are trying to write a novel, as the creative process is mostly a solitary one. Moreover, all resources are scarce, and not all resources are equal. You can write a book with a pen and paper or even a typewriter, but a computer is going to help you achieve this goal much faster. Resources alone, however, do not guarantee success. A person can own a computer, but this does not mean that she can successfully write the great American novel.

So, how can these observations help us in our exploration of political reform? Clearly, there is a connection between the goal and the kind of resources that are important. It is also evident that certain resources are not available to everyone. Moreover, some resources are more important than others. And finally, resources alone are not sufficient. Success ultimately depends on what the person who has control of the resources does with these resources.

In the context of political reform, the goal is persuasion and mobilization. The basic resources that help an advocate of reform convince other politicians to change the rules of the game are money, connections within his or her party as well as with other parties, appointment powers, media support, and/or public support.[16] These resources are important because they provide leaders with carrots and sticks to persuade, mobilize, and in some instances force other politicians to support their cause.[17] For example, leaders can use money, appointment powers, and media support to pressure politicians to support reform. Leaders can either offer other politicians these resources in return for supporting their cause or threaten to withhold them to punish politicians for opposing change. For mobilization, connections to other parties and access to the policy-making process aid advocates of reform.[18]

In the Japanese case, the resources available to leaders are related to their position in the political hierarchy. Leaders with more seniority have a larger amount of resources at their disposal to influence the policy-making process.[19] For example, if a senior politician is able to secure an influential position in a party faction, then he has money, a potentially large bloc of followers, connections with ministries, industries and opposition leaders, and access to behind-the-scenes dealings. Access to the behind-the-scenes dealings is one of the most important resources an advocate of reform can have since such backroom deals dominate Japanese politics. Without access to elite bargaining, a leader cannot build a coalition for reform. In fact, all junior politicians in Japan are doomed to fail in their pursuit of reform due to their lack of resources. Junior politicians do not have the resources necessary either to build LDP consensus or to build a coalition with the opposition. The only resource that these junior politicians have at their disposal is the media. "Going public" is a less effective strategy for junior politicians, however, given the relationship between the media and politicians.[20] Certain junior politicians might have the propensity to take risks, vision and commitment, but these attributes minus connections and access are not sufficient to force change.

Personal attributes

Although differences in resources are important, these differences only explain part of the reason why some advocates of reform succeed while others fail. The ability and willingness to use these resources in risky ways is an essential part of challenging the constraints that stand in the way of mobilizing politicians to support reform. In addition, vision and commitment help these leaders persuade politicians to go against their narrow self-interest and support reform. In short, the three personal attributes that distinguish successful advocates of reform from other leaders are their propensity to take risks, their vision, and their commitment.

Risk-taking involves challenging the constraints posed by the environment within which the leader is functioning. Recall that many observers see the international environment, the domestic institutional environment, or individual rationality as shackles inhibiting a potential reformer's ability to mobilize support for reform. Yet, some leaders break loose from these shackles and pass reform. The primary way they do is this is by taking risks – by doing unconventional things that have high or uncertain costs associated with them. Take, for example, party structure and organization, a domestic institutional constraint on any leader, especially in a parliamentary system where party discipline is strongly enforced. If members of the party elite are against reform, many politicians might consider taking up the banner of political reform equal to political suicide. Risk-takers not only are willing to take this chance, but they also see ways to overcome the constraints posed by party structure. For instance, a leader willing to take risks might bypass the normal policy-making channels within his party and gather support from opposition parties to build a coalition for reform. A particularly bold advocate of reform might go as far as breaking way from his party, a strategy used by Ozawa Ichirō, the focus of Chapter 5. Another possibility is publicly going against the position of one's party on an issue and using the media to gain public support. As we shall see in Chapter 7, Prime Minister Koizumi was a master at attacking his own party and using the media to get the public behind his policy agenda. In all these examples, leaders are challenging the constraints posed by the party by doing what most would consider impossible.

The image of reaching out for the impossible nicely captures what risk-taking entails. Max Weber first gave us this image when discussing what it takes to be a successful leader in "Politics as Vocation." He explains,

> Politics is a strong and slow boring of hard boards. It takes both passion and perspective. Certainly all historical experience confirms the truth – that man would not have attained the possible unless time and again he had reached out for the impossible. But to do that a man must be a leader, and not only a leader but a hero as well, in a very sober sense of the word ... Only he has the calling for politics who is sure that he shall not crumble when the world from his point of view is too stupid or too base for what he wants to offer. Only he who in the face of all this can say "In spite of all!" has the calling for politics.
>
> (1946: 128)

Weber places primacy on leadership, and a large part of what defines a successful leader is his willingness to take risks and challenge constraints.

Vision is the second critical personal attribute that contributes to a leader's ability to pursue political reform. Vision reflects a politician's overall understanding of how political reform fits into the larger political picture. A leader who has vision is capable of getting other politicians to look at the world differently. He can paint a picture of what the world would look like if things were changed in a certain way. A leader with vision can imagine a new future and bring it to life for others. This ability to see a changed world and express it to others can make changing the status quo less daunting for other politicians. These politicians can latch onto the vision and feel more comfortable about supporting change.[21]

Martin Luther King's Dream and Franklin Delano Roosevelt's New Deal are examples of visions for change. For instance, FDR presented the nation with a clear vision of his New Deal politics in his first inaugural address when the nation was in the midst of the Great Depression. FDR understood the crisis facing the nation and had a vision of how to overcome this crisis. In this address he proposed three plans of action. First, he advocated a greater government role in creating new jobs for the masses of unemployed. His vision is clear:

> Our greatest primary task is to put people to work. This is no unsolvable problem if we face it wisely and courageously. It can be accomplished in part by direct recruiting by the Government itself, treating the task as we would treat the emergency of a war, but at the same time, through this employment, accomplishing greatly needed projects to stimulate and reorganize the use of our natural resources.
>
> (1933: 237)

The second task was to provide relief and support for the agricultural sector of the economy. Finally, FDR proposed reforming the banking system. In his mind, accomplishing all three of these tasks required a greater role for government in the economy as well as more power for the executive to act in crisis. His vision helped the people and politicians accept these radical methods. As we shall see, such vision is critical in mobilizing support for reform of any kind.

Commitment is the final personal attribute that enhances a leader's ability to pursue political reform. Commitment is reflected in leaders' persistent pursuit of their vision and their willingness to pay a price to see this vision realized.[22] Leaders are committed if they pursue some of their ideals throughout their career with little regard of the negative consequences to themselves personally. As we shall see in Chapter 2, successful reformer Miki Takeo had a strong commitment to reform. Miki supported clean politics throughout his career. He resigned from important party and government positions to take a stand against money politics within the party more than once. He also put his prime ministership on the line when he chose not to intervene in the indictment of former Prime Minister Tanaka for his involvement in the Lockheed scandal. His commitment to reform put him in a position to exploit windows of opportunity for reform when they opened. Indeed, commitment ensures that a leader will be ready to act when the environment is conducive to reform.

The notion that a relationship exists between the personal characteristics of leaders and the leaders' ultimate success or failure in a certain task is not a new one; it is simply an idea that has dropped out of most considerations of the policy-making process. Some classic treatments of politics, however, recognize this relationship. For example, in *The Prince*, Machiavelli asserts that feared leaders, as opposed to beloved ones, are more likely to achieve the ultimate goal of capturing and maintaining power. According to Machiavelli, a leader must be willing to indulge in some vices in order to secure power. A leader who is loved is more likely to be betrayed, while one who is feared has a better chance of retaining power (Machiavelli 1985: 67). Max Weber also recognized the relationship between personal attributes and effective leadership. Indeed, one of Weber's most well-known theoretical contributions is that charismatic leaders are capable of bringing about social change (Weber 1947: 358–73). More recently, James MacGregor Burns has distinguished between the goals leaders pursue and the necessary personal attributes. When comparing reform leadership to revolutionary and transactional leadership, Burns argues

> Of all the kinds of leadership that require exceptional political skill, the leadership of reform movements must be among the most exacting. Revolutionary leadership demands commitment, persistence, courage, perhaps selflessness and even self-abnegation … Pragmatic, transactional leadership requires a shrewd eye for opportunity, a good hand at bargaining, persuading, reciprocating. Reform may need these qualities, but it demands much more. Since reform efforts usually require the

participation of a large number of allies with various reform and non-reform goals of their own, reform leaders must deal with endless division within their own ranks. While revolutionaries usually recognize the need for leadership, an anti-leadership doctrine often characterizes and taunts reform programs.

(1978: 169)

Burns concludes that given the special circumstances that surround reform, moral leadership is needed. He notes, "[reform leaders] must be willing to transform society, or parts of it, if that is necessary" (Burns 1978: 170). Political resources and skill aid him in this endeavor.

Clearly, the characteristics that are critical for effective leadership vary depending on the leader's task. For Machiavelli's prince, being feared allows him to retain power. Max Weber's charismatic leader is uniquely able to bring about social change. And John MacGregor Burns maintains that moral leaders are the most successful reformers. In an attempt to bring this theoretical insight back into our discussion of policy making, this exploration of political reform takes a similar approach. The three personal attributes that distinguish successful advocates of reform from other leaders are their propensity to take risks, their vision, and their commitment. Risk-taking directly challenges the constraints discussed at the beginning of this chapter. Vision and commitment aid an advocate of reform in persuading politicians to go against their self-interest and support political reform. These characteristics influence what politicians do with the resources available to them. Differences in the possession of these personal attributes can help explain the difference between successful and unsuccessful leaders.[23]

Alternative explanations for the passage of reform

Still, one can imagine several alternative explanations for the puzzle of reform posed at the beginning of this chapter. For example, the severity of the scandal, the length of the window of opportunity and the amount of party competition are other causal or intervening factors that could influence the passage of reform. In this section, I explore the logic of these alternative explanations. As we shall see, though, evidence from the cases that follow casts doubt on each explanation.

As mentioned earlier, the relationship between scandal and reform often has been exaggerated. A more sophisticated approach in this line of theorizing argues that reform follows more severe scandals. A more severe scandal creates greater pressure for reform as well as a more favorable environment for reform. While logical, this assertion leaves at least two critical questions unaddressed. First, how does one measure the severity of the scandal? Second, what about the favorable environment triggers reform?

There are at least three possible ways to measure the severity of scandal. These measures include the status of the transgressor(s) (MacDougall 1988), the number of politicians involved (Gaunder 1994), and the public's response to scandal (A. Doig 1988). In the chapters that follow, I will consider the severity of scandal in terms of the status and number of politicians involved. Whatever measurement is used, though, the severity of the scandal is not the decisive factor in the passage of reform. In particular, we shall see that the environment was more favorable for reform during the Kaifu and Miyazawa administrations due to the outbreak of two of the most severe scandals in the postwar period – the Recruit scandal and the Sagawa Kyūbin scandal. Reform, however, did not pass directly in the aftermath of these scandals. Instead, reform passed following Ozawa's split from the LDP five years after the Recruit scandal and a year and half after the Sagawa Kyūbin scandal.

The severity-of-scandal argument suggests that the environment created by the scandal might be more conducive to reform. Another approach to thinking about the severity of the scandal is to focus on the length of the window of opportunity opened by scandal. Specifically, one might expect that there is a higher probability of passing reform the longer a window of opportunity is open. This contention, however, assumes that the window of opportunity in and of itself results in reform. The literature on windows of opportunity does not support this assertion. A leader is necessary to exploit this window. The window independent of the leader is not decisive. Both ingredients are necessary (Kingdon 1984: 192). Certainly one could argue that leaders with more time are more able to pursue reform. In the Japanese case, reform proposals have been on the agenda for decades (Reed 1999a: 181–83). As a result all leaders have had access to developed proposal options at any given time. The key is how quickly they adopt one of these proposals and act to mobilize support for it (Kingdon 1984: 177). The environment alone does not trigger reform. Agency is also necessary.

The notion of the length of the window of opportunity being decisive in the passage of reform is best refuted by comparing the reform attempts by Kaifu following the Recruit scandal and Miyazawa and Ozawa following the Sagawa Kyūbin scandal. As illustrated in Table 1.1, in these cases the windows of opportunity were open for about the same length of time – 14 months in the case of Recruit and 15 months in the case of Sagawa. Under Kaifu's leadership, reform failed following Recruit. In contrast, due to the leadership of Ozawa Ichirō, reform passed following the Sagawa Kyūbin scandal. In these cases the lengths of the windows of opportunity were nearly identical, but the policy outcomes varied. Clearly, other variables are at play. In this book, I will illustrate that while the length of the window of opportunity is an interesting point of comparison, it, alone, does not explain the passage of reform. Instead, the leader seeking reform is decisive.

A final alternative explanation suggests that increased electoral competition leads to reform (Scarrow 1997). In her exploration of the expansion of direct democracy in Germany, Scarrow maintains that cartel parties are more willing to consider reforms that could hurt them in the long run when these parties are feeling more pressure from an increasing number of competitors.

Table 1.1 Lengths of windows of opportunity created by scandal

	Window opens	Window closes	Length	Policy result
Tanaka real-estate scandal	October 1974	July 1975	9 months	Reform passes
Recruit scandal	November 1988	February 1990	14 months	Reform fails
Kyōwa	January 1992	July 1992	6 months	No reform
Sagawa Kyūbin	October 1992	January 1994	15 months	Reform passes

Note
The dates of open windows do not necessarily correspond with the date a scandal broke. Instead, the dates of open windows reflect the point when government support began declining and the salience of reform began increasing. Closed windows are determined by a reversal of this trend or the passage of reform. The indicators for government support include cabinet support ratings, by-election results, and/or Lower or Upper House election results. The indicators for the salience of reform consist of the formation of political reform advisory councils or Diet committees, the formation of new factions/parties based on reform, and/or the formulation of reform proposals by individual politicians.

These new parties serve to highlight the fact that voters can be wooed by supporting reform (Scarrow 1997: 464).[24] While her measure of party competition is not entirely clear, one can make two inferences from her discussion. First, party competition seems to increase as elections draw closer (Scarrow 1997: 461). Absent the dissolution of the Bundestag, which has been a rare occurrence, elections are scheduled in Germany. This situation makes the build up to a national election more stable than in other parliamentary democracies. Second, electoral competition increases with the emergence of new contenders (Scarrow 1997: 464).

The contention that increased electoral competition leads to political reform is certainly a viable one in the Japanese context. Scarrow developed her argument in the German context, and she considers the German parties to be cartel parties (Katz and Mair 1995). The LDP was not a cartel party in the 1955 system; it maintained monopoly control for most of this period. Yet, a monopoly is simply a more stable form of a cartel. As a result, the same logic Scarrow uses could apply. Monopoly parties are also vulnerable to outside competition. Studies of electoral politics in Japan indicate that electoral competition was increasing from the 1980s through the turbulent period of reform in the 1990s (Cox and Rosenbluth 1993; Reed 1996b). The level of competition can be measured in a variety of ways including the LDP's vote share, the LDP's control of the Upper House, and the emergence of new or break-away parties.

The LDP's vote share in Lower House elections decreased between 1958 and 1993 as illustrated in Figure 1.1. Not surprisingly, the largest drops in vote share occurred when new parties emerged. The LDP's vote share dropped nearly six percentage points in the Kōmeitō's first election in 1967. It dropped again by five percentage points when the New Liberal Club broke from the LDP and contested as an independent new party in the 1976 election. The largest drop in vote share occurred in 1993 when the *Shinseitō*

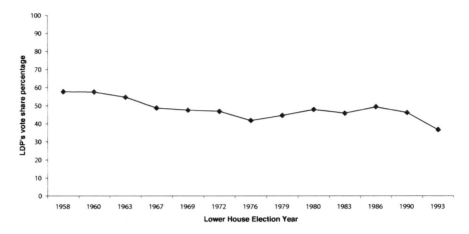

Figure 1.1   The LDP's electoral competitiveness 1958–93. LDP vote share was calculated by dividing the total votes received by the LDP by the total number of people who voted in the election.

Source: LDP vote share was calculated using raw election data from Statistics Bureau and Statistical Research and Training Institute, "Shugiingiin Sosenkyo Tōhabetsu Tōsenshasū oyobi Tokuhyōsū (Shōwa 33-Heiwa 5)" [Persons Elected and Votes Polled by Political Parties of Elections for the House of Representatives (1958–93)]. Online. Available: http://www.stat.go.jp/data/chouki/zuhyou/27-08-a.xls (accessed 5 July 2006).

and *Sakigake* broke from the LDP at the same time the Japan New Party contested its first Lower House election. In this election the LDP's vote share was only 36.6 percent. The question is, did these drops in vote share correspond with the passage of political reform? According to Scarrow's argument, we would expect significant reforms to occur at times of increasing party competition. However, no major reform bill appeared immediately before or after the formation of the Kōmeitō in 1967. The Kōmeitō, translated as the Clean Government Party, chose its name to distinguish itself from the corruption-mired LDP. However, it has had only a small, but dedicated following from the Buddhist sect Soka Gakkai since its inception. The LDP lost votes due to the formation of the Kōmeitō, but it did not feel pressure to reform.

While the elections in 1976 and 1993 share some similarities, reform policy outcomes following these elections vary. In both these elections new parties emerged as members broke from the LDP. The Lockheed scandal prompted the formation of the New Liberal Club. While only a handful of LDP members left the party, the loss of members combined with the fallout from the Lockheed scandal left the LDP scrambling for a majority in the Lower House following the election. It only obtained the majority when several candidates who ran as independents joined the LDP.

The timing for the consideration and passage of reform is off in this case, however. Prime Minister Miki oversaw the passage of revisions to the Political Funds Control Law early in his administration. This law passed prior to the outbreak of the Lockheed scandal and the turmoil this scandal produced. After the Lockheed scandal broke, the LDP did not become more receptive to reform. To the contrary, the pressure to remove the reform-minded Prime Minister Miki only increased, as we shall see in Chapter 2. The LDP might have been feeling greater electoral pressure following the Lockheed scandal which broke in late 1975 and the New Liberal Club's departure which followed shortly thereafter, but it did not respond by considering more comprehensive political reform.

The election results in 1993 do not tell the full story behind the passage of reform in 1994. The LDP arguably was feeling increased electoral pressure beginning in 1989 with the outbreak of the Recruit scandal. The party did consider reform following this and subsequent scandals, but it did not pass reform until Ozawa Ichirō risked everything by leaving the LDP to pursue reform outside the LDP. Three leaders pursued reform from 1989 to 1994 – Kaifu, Miyazawa, and Ozawa. Since these attempts occurred within a short time span, it is difficult to assess the effects of increased electoral competition. In particular, it is very difficult to determine when or if increased electoral competition reached a tipping point by looking at the LDP's steady decline in vote share over time. Because Lower House elections only occur every few years in Japan, LDP vote share is not a useful measure for assessing electoral competition during a five-year period when several reform proposals were put forth.

Control of the Upper House over time provides a second way to measure increased party competition. The LDP lost its majority in the Upper House in 1989. The Upper House is the less influential house of parliament, but its actions are not inconsequential with regard to reform. Any political reform bill must pass both the Lower and Upper House of the Diet to become law. After the LDP lost power in the Upper House in 1989, it did feel more pressure to reform. As we shall see, reform was a central issue in the Kaifu and Miyazawa administrations. No reform passed, however, until 1994 when Ozawa took up the issue. This measure of electoral competition also fails to provide compelling evidence that an increase in electoral competition was the decisive factor.

Finally, another measure of increased competition is the emergence of new or break-away parties. In the 1960s, two new parties emerged – the Democratic Socialist Party and the Kōmeitō – but politicians failed to pass reform. In 1976, the New Liberal Club broke away from the LDP on the issue of reform. However, the only reform proposal which passed during this period – the revision to the Political Funds Control Law – occurred prior to the formation of this new party in 1975 during the Miki administration. In short, the events were out of sequence. In contrast, reform did pass following the formation of the Japan New Party, the *Shinseitō*, and *Sakigake* in the early 1990s. I will illustrate in Chapter 5 that this reform passed due to leadership, not increased electoral competition. The fact that the appearance of new/ break-away parties in the 1970s and 1990s had different outcomes in terms of the passage of reform suggests that another factor was at play. I argue that leadership is decisive in the success or failure of reform.

Book outline

The chapters that follow use carefully crafted case studies to illustrate how leadership played a critical role in determining when reform occurred, given roughly similar pressures for reform. I consider four major efforts for electoral system and political funding reform during the postwar period in Japan. In each case the main focus of investigation is the leader behind reform. Three leaders considered, Miki Takeo, Kaifu Toshiki and Miyazawa Kiichi, were prime ministers. One leader, Ozawa Ichirō, pulled the strings behind the scenes in the anti-LDP coalition government in 1993. Two leaders, Miki and Ozawa, successfully saw through the passage of reform. The remaining two leaders considered, Kaifu and Miyazawa, failed. Chapters 2 and 5 consider the two successful cases of political reform in the postwar period under the leadership of Prime Minister Miki Takeo in 1975 and Ozawa Ichirō in 1994. These cases represent the only successful cases of political reform during the postwar period. There have been numerous unsuccessful cases of reform. Chapters 3 and 4 explore arguably the two most significant failed cases of reform under the leadership of Prime Ministers Kaifu Toshiki and Miyazawa Kiichi. Chapter 6 then investigates three smaller unsuccessful cases of reform led by groups of junior politicians, including the New Liberal Club, the Utopia Study Group, and the League to Restore Political Trust. These unsuccessful cases of reform by junior politicians illustrate the importance of political resources. These junior politicians, unlike the prime ministers and senior political fixer considered in Chapters 2–5, did not have access to behind-the-scenes dealings or connections within or outside their party. The lack of resources guaranteed their failure.

Pressure for electoral system and political funding reform has been nearly constant in the postwar period in Japan. The four major cases of leadership and reform considered in this book, Miki Takeo, Kaifu Toshiki, Miyazawa Kiichi, and Ozawa Ichirō, nicely illustrate the importance of leadership. As we shall see, the two successful cases occurred in a political climate that was actually less favorable to the passage of reform than in the two failed cases. Both successful reformers, Miki and Ozawa, were outsiders within the LDP. Miki was the member of a small anti-mainstream faction and Ozawa was a disaffected leader who eventually left the dominant Liberal Democratic Party to pursue reform from outside the party. In this sense, both of these leaders faced more constraints to the passage of reform. Moreover, the pressure for reform was much greater during the Kaifu and Miyazawa administrations on the heels of two of the largest scandals in the postwar period, the Recruit scandal in 1988 and the Sagawa Kyūbin scandal in 1992. These scandals implicated some of the most powerful politicians. Kaifu could have used the fact that many of his powerful patrons had been implicated in the Recruit scandal as leverage to push through his reform agenda, but ultimately he was unwilling to take this or any other risk. Miyazawa went as far as staking his entire administration on the passage of reform, but he was not willing to compromise when it became clear that his proposal was unacceptable to the opposition parties.[25] The main contention of this book is that the difference between successful and failed reform rests with political leadership.[26] An investigation of Prime Minister Koizumi and his successful effort to pass postal reform in 2005 in Chapter 7 illustrates the applicability of the theory developed in this book to Japanese politics today.

This exploration of when and why political reform was implemented throughout the postwar era in Japan demonstrates that leadership matters, and effective leadership can overcome institutional and strategic constraints. Moreover, this study suggests that different goals require different kinds of leaders. Given a favorable environment and a certain amount of resources, risk-takers with vision and commitment have a greater probability of achieving political reform. However, as we shall see, successful reformers Miki and Ozawa did not attain all their aims. Miki pushed for anti-monopoly legislation as hard as he pushed for political funding reform, yet he failed to see the passage of a new anti-monopoly law. Similarly, after electoral reform passed, Ozawa worked to build a party capable of becoming a viable opponent to the LDP, but he too failed with many of his initial disciples fleeing his dictatorial leadership style. The qualities that aided these leaders in successfully achieving reform did not help them in other areas. Clearly, success in reform does not guarantee success in all areas. Nevertheless, as Miki and Ozawa's successful pushes for political reform illustrate, individual agency can overcome constraints and lead to significant change. Indeed, the findings presented in the pages that follow force a reconsideration of the conventional wisdom on Japanese politics that consensus decision-making norms and factional power balancing produce little in the way of political leadership. Political leadership is essential to consider in any exploration of policy making in Japan.

2 Miki Takeo

An outsider stands firm inside the LDP

Just prior to Miki Takeo's selection as prime minister in 1974, *Bungei Shunjū*, one of Japan's major weekly political magazines, ran a feature article entitled "Tanaka Kakuei: His Money Connections and Personal Connections" (Tachibana 1974). The article itself was more explosive than the title as it made several allegations of wrongdoing on the part of the sitting prime minister. These allegations sparked the Tanaka real-estate scandal and resulted in Tanaka's resignation from office. Miki Takeo became the new prime minister and successfully led the passage of political reform.

The Tanaka scandal was not the first, nor would it be the last, to rock the political world. Two notable scandals in the early postwar period were the shipbuilding scandal in the 1950s and the Black Mist scandal in the 1960s (Baerwald 1967). Both these scandals involved a large number of politicians and highlighted the need to strengthen political funding, campaigning, and political ethics regulations. Minor changes to campaigning and funding laws were enacted during the 1950–60s, but Diet members were often able to kill more stringent reform proposals by linking the proposals with the need to change the electoral system, a much more contentious proposal (Curtis 1988: 161).

Indeed, what made the Tanaka scandal stand out from the shipbuilding and Black Mist scandals was the subsequent passage of reform. In 1975, the Diet passed significant changes to the Political Funds Control Law and to a lesser extent the Public Office Election Law. The goal of the revisions to the Political Funds Control Law was twofold: (1) to shift the main source of political donations away from corporations and towards individuals, and (2) to make the party, instead of factions and individual politicians, the locus for receiving political contributions. To this end, the revisions to the Political Funds Control Law established an upper limit on political contributions from corporations, unions, and industrial and other associations. For corporations, these limits were based on the level of capitalization. For unions, the ceilings were formulated based on number of members. For industrial associations the limit was derived from a formula based on annual expenditure. To encourage donations from individuals the law made such donations tax deductible (Curtis 1988: 180–83; Hrebenar 2000: 72–77).

Why did the revisions pass in 1975 when similar proposals had failed in the past? Unlike in the previous cases, the environment was ripe for reform, and even more importantly, a leader committed to reform, Miki Takeo, was prime minister in 1975. Although Miki was from the smallest faction in the Liberal Democratic Party (LDP), he was a senior politician with connections both within and outside the LDP. He also was willing to take risks, such as defying the interests of the elite members of the LDP who chose him to serve as prime minister, in order to pursue his reform agenda. Finally, his vision and commitment resonated well with the public that was disillusioned by the outbreak of political funding scandals. Miki was able to use this public support as leverage to convince fellow members of the LDP to support laws that would affect the future behavior of all politicians.

The early history of reform

The first discussions of political reform after the end of the Occupation predate the beginning of the "1955 system" of LDP dominance, the main period of investigation in this study. These discussions occurred when the political system was still in flux with a major reform proposal coming before the Diet just after the formation of the LDP during the Hatoyama administration. A brief overview of the debate under Hatoyama's leadership illustrates the long history of political reform debate within the Diet as well as the importance of mobilizing a scandal in order to garner support for reform. In this case, Hatoyama did not emphasize the connection between money politics and the need for reform. Instead, he focused on how electoral reform could facilitate the passage of revisions to the Constitution. This focus ultimately undermined the passage of his electoral reform proposal (Kusunoki 1997: 53). Nearly 20 years later Prime Minister Tanaka put electoral reform on the agenda, in the absence of scandal, with the goal of increasing the LDP's electoral strength. This reform attempt also failed. The cases of electoral reform during the Hatoyama and Tanaka administrations are considered briefly to illustrate the importance of the environment in which reform is proposed as well as the significance of the leader's approach to reform. We shall see that in comparison to Hatoyama and Tanaka, Miki faced a more favorable environment for reform. Miki's propensity to take risks, vision and commitment also were critical to the passage of reform. Miki, however, was only able to secure revisions to the Political Funds Control Law; he was not able to get electoral reform on the agenda.

The first discussions of changing the electoral system started with interested Diet members from the Liberals, Democrats and Socialists in 1951. While opposition existed in all these parties, the interested members involved in these discussions eventually created a proposal for a small district system in 1954. The shipbuilding scandal broke in this same year providing some justification for creating a small district system that would allegedly make campaigning for office less expensive (Kusunoki 1997: 52). The shipbuilding scandal revolved around the accusation that several shipping companies gave bribes to politicians and other government officials in order to secure government business and favors.[1] The LDP's secretary general, Satō Eisaku, was implicated in this scandal and scheduled to be indicted. Prime Minister Yoshida, however, stepped in on Satō's behalf and prevented the arrest (Curtis 1988: 161).

In November 1955, the small-member district bill became an important part of the Hatoyama cabinet's legislative agenda. Most observers interpreted Hatoyama's support of the bill as an attempt to secure an electoral system that would increase the number of conservatives to a two-thirds majority in order to secure Constitutional revision (Kusunoki 1997: 52–53). Hatoyama's suggestions for district division certainly seemed to support this contention as many of the district lines were drawn in favor of conservative candidates (Kusunoki 1997: 57). This redistricting plan is referred to as the "Hatomander" highlighting the connection between Hatoyama and gerrymandering (Reed and Thies 2001a: 158). Early in his battle for electoral reform Hatoyama suggested that constitutional revision and electoral reform were connected. Later he backed away from emphasizing this connection, instead claiming that small-member districts would lead to a two-party system (Kusunoki 1997: 53). In addition to maintaining that it would lead to a two-party system and elections that required less money, proponents of the bill asserted that the small-member district system would clean up elections by making the detection of illegal acts easier, as well as increase the proximity and connection between candidates and the electorate.[2] The opposition camp refuted these claims predicting that a two-party system would not emerge and that the quality of representatives would decrease (Kusunoki 1997: 55).

A big change occurred in the political system before the actual proposal for reform made it to the Diet floor. The left and right wings of the Socialist party merged and the Liberals and Democrats joined forces to form the Liberal Democratic Party. These mergers were significant because the newly created parties were strong enough to constitute two large parties. With these mergers the Japanese political system appeared to be moving to a two-party system without the proposed electoral reform (Kusunoki 1997: 56). In the end, Hatoyama removed the redistricting provisions from the bill and attempted to push through the electoral reform component. While the bill passed the Lower House, it was stymied in the Upper House due to timing. With only a short time before the close of the session, the Upper House leadership forced the LDP to choose between debating its electoral reform bill or an education reform bill that was also on the agenda. The LDP chose to focus on education reform, claiming it was more fundamental (Kusunoki 1997: 61). With this decision electoral reform died.

The consideration of electoral reform under Hatoyama illustrates that this issue is one that has been debated since the end of the Occupation and the inception of the Liberal Democratic Party. The connection between scandal and reform in this instance is a loose one though. The discussions of electoral reform began prior to the outbreak of the shipbuilding scandal, and Hato-yama was not a leader driving these discussions. Instead, the discussions seemed to be motivated by finding the right type of electoral system for Japan following the end of World War II and the Occupation.[3] Moreover, when Hatoyama did adopt the plan for electoral reform a significant amount of time had passed since the outbreak of the shipbuilding scandal. Satō Eisaku was targeted for arrest in connection with the shipbuilding scandal in April 1954. Hatoyama's proposal for reform did not come before the Lower House for a vote until May 1956, over two years later. While the proposal for a small-member district system was touted as providing a way to clean up politics, this contention was not driving the debate. The Shōwa Denkō and shipbuilding scandals gave credence to the notion that the electoral system promoted money politics; however, these scandals were not the focus of Hatoyama's push for electoral reform. Instead, electoral reform became associated with Constitutional revision due in large part to Hatoyama's initial statements to this end.

Electoral reform did not die after it failed during the Hatoyama government. The way it was pursued, however, changed. Leaders who advocated reform and actively pursued it in the Diet did not emerge. Instead, electoral reform was an issue that was left to be deliberated by advisory councils. These advisory councils were composed of approximately 12 politicians and 30 individuals outside government who were charged with making recommendations to the prime minister. Seven advisory councils met between 1960 and 1973 and each made at least one proposal for reform. Until the Tanaka administration, none of the prime ministers during this period brought one of these proposals before the Diet (Reed and Thies 2001a: 159–62).

The case of Tanaka Kakuei and electoral reform is an instance of reform being pushed during a period when a window of opportunity for reform was not clearly open. Tanaka, like Hatoyama before him, was not pushing electoral reform as a way to clean up politics. Instead, he too was an advocate of changing the electoral system in order to increase the LDP's strength. Tanaka's proposal called for a combined single-member district and proportional representation system for the Lower House with a single vote. The single vote would not allow opposition parties to reap the benefits of cooperating in single-member districts and running separately in the proportional representation portion, a circumstance that would clearly favor LDP candidates (Reed and Thies 2001a: 162). Not surprisingly Tanaka's proposal met staunch resistance from the Kōmeitō, Socialist, Communist, and Democratic Socialist parties. In fact, these parties boycotted the Diet deliberations and actively campaigned against electoral reform outside the Diet. The press backed the position of the opposition parties, painting the proposal as blatantly favoring the LDP. With pressure coming from inside and outside the Diet, the speakers of the Lower and Upper Houses pressured Tanaka to drop the bill, arguing that its consideration could undermine the rest of the LDP's legislative agenda before the nearing end to the Diet session.

Tanaka eventually consented due to the lack of full support within the LDP combined with the united opposition from the other parties (Masumi 1995: 145).

Tanaka's pursuit of electoral reform is significantly different from the other cases of reform considered in this book because he brought his reform proposal forward in the absence of scandal. Tanaka did not wait for a time when the environment was ripe for reform. The public was not disillusioned with money politics at this point and support in government was not decreasing. Tanaka was simply putting electoral reform forward in an attempt to create a system more favorable to the election of LDP candidates. One could argue that the opposition parties ran a successful campaign against reform not only due to Tanaka's selfish motives but also due to the fact that the proposal came in the absence of scandal. Ironically, Tanaka's own activities would eventually open a window of opportunity for reform, one that Prime Minister Miki successfully was able to exploit.

Reform under Miki

A window of opportunity for reform

Prime Minister Tanaka's involvement in two successive political funding scandals created a set of circumstances that were conducive to Miki's subsequent pursuit of reform. Recall that a window of opportunity for reform opens when the level of government support decreases and at the same time the salience of political reform increases. Political scandals have the unique feature of creating this set of circumstances. Two such scandals occurred in 1974.

Money politics gained salience during the July 1974 Upper House election due to questionable campaign contributions elicited by Prime Minister Tanaka. Tanaka orchestrated corporation-sponsored electoral campaigns whereby 2,000 large to medium-sized corporations were assigned specific candidates to support. The executives in these companies then carried out vote-gathering campaigns extending from within the corporation to its subsidiaries. This specific and organized effort made corporations appear to be at the beck and call of the LDP in general and Tanaka in particular (Masumi 1995: 148).

These controversial fundraising practices provided reformers with an example of money politics they could use to push for reform. Following the Upper House election, Miki Takeo resigned as deputy prime minister specifically citing his frustration with the prominent role of money in the LDP.[4] The message was that he could not support a prime minister who had manipulated corporations in such a way. Two other cabinet members, Fukuda Takeo and Hori Shigeru, followed Miki's lead and also resigned. These resignations brought attention to the role of money in politics prior to the revelations about Tanaka's questionable real-estate dealings. The public responded negatively to the corporation-sponsored campaigns only re-electing

62 LDP candidates, a figure that fell 13 candidates short of the party's official target. It also gave the LDP a slim seven-seat majority in the Upper House (Masumi 1995: 149).

Only three months after the controversy over Tanaka's campaign tactics, another scandal broke and ensured that money politics would remain salient. On 9 October 1974, *Bungei Shunjū* ran its explosive article mentioned at the beginning of this chapter detailing several questionable activities of the sitting prime minister, Tanaka Kakuei. This article pointed to Prime Minister Tanaka's involvement in reportedly illegal real-estate and construction deals. These activities included the creation of several ghost companies and the practice of "land flipping" (Masumi 1995: 152). He also was accused of tax evasion and the "improper manipulation of private business funds" (Lamont-Brown 1994: 308).

The *Bungei Shunjū* article brought the LDP's behind-the-scenes dealings out in the open, and this information outraged the public. Tanaka's way of politics had been criticized in the past, but not directly attacked. Tanaka was the head of the largest faction in the ruling LDP, a position he attained by building a strong political machine and developing *kinken seiji*, so-called "money for power politics" (Johnson 1986). Tanaka's style of politics was notorious for its backroom deals that involved the passing of large sums of illegal funds. The *Bungei Shunjū* article, however, served to turn what had been speculation into direct accusation.

The allegations against Tanaka in *Bungei Shunjū* intensified the public's outrage over money politics and led to a precipitous decline in support of the LDP, support that had been waning since the July 1974 Upper House elections. At the end of October, after the release of the *Bungei Shunjū* article, Tanaka's cabinet support rating stood at 12 percent approval and 69 percent disapproval. These figures broke the record for the lowest approval rating and highest disapproval rating since cabinet support ratings had been recorded (Masumi 1995: 153). The combination of the increased salience of money politics initially prompted by the 1974 Upper House election incident and the decreased public support illustrated by Tanaka's declining cabinet support ratings opened a window of opportunity for reform in October 1974. This window would remain open for nine months, closing with the passage of revisions to the Political Funds Control Law during the Miki government in July 1975.

In the face of the public outrage over the Tanaka scandal, the leaders of the LDP decided that Tanaka needed to resign from the prime ministership. After internal party debate over whether to hold a party presidential election, Shiina Etsusaburō, a senior member of the LDP, negotiated an agreement among the various factions to make Miki Takeo the next prime minister.[5] The selection of Miki Takeo, a lifelong reformer on the outskirts of the LDP, provides more evidence of the salience of reform. The main appeal of Miki for the prime ministership was his clean image and his long record of supporting both internal party reform and larger political system reform.[6]

A change of administration can amplify the salience of reform if the change of administration places a reformer in office. This was the case with Miki's selection as prime minister. Miki was known for advocating reformist policies and was prepared with several concrete proposals when he was inaugurated prime minister, including new regulations that placed an upper limit on business and individual contributions. Placing a reformer at the head of government does not guarantee policy success, especially when the main motivation of the prime minister's patrons is to placate the public with a symbolic gesture. Miki would face several obstacles as he tried to gain support for his reform agenda, not the least of which was getting members to transcend their own self-interest and make the restoration of the party's legitimacy a priority. Still, having a prime minister who supports reform increases the chances that reform will make it to the agenda.

Thus, with the salience of money politics and reform increasing and the support in the ruling LDP decreasing, a window of opportunity for reform was clearly open in October 1974. The change of administrations that put reformer Miki Takeo in office in December 1974 opened this window of opportunity even wider.

The passage of political reform

Miki was inaugurated on 9 December 1974. He released proposals for the revising the Public Office Election Law and the Political Funds Control Law in the very same month. The revisions to the Public Office Election Law focused on limiting publicity and increasing the public supervision of elections. The revisions to the Political Funds Control Law established upper limits on political contributions by individuals and corporations. Miki had begun formulating these proposals when he resigned from the Tanaka cabinet in July 1974 in protest of Tanaka's style of money politics.[7] Both proposals passed when they came to floor in the Lower House in June 1975; however, the Political Funds Control Law faced difficulties in the Upper House.

The LDP's slim majority in the Upper House would prove to be a formidable institutional constraint facing Miki. Following the 1974 Upper House election with Tanaka's ill-fated corporate-sponsored candidate scheme, the LDP only held 129 of the 252 seats in the Upper House. In the face of a united opposition, strict party discipline with minimal abstentions was the only way that the LDP could see its policy agenda passed in the Upper House. While the LDP was able to get some opposition support for the revisions to the Public Office Election Law, it faced staunch opposition to the proposed revisions to the Political Funds Control Law.[8] Members of the LDP were also reluctant supporters of the proposed revisions.

The controversy over the revision of the Political Funds Control Law centered around whether to place a ban or an upper limit on political contributions. When Miki came to office he stated his desire to ban corporate contributions in three years. He was forced to back away from this position, however, in order to get the support of his own party. The LDP relied heavily on corporate contributions and favored placing upper limits on the amount of contributions to a complete ban. The opposition parties that relied to a much smaller extent on corporate contributions only supported a complete ban on corporate contributions. These parties did not see any advantages to simply placing an upper limit on contributions.

Again while the revisions passed the Lower House where the LDP was stronger, the bill met staunch opposition in the Upper House. In fact, the vote was evenly split (117–117) in the Upper House with several abstentions. As a result, it was up to the Speaker Kōno Kenzō to break the tie.[9] He voted for the revisions and the bill passed.[10] With this, Miki realized two components of his reform agenda.[11]

The passage of the revisions to the Political Funds Control Law and the Public Office Election Law was an important achievement for the Miki cabinet. Securing the passage of these bills was not easy. When reflecting on the passage of this bill, the speaker of the Upper House at this time, Kōno Kenzō, points to three obstacles that stood in the Miki administration's way of realizing its policy agenda. These obstacles include the Miki administration's lack of experience in Diet management, a strong anti-Miki sentiment within the LDP, and resistance from the opposition parties (Kōno 1978: 72).

Miki's resources

The fact that Miki was a senior LDP politician with connections within and outside his party played an important role in his ability to overcome these obstacles in the case of political funding reform. Indeed, Miki's senior status afforded him several resources. Two of Miki's most critical resources were access to the internal LDP policy-making process and connections with opposition party leaders. Once Miki became prime minister he had access to even more resources, including media attention and the force of public opinion.

Access to the internal policy-making process in the LDP is a resource only available to the most senior politicians. There are several different forums within the LDP in which policy making takes place. The more formal bodies include the Policy Affairs Research Council and the Executive Council (*komon*).[12] More informal deals, however, often occur among the major power brokers in the party behind the scenes. These power brokers include faction heads and their protégés.

Miki had access to the internal policy-making process through various avenues during his career. To begin with, he was the head of a small, anti-mainstream faction. Despite its small size and outlier position, though, the faction did have a voice within the LDP. Miki also held a variety of cabinet positions during his career. He served as, among other things, minister of international trade and industry, foreign minister, LDP vice-president, LDP secretary general, and chairman of the Policy Affairs Research Council (PARC) (Masumi 1995: 166). These positions not only gave him access to the policy-making process but also allowed him to build connections within and outside the LDP.

The Miki faction's relatively weak position in the LDP provided Miki incentives to cultivate ties with the opposition parties. In many ways, the policy positions of the Miki faction were closer to that of the opposition parties.[13] Miki often aligned his faction with the opposition in an attempt to pressure the LDP to pass certain unpopular policies. This tactic is one of the few strategies available to members of smaller factions in the LDP who want to realize their political agenda (Masumi 1995: 168).

Miki's connections to the opposition helped in his bid for the prime ministership after Tanaka's resignation. Miki added to the tension brewing within the party by threatening to boycott a party election if one was held. He even opened discussions with the vice-chairperson of the DSP, Sasaki Ryōsaku, to explore the possibility of a conservative–progressive coalition among the JSP, Kōmeitō, DSP and a break-away Miki faction (Masumi 1995: 159). Although it is not clear how serious Miki was about breaking away, in the end, the party chose not to hold an open party election. Instead, it placed the decision in Shiina Etsusaburō's hands. Shiina chose Miki due to his clean image and because choosing between the other two main contenders, Ōhira and Fukuda, had the potential of leading to a party split (Johnson 1976: 31). Miki's connections to the opposition made his threat of leaving the party credible and allowed him to manipulate the situation in a way that increased his own chances of becoming prime minister.

Once he became prime minister Miki used the increased media attention and public support to push through reform. Miki's strategy was to get LDP support by using the pressure of public opinion, not the pressure of opposition support. A former member of the Miki faction highlighted the significance of Miki's resource of public support, explaining "Miki wasn't popular in the party, but he was popular with the public. The public put their faith in him" (personal interview with Itō Soichirō, 1 March 2001). As illustrated in Figure 2.1, Miki's cabinet support ratings were quite high when he entered the prime ministership, with 45 percent of the respondents indicating their support of the Miki cabinet when he came to office in December 1974. While this figure would decline approximately ten percentage points six months after his inauguration, it would stabilize at around 34 percent until the outbreak of the Lockheed scandal in February 1976 (Sorifu 1975, 1976, 1977). The level of support Miki had during the first six months he was in office was quite high in comparison to the 12 percent support rating of the Tanaka cabinet just prior to its dissolution (Masumi 1995: 153). Miki was able to use this public support to gain support within the party.

The content of his proposed bill illustrates that Miki was targeting LDP support. The bill was designed to placate the internal demands within the LDP, not the priorities of the opposition. Miki created an upper limit on contributions instead of instituting a complete ban, the preference of the

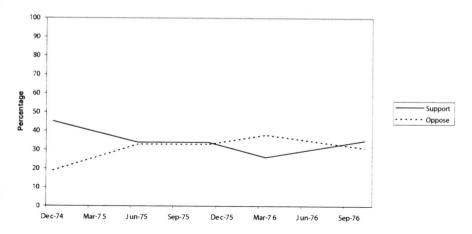

Figure 2.1 Prime Minister Miki's cabinet support ratings. This graph only shows the percentage of respondents who answered that they supported or opposed the Miki cabinet. Two other responses were available – "other" or "no answer."

Source: Data compiled from *Asahi Shinbun* cabinet support ratings reported in Sorifu Naikaku Sori Daijin Kanbo Kohoshitsu (1975, 1976, 1977) *Seron Chōsa Nenkan, 1975, 1976, 1977* (Public Opinion Research Yearbook, 1975, 1976, 1977), Tokyo: Ōkurashō Insatsukyoku.

opposition. He also included provisions on the distribution of handbills that angered the opposition but satisfied members of the LDP.

Miki used his position as prime minister to keep the focus on reform. He pointed to political funding reform as one of his three major goals in his inaugural speech. He came to office with a proposal for revisions to the Public Office Election Law and the Political Funds Control Law. Unlike other prime ministers, Miki avoided the normal party policy channels and proposed the bill directly to the Diet. His quick action allowed him to use the lingering public outrage over the circumstances that led to former Prime Minister Tanaka's resignation to pressure other members of the LDP to support reform measures.

Unlike other successful reformers such as Ozawa Ichirō in 1994, Miki did not have a strong support base in the LDP. Miki was the head of a small faction. He was appointed prime minister due to the circumstances surrounding Tanaka's resignation, not because he had a large number of followers inside the LDP. As discussed in Chapter 5, in Ozawa's case his patron–client ties proved important because he chose to leave the LDP and needed to create a new party outside the LDP. Patron–client ties are less important in Miki's case because he tried to realize change from within the party.

Although resources are necessary in a leader's pursuit of reform, they are not sufficient. Miki's resources helped him get to power. The prime ministership can be an important position because it allows a politician to bring attention to his own agenda (Shinoda 2000: 206–8). It does not guarantee the passage of reform. A leader's approach to reform is also important. Miki's willingness to put his already weak position as prime minister in jeopardy by proposing the controversial revisions to the Political Funds Control Law was an important factor in passing reform. His vision and commitment provided him with the ability to formulate the proposal and then to sell it to the public and his fellow politicians.

Miki as a risk-taker

A look at Miki's political career reveals a propensity to take risks that extends beyond the case of political reform in 1975. One example of Miki's risk-taking behavior is his multiple resignations from the cabinet. In the "1955 system" of LDP dominance, the LDP distributed cabinet seats among factions in order to maintain party harmony (Kohno 1992). Thus, even though Miki was the member of a small faction, the faction often received at least one post. Miki, however, resigned from cabinet posts three times during his career to publicly display his dissatisfaction with three different administrations. Each time Miki's goal was to draw attention to an issue where he disagreed with the mainstream LDP position. For example, Miki resigned as Director of the Economic Planning Agency in Prime Minister Kishi's cabinet to oppose the revisions to the Police Duties Law supported by the Kishi government in December 1958.[14] Miki resigned as Foreign Minister in October 1968 in objection to Prime Minister Satō Eisaku's position on the return of Okinawa. Miki went on to run against Prime Minister Satō in the LDP presidential election that followed. Finally, as mentioned earlier, Miki resigned from Prime Minister Tanaka's cabinet in 1974 due to his outrage over Tanaka's campaign strategy in the preceding Upper House election (Shinoda 2000: 62–63).

Although Miki frequently employed this strategy of resigning from the cabinet to draw attention to issues important to him, this strategy is not a common one within the LDP. Each time, the LDP could have retaliated by closing the Miki faction out of the next administration or by permanently limiting the faction's voice in the party. On a more personal level, Miki risked harming his own future within the party by resigning from cabinet posts. Even if the LDP chose not to punish the entire Miki faction by denying it cabinet positions, the party leadership could have punished Miki for his acts of defiance. Miki risked not being appointed to cabinet posts in the future. The fact that Miki received posts after his first resignation should not discount the resignations that followed. Miki was taking a risk each time he left the cabinet.

Miki also took risks in his bid to make the selection of the LDP president open to all party members. In order to emphasize the importance of granting public participation in the selection process, the first time he ran for party president Miki actually announced his intention to run in the party presidential election directly to the public. Announcing one's candidacy directly to the public was unprecedented and produced some strong reactions within the party. Many fellow LDP members labeled Miki "a strange bird," noting that he did unconventional things. When a fellow faction member reported these labels to Miki, Miki was not fazed by this and responded, "We must work with the people" (Kujiraoka 1993: 8). Miki had a different philosophy of how politics should function, and he was not afraid to challenge the constraints in place to move in the direction of change. Here, he was challenging the LDP's selection method, which was carried out behind closed doors. By making his desire to run for the top position in the party public, Miki was trying to make it more difficult for the kingmakers within the party to control the process. By defying the party leaders, however, Miki risked being further marginalized.

As prime minister, Miki took risks in the policies he pursued in addition to political reform. For example, his pursuit of revisions to the anti-monopoly law were unpopular with big business and thus were quite controversial within the LDP since it received considerable monetary support from this sector of the economy. Realizing that obtaining internal party support would be difficult, Miki looked outside the LDP and secured a deal with the opposition parties. This move outraged the mainstream, conservative forces within the LDP because these members felt obligated to honor the unauthorized deal between the LDP and the opposition orchestrated by Miki. As a result of Miki's negotiations with the opposition, the bill passed the Lower House; however, it was shelved in the Upper House (Masumi 1995: 168–71). Using the opposition to pressure the mainstream factions in the LDP to support the bill was a risky strategy because members of the mainstream had made Miki prime minister. Ignoring the position of his patrons placed his position as prime minister in jeopardy. These leaders had placed him in office and felt that they could easily remove him from office as well. Pursuing anti-LDP policies was certainly one way to provoke such a reaction.

Pursuing his controversial reform agenda once he had been made prime minister was risky in and of itself, especially given Miki's relatively weak support base in the party. Revising the Political Funds Control Law was one of Miki's top priorities. Tanaka had been forced to resign due to his questionable real-estate and construction deals. Miki was chosen to be party president because of his clean image. Many politicians, however, hoped that his clean image alone would be enough to repair the party's fallen image with the public. Former prime minister Kaifu, a member of the Miki faction at the time explained, "[a large number] of politicians were against revising the Political Funds Control Law. The main complaint from politicians inside the LDP was that 'you can't have politics without money'" (personal interview, 12 March 2001). Changing the Political Funds Control Law would impose costs on most politicians because they would be forced to adjust their campaigning. By pursuing a policy so unpopular, Miki risked his very position as prime minister. Many party members were not pleased with Shiina's choice of Miki. These members were looking for any reason to cast a poor light on Miki. Although revising the Political Funds Control Law was popular with the public, politicians who were opposed to reform tried to stir up opposition against him within the party.

One of the first of several attempts to throw Miki from office began shortly after the passage of the revisions to the Political Funds Control Law when the Lockheed bribery scandal broke. This scandal was much larger than the Tanaka scandal that had been exposed in the *Bungei Shunjū* article. In fact, this scandal opened another window of opportunity for reform, insuring that money politics remained salient even after the Miki government's initial passage of revisions to the Political Funds Control Law.[15] The scandal broke at a US Senate Subcommittee hearing. The hearing provided strong evidence that the Lockheed aircraft company bribed several senior Japanese business and government officials, including former Prime Minister Tanaka, to assert their influence on All Nippon Airways (ANA), a Japanese airline company, and Japan's Maritime Self-Defense Force to buy Lockheed's Tristar wide-body passenger jets and anti-submarine warfare aircraft, respectively (Allen 1991a; MacDougall 1988). These revelations in the United States led to the full-scale outbreak of yet another money politics scandal in Japan.

Miki's first risk in connection with the Lockheed investigation came when he declared that the government would pursue full disclosure in its investigation of this incident. The goal of the risks that Miki took in connection with the Lockheed scandal was to keep money politics salient, thereby keeping Miki's larger vision of reform on the agenda. Since many high-ranking LDP officials were implicated in the scandal, however, Miki's pursuit of a full investigation of the scandal outraged many of the top LDP elite, especially LDP vice-president Shiina Etsusaburō. In his attempt to kick Miki out, Shiina went as far as to publicly call for Miki's resignation. Miki stood his ground and responded by maintaining that he intended to see the Lockheed investigation through to the end. The press spun the incident in Miki's favor, interpreting Shiina's call for Miki's ouster as an attempt by the LDP to cover up the Lockheed scandal (Masumi 1995: 181). Indeed, Shiina's attempt to throw him from office backfired. Instead of resulting in Miki's removal from office, the campaign led to almost a 10 percent increase in his cabinet support ratings (Sorifu 1976).

Former prime minister Kaifu points out that the motivation for kicking Miki out of office went beyond the Lockheed investigation, explaining that there was a feeling inside the LDP "that it was dangerous to keep Miki in office because he might keep going in the direction like political funds" (personal interview, 12 March 2001). This fear was justified on the part of the politicians. Miki saw the passage of the revisions to the Political Funds Control Law as the first step towards cleaning up Japanese politics. The next step was to change the electoral system. Miki's initial electoral system reform proposal failed, but according to Kaifu he had not given up hope (personal interview, 12 March 2001).

The risk that proved fatal in his pursuit of the Lockheed investigation and his quest to keep reform salient was when he chose not to interfere with the indictment of former Prime Minister Tanaka. Although a precedent existed from the shipbuilding scandals of the 1950s when Prime Minister Yoshida used his influence over the prosecutor's office to prevent the arrest of the LDP secretary general Satō Eisaku, Miki chose not to intervene in Tanaka's arrest (Curtis 1988: 161). This action was a strategic, albeit risky, move by Prime Minister Miki. Tanaka was a glaring reminder of the excesses of money politics. By siding with public demands to see him brought to justice, Miki was able to increase the support for other reforms he was pushing at the time, including a party primary.

Miki's refusal to pardon Tanaka sparked another "oust Miki" movement within the LDP. This campaign was successful largely because the leaders were able to avoid being accused of a Lockheed cover up due to Tanaka's arrest (Masumi 1995: 182). Thus, this time Miki's risk of pursuing the Lockheed investigation did not pay off. He was forced to resign at the end of the Diet session in December 1976. Miki was a leader who took risks in order to pursue reform; however, as this example illustrates taking the risk alone does not guarantee policy success.[16]

Miki was quite willing to take chances in order to follow his vision and pursue his policy preferences. His risk-taking behavior during the reform process was crucial to his success. His threat to leave the party and join forces with the opposition actually resulted in his selection as the next prime minister. From this position he was able to secure the passage of the revisions to the Political Funds Control Law.[17] As prime minister, he did not shrink away from policies that ran counter to the mainstream LDP's preferences. Instead, he used his position as prime minister to pursue controversial policies that challenged the mainstream factions in the LDP. Miki had spent his entire career emphasizing the need to clean up politics. He continued to pursue reform even after he got his initial revisions to the political funding regime passed. He did not shy away from the Lockheed scandal because it involved the LDP elite. Instead, he used it as an example to push his agenda for cleaning up the political world. His push resulted in the indictment of former prime minister Tanaka.

Miki's vision

Miki's vision for reforming the Japanese political system had several different facets and evolved over the course of his political career. He had radical views about party reform, as well as political system reform, including the abolition of factions, banning corporate contributions and strengthening political ethics regulations. All of his proposals reflected his desire to clean up the political system and to restore public trust in government. Miki ardently fought to see party modernization, pushing particularly hard for the abolition of factions and the election of a party president by all party members. To clean up the political world, Miki ideally was striving for elections that do not cost money. He also wanted to reduce the influence money had on elections by banning corporate contributions. Finally, the outbreak of political scandals throughout his career, culminating with the unprecedented Lockheed scandal during his tenure as prime minister, motivated him to push for stronger political ethics regulations (Kujiraoka 1993; Kunihiro 2005; Mainichi Shinbunsha Seijibu 1975; Masuda 1976; M. Miki 1989; T. Miki 1984; Nakamura 1981).

Miki's first political action on his vision of reform came during the Ikeda administration in October 1963. Here, his goal was party reform, more specifically party modernization. He and Prime Minister Ikeda had similar views on the need for reforming the Japanese party system. In the 1960s the LDP was in its infancy and Ikeda, pointing to the problems with money and factions, reportedly warned Miki, "Politics will collapse if something is not done soon" (Kujiraoka 1993: 6). At this time Miki was active in the Party Modernization Investigative Committee. This committee submitted a report during the Ikeda administration calling for, among other things, the abolition of factions. Miki is reported as having assessed the proposal in the following way: "This proposal is not sufficient. There is still plenty left to think about. This time the thing that I think we have to implement is the abolition of factions" (Kujiraoka 1993: 6). Miki saw the abolition of factions as one of many steps necessary for realizing his vision of a cleaner political world that the public could have faith in.[18]

Putting politics in the hands of the people was one way that Miki felt public trust could be restored. In this regard, Miki pushed to make the party presidential elections open to all party members. He sought to increase politicians' accountability with the public. Involving party members in the selection of the party president was one way to do this.

Miki's vision as well as his career-long fight to see it implemented was largely responsible for making him an appealing candidate for prime minister. During less turbulent times when the political world was not being rocked by scandal, Miki and his controversial agenda for cleaning up the political world were easily and happily overlooked. When the LDP was fraught with scandal, however, a clean politician seemed like the perfect way to put a new face on the party.

Miki saw his stint as prime minister as an opportunity to realize various aspects of his vision. According to former prime minister Kaifu, who was deputy chief cabinet minister in the Miki administration, the Miki government had two goals: (1) regain the people's trust and (2) clean up money politics (personal interview, 12 March 2001).[19] These goals were completely consistent with his vision of political reform and the policies Miki had pursued throughout his career. These goals also were not abstract ones. Miki had concrete proposals for reform to back up these goals. Miki came to office with proposals already prepared, something that many politicians found quite surprising because it is uncommon for a politician to present his own bills (personal interview with Kaifu Toshiki, 12 March 2001).

Miki's vision distinguishes him from other prime ministers. In an interview in the *Tokyo Shinbun*, Kaifu contrasts Miki and then sitting prime minister Mori. In Kaifu's opinion, the main difference between Miki and Mori is that Miki had an ideal and fought to see it realized (Nishikawa 2001: 2). Politicians often evoke Miki and his pursuit of his ideals during political reform discussions. Miki's vision for a cleaner political system still resonates with Diet members as well as the public (Kujiraoka 1993: 22). Former Prime Minister Kaifu still links himself and his reform agenda to Miki and what he stood for by wearing a polka-dotted tie, Miki's personal fashion statement.

Miki's vision remains alive even after his death. The strength of this vision certainly helped him gain public support for reform during his stint as prime minister. This support in turn helped him pressure the LDP to pass revisions to the political funding regulations.

Miki's commitment

Miki's actions illustrated his commitment to his beliefs. Commitment is reflected in a politician's persistent pursuit of his vision and his willingness to pay a price to see this vision realized. By these standards, Miki's commitment to cleaning up the political world was strong. He began pursuing his ideals early in his career and fought for these ideals with little regard of the negative consequences to him personally.

Throughout his career Miki served on committees that focused on the problem of money politics and the need to reform. As we have seen, he also wrote many of his own personal proposals for several different kinds of reform, including bills on political funding, political ethics, and anti-corruption. He pushed for these proposals before, during, and after he became prime minister.

Miki actively worked to see different kinds of reform implemented. He served on Ikeda's Party Modernization Investigative Committee. He tried to change the selection of the party president by publicly announcing his candidacy. He wrote four versions of his political anti-corruption bill and continued to push for the passage of his revised package after he resigned from office. He submitted one proposal to the Executive Council (*komon*) inside the LDP during the Ōhira administration in 1979. He then submitted a revised version of this plan in 1985. Shortly thereafter he became sick and was hospitalized. His hospitalization did not deter him from pursuing his vision. He ran and was elected to his nineteenth term in office from a hospital bed (Kujiraoka 1993: 18–19).

Miki not only persistently pursued reform. He also made personal sacrifices to conduct politics in a manner consistent with his vision. Itō Soichirō, a senior member of the Lower House and former member of the Miki faction, characterized Miki's leadership as *seiketsu* (clean/pure). According to Itō, Miki once sold a second home in Karuizawa in order to raise funds for his faction. He was committed to doing things the legal and clean way (personal interview, 1 March 2001). Miki was willing to make personal sacrifices in order to do politics his way.

Miki's high level of commitment to reform aided him in his pursuit to see the passage of the first major revisions to the Political Funds Control Law during the postwar era. Miki made these controversial revisions the center-piece of his policy agenda. Once Miki became prime minister, two of the first three bills he proposed were directly tied to his career-long crusade to clean up the political world. These bills were the revisions to the Political Funds Control Law and the anti-corruption additions to the Public Office Election Law. These bills were highly unpopular both within the LDP and with the opposition. Miki, however, saw his appointment as prime minister as an opportunity to pursue reform from a highly visible position. Miki did not follow the lead of the stronger factions that had placed him in power. He, instead, acted in a way consistent with his beliefs when he assumed the position of party president. He got these controversial reform measures passed in large part because he was able to mobilize the public's frustration over the circumstances that led to the resignation of Tanaka. This success did not come without its costs. Miki's pursuit of reform scared many politicians and led them to organize the first oust-Miki campaign. Miki was not thrown from office, but his already weak position became even weaker. These circumstances did not weaken his commitment to reform.

Miki's pursuit of the Lockheed scandal during his tenure as prime minister illustrates his persistence and his continued willingness to pay a potentially large cost to see further elements of his vision of a cleaner political system realized. When criticized for his pursuit of Tanaka's arrest and trial Miki responded, "I have to get this through. I must do so even if it leads to my death" (Shinoda 2000: 100–101). While taking an active approach to a thorough investigation of the scandal did not literally lead to Miki's death, figuratively speaking it brought on a campaign to see Miki removed from office.

Miki tenaciously fought to realize various kinds of political reform through-out his career. The goal of these reforms was to clean up the political world and restore the public's trust in politics. Many of the measures he pushed did not pass, including the public management of elections, the strengthening of the *renza-sei* (accomplice regulations) and punishments for violations of the election law, increasing the swiftness of court action and the abolition of factions. But, many significant reforms did pass over the course of his career, including the revisions to the political funding regulations, the ban on every-day contributions from constituents, and the changes made to the LDP's party presidential election. The one thing that did not vary over the course of his career was his continued pursuit of his goals, regardless of the barriers that stood in his way.

The role of scandal in the 1970s

An alternative explanation for reform suggests that politicians are more likely to pass reform in the wake of more severe scandals. Three scandals are relevant in the investigation of reform in the 1970s. These scandals include the 1974 Upper House election incident, the Tanaka real-estate scandal and the Lockheed scandal. The Lockheed scandal clearly was the most severe scandal of the three measured in terms of the number of politicians arrested or implicated in the corrupt activity. As discussed earlier, the 1974 Upper House election incident centered on Prime Minister Tanaka's attempt to encourage corporations to sponsor specific candidates. The main repercussions in this case came in form of the LDP's poor performance at the polls during this election. The allegations in the Tanaka real-estate scandal also were limited to Prime Minister Tanaka. He was not arrested for the alleged misdeeds in this case; however, he was forced to resign from office due to the negative repercussions following the article that appeared in *Bungei Shunjū*.

In contrast, the Lockheed scandal was much broader in scope. This scandal broke at a hearing of the US Senate Subcommittee on Multinational Corporations. As we saw earlier in this chapter, at this hearing Lockheed officials revealed that their company had bribed several senior Japanese business and government officials to assert their influence on the domestic carrier All Nippon Airways (ANA) and Japan's Maritime Self-Defense Force to purchase Lockheed's products (Allen 1991a: 154; Calder 1988: 111; Johnson 1986: 13–14). Specifically, A.C. Kotchian, the vice-chairman of Lockheed, implicated eight Japanese politicians in his Senate testimony (Johnson 1986: 15). The most prominent figure was former Prime Minister Tanaka Kakuei. He was accused of accepting a total of 500 million yen in bribes in return for encouraging both ANA and the Defense Agency to buy Lockheed aircraft during his tenure as prime minister (Allen 1991a: 154). In addition to the former prime minister, Hashimoto Tomisaburō, former LDP secretary general and former minister of transportation, and Satō Takayuki, former parliamentary vice-minister of transportation, were deeply implicated in the scandal. Tanaka, Hashimoto, and Satō were indicted and later found guilty of accepting bribes and sentenced four, two and one-half, and two years in prison respectively (Allen 1991a: 156–57). The other politicians implicated in the Lockheed case avoided indictment. These politicians were referred to as "gray officials" because they were seen as having committed moral as opposed to criminal violations. Although a committee in charge of part of the Lockheed investigation reportedly composed a listed of 14 "gray officials," they only released five names (Asahi Shinbunsha 1977: 267).[20]

The Lockheed scandal was not limited to the political realm. Three other actors played a role in the incident – the Marubeni Trading Company, All Nippon Airways, and Kodama Yoshio, a political fixer with ties to the underworld. Three agents from Marubeni were convicted of bribery and violations of the Foreign Exchange Control Law as the trading company acted as a go-between for Lockheed and the political officials. ANA chairman Wakasa Tokuji and five other ANA employees were indicted and convicted for accepting bribes; however, all their sentences were suspended (Allen 1991a: 157). Finally, although Kodama Yoshio was suspected of securing the deals on Lockheed's behalf, the evidence against him was weak. Due to this fact, the prosecutor only charged him with tax evasion and violations of the Foreign Exchange Control Act. In the end, he was convicted on the charges of tax evasion and received a three and one-half year prison sentence and a 700 million yen fine (Allen 1991a: 159).

Clearly, the Lockheed scandal was a more severe scandal than the 1974 Upper House election incident and the Tanaka real-estate scandal in terms of the number and status of politicians implicated and/or arrested in relation to the incident. Revisions to the Political Funds Control Law, however, occurred prior to the outbreak of the Lockheed scandal. This fact illustrates that the severity of the scandal does not determine the passage of reform. If this were the case we would expect reform to pass following Lockheed, not before it. The difference, as we have seen above, was not related to the severity of the scandal that opened the window of opportunity; it rests in Miki's leadership, specifically his willingness to take risks, vision, and commitment.

Conclusion

Miki is a case of a successful reformer. His success is related to both the environment in which he came to office and the resources and personal attributes he brought to bear on the policy-making process. Table 2.1 summarizes each of these factors. The financial scandal that forced Tanaka to resign from office opened the window of opportunity for reform; however, it did not guarantee the subsequent passage of reform. A scandal is a necessary but insufficient condition for the passage of political reform. In this case the real-estate scandal only involved one high-level politician, Prime Minister Tanaka, making it much less severe than the Lockheed scandal which followed. The severity of the scandal was not key in the passage of reform; leadership was. Moreover, the case of Miki illustrates that the length of the window of opportunity does not have to be particularly long. In fact, Miki's success lends credence to Kingdon's assertion that leaders are more likely to be successful if they have a proposal ready and are able to act quickly once a window opens. Ultimate success depends on the presence of a leader with certain resources and personal attributes to capitalize on the open window.

Miki Takeo was such a leader. The resources Miki accumulated over the course of his career helped him secure the position of prime minister. The fact that Miki was a senior faction head placed him in the running for the prime ministership. His vision, however, distinguished him from the other potential candidates. He had pursued political reform throughout his political career and long advocated radically changing the system that fostered

Table 2.1 A summary of Prime Minister Miki's reform attempt

Overall length of the window of opportunity	9 months (October 1974 to July 1975)
Length of the window of opportunity while the leader is in government	7 months (December 1974 to July 1975)
Magnitude of the scandal that opens the window	Medium
Level of resources	High
Risk-taking	High
Vision	High
Commitment	High
Outcome	Revisions to the Political Funds Control Law

money politics. These views made him an appealing candidate to the more powerful leaders in the LDP who were trying to control the damage the party had incurred from the Tanaka scandal. The party leaders who helped place Miki in office, however, did not count on Miki actually realizing his reform agenda. These politicians hoped that Miki's symbolic placement in the prime ministership would in and of itself be sufficient. Miki's willingness to take risks and his commitment to see his vision realized aided him in his quest to pass reform.

Miki frequently challenged the constraints in place. This strategy was the only one available to him as the head of a small anti-mainstream faction. This strategy proved effective in the pursuit of political reform. He was not deterred by the fact that his more powerful patrons preferred symbolic reform, if any at all. He simply increased the pressure on them to pass concrete reform by using the media and mobilizing voter support (Ōtake 1996: 290). Miki came to office with a reform proposal and quickly got it on the agenda before the public's outrage over money politics had waned. Under these circumstances politicians found it difficult to oppose reform as they risked a backlash at the polls.

Miki did not do things the conventional way. One of the main ways that Miki challenged the constraints in place was by refusing to seek consensus (*nemawashi*). According to an assistant, "Mr. Miki was neither good at *nemawashi*, nor fond of doing it" (Shinoda 2000: 92).[21] One hypothesis is that creating a sense of urgency might be one way of getting around the need to build consensus. Miki was able to create this sense of urgency after the Tanaka real-estate scandal. Acting quickly after this scandal made reform salient, enabling him to gain support for political funding reform.[22] In short, Miki's willingness to take risks, his vision, and his commitment all helped him capitalize on the window of opportunity opened by the Tanaka scandal and secure the passage of reform.

3 Kaifu Toshiki
Mr. Clean plays it safe

The case of Prime Minister Miki in Chapter 2 illustrates the importance of individual agency in the passage of reform. However, skeptics might not be convinced. An alternative explanation would be that the public was outraged by the circumstances that led to Tanaka's resignation. Unable to ignore this pressure, politicians passed reform. In this explanation, the argument is: leader or no leader, politicians pass reform following scandals. This argument, however, does not hold up next to the evidence when all electoral system and political funding reform attempts in postwar Japan are considered. One example of scandal failing to lead to political reform is the Recruit Cosmos scandal, a large stocks-for-favors scandal in the late 1980s. The following discussion reveals that reform was not realized during this period because the prime minister in office when the Recruit scandal broke, Takeshita Noboru, did not have the desire to implement reform, and his successor, Kaifu Toshiki, did not take any significant risks to push reform through the Diet. The Recruit scandal and the actions of Kaifu Toshiki represent a case of a leader's unsuccessful pursuit of reform. Scandal alone is not enough to secure the passage of reform. A leader is required to take advantage of the conditions created by the scandal.

Takeshita's symbolic response to scandal

A window of opportunity for reform

The Recruit scandal erupted in June 1988. This scandal involved executives of the Recruit Group, an up-and-coming conglomerate involved in various areas including real-estate and job placement, who were accused of engaging in extensive stocks-for-favors deals with prominent politicians from almost every political party, bureaucrats, and members of the business community. Most of the questionable activities involved Recruit executives distributing shares of a Recruit subsidiary, the Recruit Cosmos Company, to various officials before the stock was floated on the stock market (Kearns 1990; Yayama 1990). When the stock was floated, the recipients made a substantial profit. Recruit's goal in distributing these pre-floatation stocks was to increase its access and influence in the political arena (Kearns 1990: 64). It is technically legal for politicians to receive stock tips or pre-floatation shares of a stock at a reduced rate, but the amount of the donation must conform to the limits on contributions (Kearns 1990: 64; Curtis 1999: 76). Using stocks instead of money as contributions, however, made the transactions easier to trace, aiding the media's ability to uncover the scope of the company's activities as well as pinpoint the politicians potentially involved in the suspected stocks-for-favors deals.

The number of high-ranking officials implicated in the scandal ranks it as one of the largest scandals in Japan's history. Sixteen people were indicted and 43 business people, journalists, bureaucrats, and politicians, including Prime Minister Takeshita Noboru, were ultimately forced to resign due to their alleged involvement in this scandal.[1] Many more politicians received shares from Recruit and suffered from a veil of suspicion that surrounded their association with this company. Still, the majority of the legal repercussions fell in the private sector. Only two Diet members along with two bureaucrats, the former vice-ministers of education and labor, were arrested on charges of bribery (Allen 1991b: 164).[2] While few politicians were indicted, many prominent politicians were implicated, including the former prime minister, Nakasone Yasuhiro, the sitting prime minister, Takeshita Noboru, and future prime minister, Miyazawa Kiichi.

The Recruit scandal exposed several weaknesses in the political funding regulatory regime. First, it illustrated the problem of determining what constitutes a contribution. The implicated politicians were given stocks, not money. Whether stocks were monetary contributions was a contested notion, at least among politicians.[3] Secondly, it exposed a loophole in the reporting requirements outlined in the Political Funds Control Law. Politicians avoided reporting the contributions from Recruit to the Home Ministry by dividing the contributions among the various political groups associated with them, exploiting the fact that while the law limited the amount that could be given to a single political group, it did not limit the total number of groups a politician could have. Finally, the handling of the Recruit scandal called the punishment provisions into question, as many politicians implicated in the scandal avoided prosecution by letting their administrative assistants take the fall for them (Hirose 1989: 74–77).

By November 1988, the Recruit scandal had opened a window of opportunity for reform.[4] This window would remain open for 15 months, only closing with the LDP's ability to maintain its majority in the February 1990 Lower House election. The Recruit scandal played a key role in opening the window of opportunity. As the scope and scale of the scandal unfolded over a year and a half, the salience of reform increased and government support declined. The continuous stream of revelations of involvement made the Recruit scandal difficult to sweep under the carpet and contributed to its prolonged salience. The involvement of the former vice-minister of labor was revealed in late October 1988, and the revelation of misconduct by the former vice-minister of education followed shortly thereafter. In December 1988, Prime Minister Takeshita inaugurated his "Clean Politics Cabinet" only to see two members forced to resign within a month due to their involvement with Recruit.[5] In January 1989, the Speaker of the Lower House, Hara Kensaburō, announced that he too had received contributions from Recruit (Minkan Seiji Rincho 1993: 233). Then, the first major opposition party member, the chairman of the Democratic Socialist Party (DSP), Tsukamoto Saburō, resigned in February 1989 simply because he received legal donations from Recruit. The resignation of Tsukamoto illustrates how intense the negative stigma of accepting any money from Recruit had become. In March 1989, Recruit was accused of distributing 39 million yen in hush money to several high-ranking officials when the investigation began in an attempt to prevent the full extent of their activities from coming to the surface. On 25 April 1989 Prime Minister Takeshita resigned after the fact that he had received large contributions from Recruit was revealed. Then, after months of refusing to appear before the Diet Investigative Committee, former Prime Minister Nakasone testified in May 1989 (Minkan Seiji Rincho 1993: 235).

In addition to this constant stream of revelations, Diet activity concerning reform also increased during this period, indicating the increased salience of reform. Following former Prime Minister Nakasone's testimony, the LDP submitted a general proposal to revise the Public Office Election and Political Funds Control Laws to the Diet. The Diet did not take any immediate action; however, the Electoral System Advisory Council reconvened for the first time in 17 years to explore the issue further.

A study group of young reformers calling themselves the Utopia Study Group also emerged and began a public campaign for reform. These members boldly publicized their true annual expenditures in an attempt to illustrate how costly a politician's life can be and to emphasize the need for reform. The activities of these politicians, further explored in Chapter 6, also increased the salience of reform.

While the salience of reform was high, government support began to decline following the outbreak of Recruit. The various support ratings and election results reflect this dwindling government support. As Figure 3.1 illustrates, Prime Minister Takeshita's cabinet support ratings began declining as the scope of the scandal became apparent. By November 1988 a window of opportunity for reform was clearly open with Prime Minister Takeshita's disapproval rating exceeding his approval rating for the first time since he entered office. At this point in time only 36.4 percent of respondents to a *Yomiuri Shinbun* survey expressed their support of the cabinet, while 43 percent opposed it (Sorifu 1989). Prime Minister Takeshita's support ratings continued to fall from this point, hitting an all time low of 3.8 percent prior to when he announced his intention to resign on 25 April 1989 (Sakamoto 1999: 74). Performance in local elections also reflected public disgust with politics as usual. The LDP suffered a considerable defeat to a Socialist in an Upper House by-election in Fukuoka in February 1989 ("Takeshita Hears

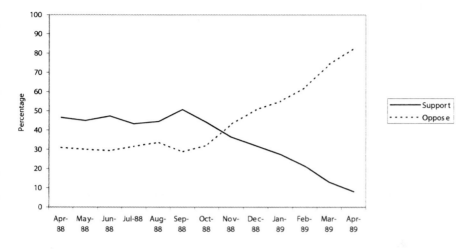

Figure 3.1 Prime Minister Takeshita's cabinet support ratings. This graph only shows the percentage of respondents who answered that they supported or opposed the Takeshita cabinet. Two other responses were available – "other" or "no answer."

Source: Data compiled from *Yomiuri Shinbun* cabinet support ratings reported in Sorifu Naikaku Sori Daijin Kanbo Kohoshitsu (1989, 1990) *Seron Chōsa Nenkan, 1989, 1990* (Public Opinion Research Yearbooks, 1989, 1990), Tokyo: Ōkurashō Insatsukyoku.

the Thud of the Axes": 29). This loss was followed by a poor performance in the March 1989 prefecture governor election in Chiba with the LDP candidate barely winning after previously holding a very secure seat ("Down on the Farm": 40). Dissention within the LDP was also on the rise. In March 1989, members of the LDP called for Takeshita's resignation at the Tokyo General Assembly (Minkan Seiji Rincho 1993: 235).

Clearly, the Recruit scandal opened a window of opportunity for reform. As more and more politicians were implicated in stocks-for-favors deals with Recruit, the salience of political reform began increasing. Not unrelated, both the LDP's and its prime minister's support ratings began sinking. Ultimately, the LDP suffered a huge defeat in the July 1989 Upper House election, but even before this defeat the party was facing a legitimacy crisis. The defeat in the Upper House election only served to open the window for reform even wider. With the window of opportunity for reform open, the next ingredient needed for successful political reform was the presence of a leader with the resources and personal attributes to exploit the window.

Three actors had the position and/or desire to implement reform once Recruit opened the window of opportunity for reform: the sitting prime minister, Takeshita Noboru, his successor Kaifu Toshiki, and the Utopia Study Group, a group of junior politicians within the LDP who formed with the single purpose of realizing reform. This chapter explores how Takeshita and Kaifu responded to the opportunity for reform provided by the outbreak of the Recruit scandal. The actions of the Utopia Study Group will be discussed in Chapter 6, which explores how the lack of seniority can impede policy implementation in Japan.

Takeshita's failed leadership

Takeshita was prime minister when the Recruit scandal broke. Although Takeshita did pursue political reform to a certain extent, these actions were largely symbolic. The goal was to diffuse the scandal once it surfaced by appearing to take the problems exposed by Recruit seriously. Takeshita also had personal motivations for containing the repercussions from Recruit and sweeping it out of the public eye as quickly as possible since he was one of the many officials implicated in the scandal. Taking action on reform, or at least appearing to do so, was a strategy to redeem his reputation with the public.

Takeshita's first symbolic response to reform came five and a half months after Recruit surfaced and two and a half months after the first prominent national level politician was implicated, when he asked the chairman of the Electoral System Committee to investigate three aspects of reform – apportionment, political funding, and the electoral system. A bipartisan committee on political ethics was also established. Takeshita's plan was to set up a Committee on Political Reform in the LDP, reopen the Electoral System Advisory Council, which had been inactive for nearly 17 years, and consult intellectuals in a *kenji kaigi* (research group) (Iio 1999: 41).[6]

Takeshita's rhetoric reflected the fact that he was aware that the public expected politicians to take some action. For example, on 1 January 1989, Takeshita went as far as pronouncing 1989 the year of reform (Minkan Seiji Rincho 1993: 233). Declaring one's commitment to reform, even establishing investigative committees to explore the issues, does not mean that a politician is truly committed to realizing reform, though. In Japan, where scandals are quite common, these types of actions are ways to placate the public in the short-term until another issue emerges and overshadows the problems exposed by the scandal. In the case of Takeshita, despite his apparent action on reform, he was not truly committed to reform. He, himself, was deeply involved in the Recruit scandal and as head of the largest faction in the LDP had mastered the exploitation of the loopholes and ambiguities in the current law. Thus, he had incentives to close the window of opportunity for reform as quickly as possible. His actions were "symbolic" – meant to placate the public, not to change the system under which he had thrived (Edelman 1964; Mazur 1995)

In addition to establishing investigative committees and declaring 1989 the year of reform, Takeshita did take some modest legislative action regarding reform. Specifically, he submitted proposals to revise portions of the Public Office Election Law and the Political Funds Control Law. The proposed changes were marginal, increasing the restrictions on election posters and the types of contributions that can be made by personal support groups and candidates during the official election period, prohibiting such trivial things as the donations of flower wreaths and other types of condolence or congratulatory gifts (Iio 1999: 39–48). Even these minor proposals were not passed by the end of the session. Takeshita announced his intention to resign to take responsibility for the Recruit scandal prior to submitting the proposals to the Diet. The submission of the proposals was an attempt to placate the public; however, it is clear that these proposals had no chance of becoming law during the current session. The goal was to appear to be taking some action. These proposals were tabled and brought up for further debate and discussion in the next session.[7]

The LDP did pass a very general outline for reform that was supposed to serve as a basis for future discussion. Even though this outline was quite basic, it produced considerable debate in the party. The main areas where reform was suggested included (1) political ethics, (2) political funding (contribution limits and transparency), (3) electoral reform (reapportionment and electoral system), (4) Diet reform (increase the efficiency and comprehensibility of the advisory council system), (5) party reform (factions), and (6) decentralization of the national government to the localities. While the areas of reform were clear, the content of reform proposed in the outline was vague. For example, although the outline stressed the importance of implementing a single-member district (SMD) electoral system, it did not discuss the specifics of how to establish such a system. It also did not firmly commit to establishing a pure SMD system. Instead of proposing concrete legislation, the LDP submitted this outline as a guideline for future debate. Diet members decided to continue investigating various types of political reform in order to develop more specific plans for reform. For many members of the LDP these promises to act constituted postponing action with the intention of doing nothing in the future (Iio 1999: 39–48; Tanaka 1997: 18–32).

Takeshita did not completely ignore the scandal; however, he chose the weakest of three possible options. These options were (1) symbolically pursuing reform, (2) implementing cosmetic changes, or (3) passing political reform that overhauled the current laws regarding political funding and/or the electoral system. The symbolic pursuit of reform involves taking action on reform without the intention of implementing reform (Mazur 1995: 6). Such action can entail anything from establishing investigative committees, holding committee debates over potential proposals, and even placing proposals on the agenda. If proposals are made, however, they are not meant to be passed because they either will never be put up to a vote or they clearly are not capable of receiving majority support. Politicians frequently talk about reform; the passage of actual reform is much rarer.

The second option, the implementation of cosmetic reform, can be an extension of a symbolic response or an action in and of itself. Politicians might seek to make minor changes to the law or they may resort to these actions if the symbolic pursuit of reform does not work to close the window of opportunity for reform. Those who want to close the window of opportunity for reform prefer the first or second option.

In contrast, leaders who truly seek change push for the third option, the implementation of political reform. This option is the hardest and most unlikely outcome, for the reasons outlined in Chapter 1. Changing the rules of the game involves a high level of risk and uncertainty. A leader who advocates reform is needed to convince other politicians that political reform is the best course of action.

Takeshita chose the first option, the symbolic pursuit of political reform. He reconstituted the Electoral System Advisory Council and established LDP committees to pursue reform. However, the Advisory Council had not even met by the time Takeshita was forced to leave office. Immediately after he announced his intention to resign, Takeshita submitted two proposals to the Diet, one regarding revisions to the Public Office Election Law, the other regarding revisions to the Political Funds Control Law. Since he did this within a year of the outbreak of Recruit, one could argue that he acted quickly once a window of opportunity for political reform opened. However, as mentioned above, these proposals only contained minor revisions and did not address the problems exposed by the Recruit scandal.

Takeshita was not a leader seeking political reform. He simply happened to be in office when the Recruit scandal broke. He did not have a vision of reform. Nor was he committed to seeing reform passed. Instead, he was an old-style politician who supported maintaining the status quo. His goal was to diffuse the situation. He wanted to appear to be taking the problems exposed by Recruit seriously. He submitted his modest proposals just five days before the official close of the Diet investigation of Recruit and then left office ten days later due to his own implication in the scandal. The Diet session closed a month after submission with the proposals still on the table. This strategy did not involve risk-taking. Quite to the contrary, Takeshita went out of his way to minimize the consequences of any actions taken on reform.

The window of opportunity remains open

After Takeshita's resignation, the LDP adopted the same strategy as after the Tanaka scandal in 1974, choosing a politician with a clean image, Uno Sōsuke, to be prime minister. However, only a few days passed before Uno's image was dirtied with revelations of an extra-marital affair.[8] He resigned six weeks after his inauguration to take responsibility for the LDP's extremely weak performances in the Tokyo Assembly and Upper House elections in July 1989. Following the Upper House election, the LDP tried to choose another politician with a clean image, appointing Kaifu Toshiki, a member of the smallest faction known for being committed to reform, to lead the party until the storm over the Recruit and Uno scandals blew over. A change of administration can open a window of opportunity even wider. In this case, the change of administration did not involve a change in parties, but it did result in a more reform-minded politician taking the helm.

When Kaifu took office, reform was still salient due to the constant stream of revelations concerning the Recruit scandal. Takeshita had not been able to close the window. Instead, he was forced to resign to take responsibility for the scandal. Two politicians had been indicted, and several other politicians were suspected of receiving large sums from Recruit, but they were not charged due to lack of evidence. The public felt that the possible misconduct of these actors needed to be pursued further and that those guilty of wrongdoing should be punished (Curtis 1999: 75–76).

Public support was also waning when Kaifu took office. When Takeshita left office on 3 June 1989, his cabinet support ratings were abysmal, having sunk to 74 percent disapproval by the end of March 1989 (Minkan Seiji Rincho 1993: 235). The Uno sex scandal, although unrelated to political funding, only served to further the sense that the LDP was full of dirty politicians who could not be trusted. The public was clearly angry.

The results of the July 1989 Upper House election reflect this declining public support of the LDP. The LDP only won 36 of the 126 seats up for re-election where it previously had held 72 seats, causing it to lose the majority in the Upper House for the first time since 1955 (Sakamoto 1999: 74). After the election the LDP only held 109 of the 252 seats in the Upper House (Sakamoto 1999: 169, fn. 54). The LDP also experienced an overwhelming defeat in the July 1989 Tokyo Assembly election, reducing the number of seats it held from 63 to 43 seats. The JSP was the beneficiary of the LDP electoral losses in both the Upper House and Tokyo Assembly elections. After the 1989 elections, the JSP held 73 seats in the Upper House, constituting 29 percent of the total seats, and increased its seats in the Tokyo Assembly three-fold if the candidates it recommended but did not officially support are included (Masumi 1995: 434–35).

These electoral defeats were quite significant. To begin with, the election losses are indicators of declining LDP support. While the Recruit scandal initially opened a window of opportunity for reform, these election results ensured that the window remained open. In fact, one could argue that the poor showing by the LDP opened the window of opportunity for reform even wider by increasing the pressure on the LDP to act on reform. While opening the window of opportunity for reform even wider, though, the loss of the majority of the Upper House meant that the LDP was facing greater institutional constraints for the passage of legislation in general and political reform in particular. Without a majority in the Upper House, the LDP would be more constrained to give heed to the reform preferences of the opposition parties, since such legislation must be passed by both the Lower and Upper Houses of the Diet. The JSP in particular was in a position to exploit this added leverage given its overall strong performance in both elections, as well as the fact that it had outpolled the LDP in the PR portion of the Upper House vote. With the JSP doubling its seats in the 1989 Upper House elections and the seat share of the Kōmeitō, Democratic Socialist Party and the Japanese Communist Party decreasing, it appeared that the party system was leaning more towards a two-party system with the LDP and the JSP as the major contenders, something that caused great alarm within the LDP (Masumi 1995: 435).[9] With few options in the face of the declining public support reflected in these electoral outcomes, the LDP selected a reformer, Kaifu Toshiki, as prime minister.

Kaifu's attempt to realize reform

Kaifu was inaugurated prime minister on 8 August 1989. At this time a window of opportunity for political reform was open. The key for Kaifu was for him to act quickly before the salience of reform decreased and/or public support increased. When Kaifu came to office there was a constituency for reform. Many members in the LDP believed that if they did not do something, either cosmetic or substantive, then they would continue to feel the repercussions at the polls as was the case in the July 1989 Upper House election. This belief was strongest among younger Diet members whose seats were less secure (Ōtake 1996).

During his first year or so in office, Kaifu was in close consultation with the secretary general of the LDP, Ozawa Ichirō. Ozawa was a member of the largest faction in the LDP, the Takeshita faction. The Takeshita faction sponsored Kaifu's bid to become prime minister. Kaifu chose Ozawa to be secretary general, in part, out of debt to his kingmaker, Takeshita. Ozawa is known and generally not trusted by the public for his radical views on the Constitution. He is in favor of changing the Constitution so that Japan and its military can play a larger role in international affairs. This view made him many enemies in the party or at least there were many people who were wary of being associated with him (Williams 1996: 294).

Ozawa and Kaifu worked closely to develop a plan for political reform. Ozawa, however, had his own reasons for pursuing reform, reasons that went far beyond diffusing the Recruit scandal. He wanted a particular type of reform – electoral system change. Changing the electoral system was not the most logical remedy to the problems exposed by a political funding scandal such as Recruit. The public was demanding strengthening the limits on contributions, making the regulations of stocks as donations more explicit, and increasing the transparency in the funding process. The LDP, however, had long pointed to the electoral system as the root of the political funding problems. The general argument was that the multiple-member district (MMD) system fostered competition between members of the same party as any party would have to win an average of two seats in the 130 multi-seat districts in order to retain a majority. Critics cited competition among fellow party members as the main cause of the factional system within the LDP and other opposition parties. In the LDP, each faction strove to get as many members elected as possible in order to get a member of its faction elected prime minister. LDP candidates in the same district could not compete based on policy since they were members of the same party. As a result, competition centered on the distribution of favors and projects. The intense competition based on patronage that resulted required large amounts of money. Individual members needed personal support groups in their districts in order to compete against fellow party members, and the factional leaders needed large sums in order to attract patrons. This pressure to raise funds on an individual and factional level was often pointed to as a main cause for the pervasive corruption (Ozawa 1994: 63).

The favored solution by several members in the LDP, including Ozawa, was the implementation of an SMD system. This solution was preferred for one of two reasons: (1) it had a low probability of actually passing; (2) if it passed, such a system favored the dominant LDP. Drawing on conventional wisdom, politicians who supported a move to a pure SMD system pointed out that this type of system would eliminate intra-party competition and move Japan to a two-party system. Many politicians argued that a first-past-the-post system would require fewer financial resources because intra-party factional competition would be eliminated (Ozawa 1994: 66–67). These politicians did not consider the possibility that running against a viable candidate from a competing party also could require large sums of money. The questionable claim that an SMD system would cost less money was promoted to the point that many politicians, and even the public, began to accept the argument without question.

Ozawa actively advanced the notion that an SMD system would remedy money politics in Japan. However, his true motivation for supporting an SMD system was more complicated. He, too, favored a pure single-member district system because he believed that it would result in a two-party system. However, the advantages he saw from an SMD system transcended the possibility that it might lessen the financial burden on politicians. He believed that a two-party system would allow him to realize his vision of a new Japan capable of playing a larger role in the international arena (Desmond 1995: 126–27). Ozawa claimed that Japan's inconsequential role in international politics was linked to a lack of leadership (Ozawa 1994). This lack of leadership was a function of the electoral system. The multiple-member district system allowed the survival of several smaller parties, parties that Ozawa claimed were satisfied with their comfortable position in the opposition (Ozawa 1994: 64). Moreover, over the years the LDP had solidified its position as the dominant player in this system. Its secure position produced certain inefficiencies, as well as a strong preference for the status quo. Ozawa believed that an SMD system would enhance Japan's leadership capabilities by moving Japan toward a two-party system. If the LDP had a viable competitor capable of replacing it in office, its accountability would increase and so in turn would its sense of responsibility (Ozawa 1994). Using this logic, Ozawa convinced Kaifu initially to consider a pure SMD system in October 1989 (Minkan Seiji Rincho 1993: 239). As we shall see, though, by

December 1990 Kaifu had rejected Ozawa's pure SMD plan and proposed a mixed SMD/PR system instead (Reed and Thies 2001a: 164; Sakamoto 1999: 104–8).

The opposition parties were vehemently opposed to an SMD system. Many of these smaller parties were afraid of disappearing under such a system (Sakamoto 1999: 180, fn. 16). The LDP lost its majority in the Upper House in 1989. As a result, the opposition had a larger voice in determining what kind of reform had a chance of passing; at least these parties could block the LDP from implementing a pure SMD system. Indeed, the opposition was quite active during this time. Cooperation among opposition parties, however, was sporadic. Four of the opposition parties (JSP, DSP, Kōmeitō, and Rengō) worked together on developing a counter-reform policy proposal, but these negotiations broke down after one month in December 1989 (Minkan Seiji Rincho 1993: 238–39). The opposition began cooperating again regarding Diet reform in late June 1990 (Minkan Seiji Rincho 1993: 242–43). This activity did not put much pressure on the LDP, however. The LDP's position in the Lower House remained secure, especially after the LDP's strong performance in the February 1990 Lower House election.

The fact that the opposition parties could block a pure SMD system actually made it easier for members of the LDP to support this option. Knowing that an SMD system would never pass, the members of the LDP could appear to be supporting reform without actually having to deal with the consequences of realized reform.

As the Electoral System Advisory Council and the LDP's Head Office of Political Reform (*Seiji Kaikaku Honbu*) were debating proposals for electoral system and political funding reform, Kaifu dissolved the Lower House in February 1990 because the four-year maximum time span between elections was approaching. In the election following the dissolution, the LDP did surprisingly well, winning 286 of the 512 seats. After the election, Kaifu's support ratings hit a career high exceeding 50 percent, an extremely high level of support for a Japanese prime minister (Minkan Seiji Rincho 1993: 241).

Kaifu still actively pursued political reform after the 1990 election, but the LDP's strong performance in the Lower House election took away the momentum for political reform, effectively closing the window of opportunity for political reform. Interpreting the success in the 1990 election as an indication that public opinion had recovered from the Recruit scandal, the anti-reformers within the LDP were eager to focus on other issues. The investigative committees continued their work on reform, and Kaifu earnestly reiterated his determination to see reform enacted in April 1990, setting the deadline for a definite plan by fall 1990. In May, he visited the leaders of each faction and demanded their cooperation on electoral system reform, but the leaders were noncommittal, simply taking a cautious stance (Minkan Seiji Rincho 1993: 241).

Despite the fact that Kaifu did not get overwhelming support from the other faction leaders, he announced that he would have a definite plan for reform by November. In September, LDP secretary general Ozawa announced plans to introduce a bill to the Diet in April 1991. Two days later Hata, the chairman of the Electoral System Investigative Committee, indicated his support for Kaifu by announcing plans to have an outline for reform by November. Hata also announced his support for a special session of the Diet to enact reform. However, many members of the party elite, including the party vice-president, Kanemaru Shin, and the leader of the largest faction, Takeshita Noboru, opposed a special session for reform (Minkan Seiji Rincho 1993: 249).

As Kaifu tried to push forward with reform, he met more and more resistance in the LDP. In the beginning the vocal opposition to reform was not as strong. Most anti-reformers were keeping their opposition hidden in hopes that the movement for reform would lose momentum, and they would never have to reveal their opposition. Kaifu's persistence, however, forced those opposed to reform to take sides and become more vocal. Once this occurred, the LDP began to split into reform and anti-reform camps with the lines of demarcation transcending factional lines. That is, support or opposition to reform was not determined by factional affiliation. For example, by early 1991 the junior members of the LDP divided into two groups that transcended their patronage-related factional affiliations: a reform faction and an anti-reform faction. The reform faction under the leadership of Ishiba Shigeru formed the Young Diet Members for Political Reform (Ōtake 1996: 273). The anti-reform group under the leadership of Etō Seiichi established the League of Legislators for Political Reform, the misnomer illustrating how difficult it was for these Diet members to oppose reform publicly (Minkan Seiji Rincho 1993: 247).

Despite the internal party disagreement over reform, Kaifu met his deadline for having a concrete plan of action by November. On 27 November 1990 the LDP's Head Office of Political Reform submitted its outline for a combined SMD/PR system to the LDP. This plan called for a total of 471 seats with 300 elected under a single-member district system and 171 chosen through proportional representation.[10] After considerable debate, the members of the LDP adopted this plan as party policy on 25 December 1990, adding one major amendment that changed it from a one vote to a two-vote system (Minkan Seiji Rincho 1993: 247).

Even after the party accepted the outline, voices of discontent concerning the decision were heard at the Policy Affairs Research Council (PARC) deliberations. Groups within the LDP, such as the anti-reformers in the misleadingly named League of Legislators for Political Reform, aimed at obstructing these proposed revisions and began meeting with leaders from each faction and other prominent LDP officials such as party vice-president Kanemaru Shin who had already expressed his opposition to opening a special session of the Diet. The anti-reformers hindered party approval of a reform package, but eventually Kaifu pushed the package through the LDP Executive Council (Sakamoto 1999: 106). In fact, Executive Council chairman Nishioka Takeo had to cut off discussion to force a party decision on 29 June 1991. The Miyazawa, Mitsuzuka and Watanabe factions were outraged by this decision and began collecting names in an attempt to repeal the decision. Their efforts failed, as the bill went to the Diet on 5 August 1991 (Minkan Seiji Rincho 1993: 253).

Kaifu's failure to reach party consensus, however, proved detrimental when the LDP's proposal reached the Diet. Key party leaders were not in favor of reform, so they allowed a large contingent of LDP anti-reformers to sit on the Diet electoral reform committee. In fact, nearly half of the 28 LDP members on the committee were anti-reformers (Sakamoto 1999: 107). These anti-reformers made their opposition to their own party's bill quite clear in committee deliberations. Of the seven LDP members who spoke about the bill in committee, five expressed their opposition. Former Finance Minister Miyazawa went as far as publicly announcing that he opposed a combined system and supported reapportionment of the MMD system instead (Minkan Seiji Rincho 1993: 255). The LDP elite also stipulated that the proposal submitted by the LDP could not be amended in the Diet, making it impossible for the party to compromise with the opposition that was clearly opposed to a proposal so heavily weighted toward SMD instead of PR seats. Given the amount of disagreement over the proposal, the chairman of the Special Committee on Electoral Reform "discarded" the bill on 27 September 1991, meaning that the proposals were never even brought to a vote on the Diet floor. Kaifu resigned on 4 October 1991, taking responsibility for the failure of reform (Sakamoto 1999: 104–8).

After he announced his intention to resign, but before the LDP's next presidential election, a frustrated Kaifu threatened to dissolve the Lower House of the Diet (Shinoda 2000: 70–71). A dissolution so close to the failure of reform would serve as a public referendum on the LDP's inability to agree on reform. Indeed, a severe setback at the polls could put enough pressure on the LDP to seriously consider political reform in the Lower House. In the end, Kaifu's words turned out to be an empty threat. He chose not to take this risk.

Why Kaifu failed

Kaifu is an example of an unsuccessful advocate of reform. He was and continues to be ideologically committed to reform; however, he failed to realize change in the early 1990s. No single factor explains his failure. Indeed, many things combined to work against him. In particular, Kaifu's slow pursuit of reform along with his unwillingness to risk defying the wishes of his patrons led to his ultimate failure.

Kaifu's resources

Kaifu was a senior politician when he was appointed prime minister in 1989. He had been elected ten times. He was a member of the smallest faction in the LDP, the Kōmoto faction, formerly the Miki faction. In fact, Kaifu's position in the party was quite similar to his political mentor, former Prime Minister Miki Takeo, the reformer explored in Chapter 2, in that they were both placed in office by patrons of stronger factions.

Still, Kaifu, like Miki before him, had the basic set of resources needed to pursue reform. Throughout his career he had served in several party and parliamentary positions, including Lower House Legislative Management Committee chair (1972), Prime Minister Miki's deputy chief cabinet minister (1974), and minister of education (1976) (Toyoda 1983: 250–54). These positions provided him with connections both within and outside the LDP. Because he was a member of the smallest faction, though, his patron–client ties were not that extensive. As with Miki, very few politicians felt beholden to follow Kaifu's wishes out of a sense of obligation.

The position of prime minister afforded Kaifu with even more resources. Although prime ministers in Japan are institutionally weak, the position does come with some significant informal powers (Shinoda 2000).[11] As we saw in Chapter 2, Miki was able to use the added media attention he received to keep the salience of reform high as well as exert pressure on his fellow politicians to pass reform. His popularity allowed him to garner a large amount of support for reform. Kaifu also had a high level of popular support. As Figure 3.2 illustrates, Kaifu's cabinet support ratings increased after he was inaugurated prime minister. While his support sat at 38 percent when he entered office, it reached as high as 60.1 percent in August 1990. For the majority of the time he was in office, his cabinet ratings fluctuated between the high forties and the low sixties. Most significantly, his support levels were on the rebound when he submitted his reform proposal to the Diet in August 1991, registering 57.9 percent (Sorifu 1992). Despite this high level of support for his cabinet, Kaifu, unlike Miki, was not able to use his popularity to pressure his fellow LDP members to support reform. The difference between Miki and Kaifu rests in their personal attributes. Kaifu's personal attributes influenced the way he chose to use – or in some cases *not* use – both his formal and informal resources.

Kaifu as a non-risk-taker

The main reason that Kaifu failed to realize reform was that he was not willing to challenge the constraints standing in the way of reform. Two related constraints were those presented by the LDP in general and the power configuration within the party specifically. Kaifu was an outsider within the party. He was from a small faction and did not hold as much influence as other members of the LDP. Instead of employing strategies of other outsiders

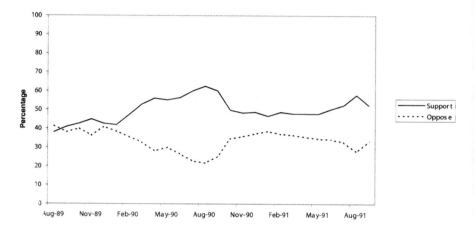

Figure 3.2 Prime Minister Kaifu's cabinet support ratings. This graph only shows the percentage of respondents who answered that they supported or opposed the Kaifu cabinet. Two other responses were available – "other" or "no answer."

Source: Data compiled from *Yomiuri Shinbun* cabinet support ratings reported in Sorifu Naikaku Sori Daijin Kanbo Kohoshitsu (1990, 1991, 1992) *Seron Chōsa Nenkan, 1990, 1991, 1992* (Public Opinion Research Yearbooks, 1990, 1991, 1992), Tokyo: Ōkurashō Insatsukyoku.

within the LDP, such as seeking opposition support as Miki did in the case of the anti-monopoly bill or going public as Miki did with the political reform package, Kaifu took reform through the normal policy channels within the LDP. The only risk in doing this was that reform would fall between the cracks and not pass.

Taking a proposal through the normal policy-making channels is time consuming. Perhaps, Kaifu felt that this strategy had the best chance of securing party consensus, reasoning that if the LDP's Head Office of Political Reform, the PARC, and the Electoral System Advisory Council discussed these issues long enough, those opposed to reform could be persuaded to compromise.

Kaifu chose to develop a new reform proposal. He did not have to do this, however. Electoral reform had been on the Home Ministry's agenda for decades; thus, a variety of different proposals for electoral system and political funding reform already existed. Kaifu could have expanded these proposals, adjusting them to fit his policy preferences. Instead, Kaifu chose to let the party debate a new proposal. This process proved to be a long, cumbersome one. In fact, it took Kaifu over a year to formulate a proposal that had LDP backing. By the time Kaifu submitted his bill in 1991, the sense of crisis had passed. The LDP's strong performance in the 1990 Lower House election was interpreted as indicating that the public's outrage had weakened.

The LDP felt much more secure in its position and its mandate to lead, as well as its ability to get away with misconduct. Persuading incumbents to support change if no legitimacy crisis exists is quite difficult.

Timing is important in determining the success of advocates of reform. Windows of opportunity for political reform are not open forever. Reformers must have a proposal ready when the window opens. If they take the time to formulate a new proposal, then the sense of urgency created by the outbreak of a scandal will have passed. Just as reformers have incentives to take advantage of windows of opportunity, those opposed to reform have incentives to close them. These anti-reformers work to create a perception that the problem has been handled (Kingdon 1984). Advocates of reform must take advantage of the window of opportunity quickly or another politician may succeed in turning the focus elsewhere. In this case, acting quickly meant taking the risk of alienating the patrons who had put Kaifu into the prime ministership and forcing the LDP to adopt a reform proposal more quickly. Kaifu was not willing to take this drastic action.

In retrospect, Kaifu recognized the effect that the 1990 Lower House election had on the ultimate failure of reform. Kaifu explained, "The LDP won too big. [As a result,] reform failed. The fever for reform declined" (personal interview, 12 March 2001). Kaifu believed that the LDP won because it promised reform. This electoral mandate made it the LDP's responsibility to enact reform (personal interview with Kaifu Toshiki, 12 March 2001). The LDP's big win, however, had quite the opposite effect on politicians. The victory indicated that the public was less angry with the LDP. In this sense, the election was the end of reform.

Kaifu's safe, slow action had certain consequences. Other issues also appeared on the agenda and began to overshadow the debate over political reform. Most prominent among these events was the outbreak of the conflict in Iraq, which forced Japan to deal with the ambiguity of its Constitutional provisions concerning its self-defense forces, the main question being whether Japan could send a peace-keeping operation to the area. Iraq invaded Kuwait in August 1990, the LDP submitted a Peace-Keeping Operations (PKO) bill to the Diet in October, and the bill was rejected in November. After the PKO bill was rejected, the LDP spent a large amount of time drafting a new proposal. The new PKO proposal was placed on the agenda at the same time that Kaifu's political reform package was being debated. Kaifu was forced to prioritize policies, knowing that he would not be able to get opposition cooperation on both these controversial proposals. He chose the PKO bill (Sakamoto 1999: 107).

One potentially risky strategy that Kaifu considered using to convince his party of the public demand for reform was a second dissolution of the Lower House of the Diet, one immediately following the failure of his reform package in committee. The dissolution of the Lower House of the Diet is one of the few formal powers a Japanese prime minister possesses. In parliamentary systems, prime ministers usually use this power to call new elections when their party is likely to perform strongly. Prime ministers, however, theoretically can use this power to send a message to their party when the two sides fail to agree on policy priorities. In Kaifu's case, a dissolution of the Diet provoked by a failure to act on reform would have resulted in an election and provided the public with a chance to voice an opinion on reform. As we shall see in Chapter 7, Prime Minister Koizumi successfully used this power and dissolved the Lower House to isolate anti-reformers in the LDP and build more support for his agenda by supporting pro-reform candidates in the new election.

A new election had the potential of providing Kaifu a public mandate for reform. Renewed public support would have increased his chances of realizing reform. Even though the LDP had done well in the February 1990 elections, a repeat strong performance was far from guaranteed. The public was fickle and known for keeping the LDP's power in check, at least at the margins, when it felt that the party was abusing its position. Thus, the prospect of an election so soon after the 1990 victory and the failure of reform was an ominous one for many members of the LDP. A legitimate threat to dissolve the Diet might have convinced some LDP members to reconsider their position on reform. In the end, however, Kaifu chose not to dissolve the Diet.

At least two constraints influenced Kaifu's decision not to dissolve the Lower House. Factional politics in the LDP presented the first constraint. When asked why he did not take this action at this time, Prime Minister Kaifu explained, "If I had a free hand, I would have [dissolved the Diet]" (personal interview, 12 March 2001). Three factions, the Mitsuzuka, Watanabe, and Miyazawa factions, were adamantly opposed to the dissolution because they feared that among other things it would result in the re-election of Kaifu as party president due to his popularity with the public. The strong opposition from these factions convinced the largest faction that had backed Kaifu as prime minister, the Takeshita faction, to pressure Kaifu to refrain from dissolving the Diet (Sakamoto 1999: 180, fn. 20). Kaifu felt this pressure and believed that his hands were tied. He was not willing to risk the wrath of his patrons. Instead, he chose not to dissolve the Diet and not to run in the next party presidential election to take responsibility for the failure of reform (Sakamoto 1999: 108).

The fact that the LDP no longer held a majority in the Upper House of the Diet presented a second potential constraint. Even if a new election changed the composition in the Lower House, providing Kaifu with a more favorable environment for reform, Kaifu and the LDP would still face resistance from the opposition parties, which together constituted a majority in the Upper House. All opposition parties rejected a pure SMD system. Kaifu's proposal contained a PR element that would allow for some continued minority representation. Getting enough opposition party support in the Upper House, however, might have required additional concessions. This additional constraint that remained regardless of a dissolution of the Lower House might have influenced Kaifu's decision. Still, one can imagine that a public mandate for reform could weaken this constraint, making it more difficult for opposition parties in the Upper House to block reform.

Kaifu was not willing to reach out for the impossible. Dissolving the Lower House would not have guaranteed the passage of reform, especially given the LDP's minority status in the Upper House. A dissolution, however, could have weakened some of the constraints Kaifu faced by illuminating strong public support or increasing the number of pro-reformers in the Lower House. Kaifu could then reintroduce his legislation in a new environment that potentially was more favorable. Kaifu was unwilling to take this risk, though. If he dissolved the Diet, he risked alienating himself from the other members of his party and losing any future influence in policy matters. His decision suggests that he preferred failing to following through on reform and resigning from office to being a permanent pariah in his own party.

Although Kaifu did not take the risk of dissolving the Diet, he defied the party elite by bypassing the LDP Executive Council and sending his proposal to the Diet floor. The LDP elite prevailed this time as well, as they allowed party members to express their opposition to the LDP's official bill in committee. They also refused to move an inch in negotiations with the opposition. Due to his weak position in the party, Kaifu was unable to stop this attack orchestrated by the more powerful power brokers in the party. As mentioned above, the only formal power that Kaifu had to counter the failure of the bill in committee was the dissolution of the Diet. An electoral mandate for reform was quite possibly the only thing outside the outbreak of another scandal that could increase the salience of reform. In the end, Kaifu decided that dissolving the Diet was too risky for the party as a whole, not to mention for his future in the party. Instead, he left power relatively quietly, defeated in his attempt to realize reform.

Kaifu's insufficient vision

Kaifu did not have a precise vision of reform. His support of reform was more symbolic than concrete. He did have an image of a clean politician, an image he fostered throughout his career. However, he did not have a clear vision of what reform would look like or what it would take to get reform implemented.

Instead of vision, Kaifu fostered a symbolic support of reform. Kaifu emphasized his connections to Miki in an attempt to bolster his credibility as a clean politician in pursuit of reform. Many of his actions were symbolic. For example, Kaifu almost always donned a polka-dotted tie, a fashion trait that had been Miki's trademark. Kaifu was a member of the Miki faction and had served as Deputy Chief of the Cabinet under Miki. In addition to being Kaifu's mentor, Miki was also quite popular with the public, even after his tenure as prime minister and his death. Kaifu hoped to benefit from Miki's popularity by such symbolic actions. Shortly after his appointment to the prime ministership he visited Miki's grave. These actions sent a message to the public of Kaifu being a loyal follower of the former reformer. Kaifu, however, did not back these symbolic acts with a concrete vision for reform.

Further evidence of Kaifu's lack of vision is found in the fact that he switched the type of electoral system he supported during the middle of his term in office. During the first part of his administration, following Ozawa's preferences, Kaifu supported a pure single-member district system. Later, he changed his position and endorsed a mixed system proposed by the advisory council.[12] The opposition was resolutely against any system that had an SMD component to it; thus, switching support to a mixed system did not improve the chances of opposition approval. The mixed system also veered from Ozawa's vision of reform, a pure SMD system. It is not clear what motivated his changed position; however, it is clear that he was not leading the process with his vision. First, he adopted Ozawa's; then, he accepted the advisory council's revisions.

Kaifu's questionable commitment

Kaifu did have a history of supporting reform. He served on an LDP committee that reviewed the party's presidential electoral system in 1973. He was part of Miki's cabinet and supported Miki's efforts to pass his political reform package. His focus after Miki's reform package passed, however, veered in other directions. He served on various committees, including commerce and tax-related ones (Toyoda 1983: 250–60).

Kaifu capitalized on his "Mr. Clean" image to gain support for the prime ministership after the Recruit stocks-for-favors scandal and the Uno sex scandal. He drew on his experience in Miki's cabinet to bolster his legitimacy as a reformer. And, he did keep reform on the agenda throughout his administration. Kaifu, however, was not willing to pay a price to see reform enacted. In this sense, Kaifu's commitment to reform was inadequate. If he dissolved the Diet in an attempt to pressure the LDP to act on reform, he risked antagonizing his patrons and being alienated within the party. Even though he lost his position as prime minister, he was able to retain a potentially vocal role behind the scenes. Kaifu saw dissolving the Diet as more costly for him personally. If the LDP performed poorly in an election after the dissolution, then the party might have been pressured to support reform. Forcing the party's hand, however, could have cost Kaifu any potential future influence in the party. Kaifu was not willing to pay this personal price to see reform enacted.

The role of scandal and electoral competition

Kaifu's failure to pass reform refutes the competing contentions that the severity of scandal or increased electoral competition lead to reform. The Recruit scandal certainly ranks as one of the most far-reaching scandals in

Japan's postwar political history. The number and status of politicians arrested in the Recruit scandal was not as great in comparison to the Lockheed scandal discussed in Chapter 2. Only two politicians were arrested in connection with the Recruit scandal and neither was of the same stature as former Prime Minister Tanaka. The number of politicians and outside officials implicated in the Recruit scandal, however, greatly outnumbered the "gray officials" connected to the Lockheed scandal. As mentioned earlier, 43 politicians, bureaucrats, journalists and business people, including Prime Minister Takeshita, were forced to resign due to their involvement in the scandal. Politicians who had accepted legal contributions from Recruit even felt negative repercussions due to the company's tarnished reputation. All told, the Recruit investigations spanned 260 days and resulted in 16 indictments, mainly in the private sector (Allen 1991b: 164). The broad scope of the scandal makes it comparable in terms of severity with the Lockheed scandal.

Despite the fact that the scandal negatively impacted the ruling and opposition parties as well as the bureaucracy, politicians did not pass reform directly following this scandal. Instead, as we have seen, Takeshita only symbolically pursued reform in hopes of waiting out the scandal's salience. Kaifu did bring a proposal before the Diet, but his unwillingness to dissolve the Diet when it refused to vote on the issue led to the eventual demise of his reform proposal. The Recruit scandal, like Lockheed before it, presents a case of a far-reaching scandal that does not result in the passage of reform.

The LDP experienced heightened electoral competition following the outbreak of the Recruit scandal, but this factor also failed to result in the passage of reform. The 1989 Upper House election results provide one indication of this increased competition. In this election, the LDP lost its majority for the first time, only reclaiming 109 seats (Allen 1991b: 165).[13] Although the scandal-tainted LDP also lost votes in the 1990 Lower House election, its seat loss was not as large. The loss in votes for the LDP did not necessarily result in implicated candidates losing their seats due to the multiple-member district electoral system, where candidates in a five-member district, for example, only need to retain enough support to secure a fifth-place finish. The important point is that even though many of the implicated candidates retained their seats, most lost votes, as did the LDP as a whole (Reed 1999b: 145). The LDP's overall loss in vote share in the Lower House election when compared to the previous election in 1986 was 3.3 percent.[14] Such fluctuation was not uncommon during postwar elections. This vote share lost reflects the Socialist Party's inability to capitalize on the public's frustration with the LDP as it had done in the Upper House election, due in part to the differing electoral system (Reed 1999b: 146–47). As a result, the LDP maintained its majority in the Lower House following the 1990 election. With its majority secure, for the moment at least, the LDP felt less pressure to reform. The overall ambivalence of the LDP to the public's outrage over Recruit is best exemplified by the fact that Prime Minister Kaifu appointed six Diet members to his cabinet who had been implicated in Recruit (Allen 1991b: 165–66). The LDP considered reform proposals following Recruit; however, it did not pass reform even though the 1989 Upper House and 1990 Lower House elections suggested that the party was facing increased public dissatisfaction. As we have seen above, the decisive factor in the failure of reform was the absence of a leader who was willing to take a risk to capitalize on this public dissatisfaction.

Conclusion

Kaifu failed to realize reform due to his unwillingness to take risks, as well as a lack of commitment and vision. Some might point to Kaifu's weak position in the party as explaining his ultimate failure. A comparison with former Prime Minister Miki, however, refutes this alternative explanation for Kaifu's failure. Miki and Kaifu were from the same small faction within the LDP and both of these politicians owed their appointment to the prime ministership to the support of larger, more influential factions. In this sense, Miki had an equally weak position within the LDP, yet he successfully realized reform. The difference between these two leaders' quests for reform rests in how they manipulated their similar positions. Miki took risks, acted quickly on his vision, drew on proposals he had formulated due to his long support of reform, and rallied public support to pressure the LDP into action. Kaifu moved slowly and took the issue of reform through the normal policy-making channels in the LDP. This non-risky approach contributed to his ultimate failure.

Table 3.1 compares the reform attempts by Prime Ministers Miki and Kaifu. As Table 3.1 reveals both leaders had windows of opportunity for reform similar in length. The windows had been open for differing amounts of time before each leader came to office, though. Specifically, the window of opportunity for reform opened eight months prior to Kaifu's inauguration as prime minister. In contrast, the window opened two months before Miki was named prime minister. Miki, unlike Kaifu, however, had a proposal for reform prepared before he entered office despite the shorter lead time. The severity of the scandals that opened the windows of opportunity for each leader also seemed to favor the passage of reform during the Kaifu administration, not the Miki cabinet. As we have seen in this chapter, the Recruit scandal was far reaching in nature, implicating high-level politicians from various parties. In comparison, the Tanaka real-estate scandal only involved the sitting prime minister's participation in money politics. Given the greater severity of the Recruit scandal, one might expect reform to pass after this scandal, not the Tanaka real-estate scandal. However, the opposite was the case in large part due to the varying approaches to reform of the two leaders.

As illustrated in Chapter 2, Miki took a non-conventional approach to gathering support for his policies. He often went outside the LDP and looked

Table 3.1 A summary of the reform attempts by Prime Ministers Miki and Kaifu

	Prime Minister Miki	*Prime Minister Kaifu*
Overall length of the window of opportunity	9 months (Oct. 1974 to July 1975)	14 months (Nov. 1988 to Feb. 1990)
Length of the window of opportunity while the leader is in government	7 months (Dec. 1974 to July 1975)	6 months (Aug. 1989 to Feb. 1990)
Magnitude of the scandal that opens the window	Medium	High
Level of resources	High	High
Risk-taking	High	Low
Vision	High	Low
Commitment	High	Low
Outcome	Revisions to the Political Funds Control Law	No reform

to the opposition for support of his positions in order to get the attention of the members of his own party. In the case of his proposal for revisions to the political funding regulations, however, he did not have opposition support. Instead, Miki maintained his unpopular position and tried to get support from the LDP by "going public" and using public support of reform to pressure his fellow party members. This strategy worked in part because Miki came to office with a self-written bill to revise the Political Funds Control Law. This proposal was the result of Miki's years of dedicated work on reform. He began formulating this proposal when he resigned from the Tanaka cabinet in protest of money politics just prior to his own appointment as prime minister. Once prime minister, he submitted this bill immediately, before the government had recovered from the damage done by the Tanaka scandal, making it more difficult for his fellow LDP members to oppose the bill.

Kaifu took a different, more conventional approach to reform. Kaifu also came to office when the LDP was steeped in controversy due to the outbreak of the Recruit scandal followed by the Uno sex scandal. Kaifu entered office promising reform, but he was not willing to act quickly and pressure his patrons who were not in favor of reform. Kaifu knew that there was a large amount of internal dissent over reform. He chose the conventional approach of long internal party deliberations and external deliberative council recommendations in order to build party consensus. He was not willing to force party compliance, like Miki had done, by working to translate public calls for reform into pressure for reform. His ultimate unwillingness to take risks became apparent when he refused to dissolve the Diet after his reform proposal died in committee. Dissolving the Diet would have allowed voters to express their opinion of the politicians' failure to pass reform at the polls.

A poor performance by members of the LDP might have convinced reluctant politicians to change their positions and support reform. Kaifu, however, chose to obey the wishes of his patrons and refrain from using his powers as prime minister to dissolve the Diet. This unwillingness to take risks ultimately led to his failure to see the passage of reform.

4 Miyazawa Kiichi

An anti-reformer caught in "reform fever"

Following Prime Minister Kaifu's resignation, the LDP selected Miyazawa Kiichi to the premiership. This choice reflected the decreased salience of money politics. Instead of looking for another clean politician, the LDP returned to its traditional way of selecting a prime minister based on seniority and factional power politics. The return to this approach meant that the main contenders were old-guard politicians, many of whom had been implicated in scandals in the past, including Miyazawa Kiichi.

The Takeshita faction, the largest faction in the LDP, had the strength to hand-select Kaifu's successor. The two premier leaders of the Takeshita faction, Takeshita Noboru and Kanemaru Shin, tried to convince Ozawa Ichirō to take the post. Ozawa had served as secretary general during the Kaifu administration and was credited for running the administration from behind the scenes. He was Kanemaru's protégé and thought to be in line to take over the Takeshita faction when Kanemaru retired. Since Ozawa was only forty-nine, however, many in the LDP considered him too young to be prime minister. While high up in the party and quite influential in his own right, if he had become prime minister at this time he would have been under the control of some of the more senior members of the party. Many speculated that Ozawa wanted to wait to take the top position in the party until a time when he would be less beholden to his patrons. Officially, Ozawa declined the Takeshita faction's endorsement due to health reasons, recently having suffered a heart attack.

Instead of vying for the position, Ozawa was put in charge of choosing the candidate that the Takeshita faction would support in the party race. Given the size and influence of the Takeshita faction at the time, this task was equivalent to choosing the new prime minister. After personally interviewing the three top contenders, Watanabe Michio, Mitsuzuka Hiroshi, and Miyazawa Kiichi, Ozawa chose Miyazawa. Ozawa chose Miyazawa because he willingly accepted Ozawa's priorities – the passage of the Peace-Keeping Operations (PKO) bill and electoral system reform. Miyazawa accepted these priorities even though he had been a vocal opponent of political reform during the Kaifu administration. He was willing to change his position, however, in order to become prime minister. Miyazawa's readiness to accept

Ozawa's agenda was seen as an indication that he could be controlled once in office (Schlesinger 1997: 211–14).

The selection of Miyazawa as prime minister reflected the LDP's willingness to support politicians implicated in scandal. Miyazawa Kiichi had been forced to resign from a cabinet position in 1988 during the Takeshita administration because he received questionable shares from the Recruit company. The Recruit scandal implicated a large portion of the upper echelon of the LDP, and many speculated that most of the implicated senior members had lost their chance of joining the cabinet or becoming prime minister. With renewed confidence in its public support after the 1990 Lower House election, however, the LDP dispensed with the strategy of placing a clean politician at the helm and chose someone who had been publicly accused of abusing funding regulations. Miyazawa then went a step further and placed four politicians who had been implicated in the Recruit scandal in his first cabinet. He also appointed party members who had been implicated in the Recruit and Lockheed scandals to influential party positions. Choosing a prime minister who had been implicated in Recruit opened the door for future cabinet and prime minister appointments of other LDP politicians who had been implicated in scandal. It also signified the LDP's return to the money politics which had fueled its machine throughout the postwar period (Pitman 1991: 16).

When Miyazawa became prime minister, he found himself in a weaker position than Kaifu had been in. To begin with, Miyazawa did not win the party presidency by a margin as wide as had been expected, only receiving 285 of the 496 votes.[1] What was surprising and unsettling for Miyazawa was that several LDP politicians who had promised to support Miyazawa changed their minds on election day. A large portion of these defectors were members of the Takeshita faction. By having some of the members of the Takeshita faction vote for Miyazawa's opponent, Watanabe, the faction was sending Miyazawa a message – he owed his position to the faction, and the faction could withdraw its support if he did not cooperate ("Getting to Know Mr. Miyazawa": 33). Even though the Takeshita faction had chosen to support Miyazawa, their support was anything but enthusiastic. Members of the Takeshita faction voted for Miyazawa due to faction fiat, while factional leaders supported Miyazawa because they thought he would be the easiest of the candidates from other factions to control.

Miyazawa and political reform

Although Ozawa had picked Miyazawa due to his willingness to support electoral reform, once Miyazawa became prime minister, he was much more interested in international affairs than in electoral system change. As a result of both Miyazawa's lack of commitment to reform and the decreased salience of the issue, very little action occurred following Miyazawa's inauguration as prime minister in October 1991 (Schlesinger 1997: 212). Miyazawa eventually was forced to consider political reform when two separate scandals opened windows of opportunity for reform in 1992. These scandals renewed demands for reform both within and outside the LDP. Miyazawa felt the pressure of "reform fever" and promised to pass electoral reform. Ultimately, however, Miyazawa failed to pass reform. This chapter contends that Prime Minister Miyazawa Kiichi failed to realize reform in 1993 because he did not have a vision of reform nor a commitment to it; therefore, not surprisingly, he was not willing to take risks to see reform passed.

Although Miyazawa ultimately failed to enact reform like his predecessor, Kaifu Toshiki, whose attempt to pass reform was the focus of the previous chapter, the reasons for the two leaders' failure differ in some important ways. Unlike in the Kaifu case, the environmental conditions were much more favorable for the passage of reform under Miyazawa. Specifically, the window of opportunity for reform basically remained open from January 1992 to the end of Miyazawa's term. The element that was missing was effective leadership. Miyazawa, even more than Kaifu, lacked the personal attributes needed to push reform. Miyazawa did not take risks to seek the passage of reform nor did he use any innovative tactics in an attempt to build a coalition for reform. Both Kaifu and Miyazawa felt constrained by those who had placed them in office. As a result, they tried to realize reform through the accepted decision-making channels within the LDP, a tactic that proved unsuccessful in both cases.

Miyazawa's commitment and vision were also weak. Kaifu was a career reformer, while Miyazawa preferred the role of foreign diplomat. Unlike Kaifu, Miyazawa had little desire to change the electoral system or to tighten the political funding regulations; his policy priorities lay in other areas. When it was clear that the fate of Miyazawa's administration rested on the passage of reform, he tried to create a consensus within the LDP in order to present a bill to the Diet. He did not have a vision of reform, though. Instead, under the influence of the LDP leadership, he proposed a bill that had little to no chance of receiving opposition support. Not surprisingly, due to his lack of leadership, this bill failed.

A window of opportunity for reform

Two successive scandals made it impossible for the Miyazawa administration to ignore the issue of political reform. To begin with, a case of bribery referred to as the Kyōwa scandal surfaced in January 1992. The scandal unfolded when the Tokyo Prosecutor's Office arrested Abe Fumio, a member of Prime Minister Miyazawa's own faction, on charges of bribery. Abe was accused of accepting 80 million yen in return for helping the Kyōwa steel company secure projects in Hokkaido. While at least four other members of the Miyazawa faction received money from Kyōwa, Abe was the only member arrested. Over the course of his dealings with Kyōwa, Abe reportedly received over 80 million yen from the company in return for supplying the company with favors, such as giving Kyōwa a tip on what lands would be used in the construction of a main road in Hokkaido and helping Kyōwa procure inexpensive government loans ("Japan: Lockheed, Recruit and now ... ": 32).

Declining public support ratings and the increasing salience of reform that followed the outbreak of the scandal indicate that Kyōwa opened a window of opportunity for reform in January 1992. This window would remain open for six months, closing with the LDP's solid performance in the Upper House election in July 1992. The Kyōwa scandal played a significant role in opening the window of opportunity. To begin with, public support for the Miyazawa cabinet fell rather dramatically following the revelation of the Kyōwa scandal, dropping from 56 percent when Miyazawa took office to 40 percent immediately following the outbreak of Kyōwa. As illustrated in Figure 4.1, opposition to the Miyazawa cabinet exceeded support from January 1992 on, clearly signaling the opening of a window of opportunity for reform from the standpoint of declining government support. In fact, support continued to drop following the scandal and was below 30 percent in early March 1992 (Sorifu 1992). Further indicating the public's frustration with the scandal-ridden LDP, the LDP lost two Upper House by-elections in February and March 1992 (Minkan Seiji Rincho 1993: 257).

Miyazawa was not actively pursuing comprehensive reform prior to the outbreak of the Kyōwa scandal. In fact, he completely abandoned electoral reform, choosing instead to focus on the over-representation of rural districts

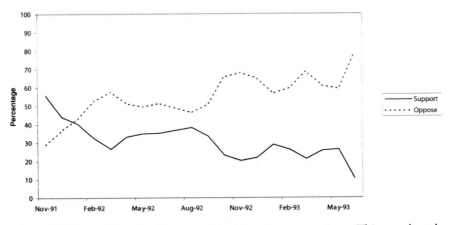

Figure 4.1 Prime Minister Miyazawa's cabinet support ratings. This graph only shows the percentage of respondents who answered that they supported or opposed the Miyazawa cabinet. Two other responses were available – "other" or "no answer."

Source: Data compiled from *Yomiuri Shinbun* cabinet support ratings reported in Sorifu Naikaku Sori Daijin Kanbo Kohoshitsu (1992, 1993, 1994) *Seron Chōsa Nenkan, 1992, 1993, 1994* (Public Opinion Research Yearbooks, 1992, 1993, 1994), Tokyo: Ōkurashō Insatsuk-yoku.

and the need for reapportionment. At the inauguration ceremony of the newly appointed chairperson of the LDP's Head Office of Political Reform on 18 December 1991, Miyazawa made his stance on political reform quite clear. While he acknowledged that the public was demanding politics that did not cost money and increased transparency in political finance, he stated that he felt that reapportionment should take precedence over changing the electoral system. Changing the electoral system was an issue that needed to be considered over the long term, while reapportionment in the Diet was something that could be addressed immediately (Taniguchi 1999: 101). In essence, Miyazawa was trying to change the direction of political reform. Under Kaifu, political reform had meant electoral reform. Miyazawa was shifting the focus of political reform to reapportionment.

After Miyazawa placed the emphasis on reapportionment, the newly appointed chairperson of the LDP's Head Office of Political Reform, Hasegawa Takashi, reinforced Miyazawa's policy position in an interview with the *Asahi Shinbun* on 25 December 1991, stating:

> Even if we submitted the three bills that died under Kaifu, they would not pass due to opposition from all the opposition parties. I would like to pay special attention to single-member districts as a future issue, but political reform is not just about electoral reform. There isn't anything to do except act on the easy to implement issues out of the numerous issues on the table.
>
> (Taniguchi 1999: 101–2)

The interviewer then asked if reapportionment was one of these issues. The chairman replied, "it will probably become that way. The members of the opposition have submitted a proposal on this, haven't they?" (Taniguchi 1999: 102). Leaders from the Socialists and the Kōmeitō announced on a major television network (NHK) program two days later that reapportionment was the number one priority in the following year (Taniguchi 1999: 102).[2]

Reapportionment would not remedy money politics. This problem was attributed to the multiple-member district electoral system that forced members of the same party to compete against each other, thereby increasing the pressure on politicians to raise funds. A relationship between the problem (money politics) and the proposed solution (reapportionment) did not exist. Miyazawa was trying to sell fixing the current system instead of creating a new one. Reapportionment speaks to representation; it does not in any way deter the corruption problems that were coming to the surface. Its proponents argued that more equal representation would enhance democracy.

The amount of attention the Miyazawa administration paid to political reform increased after the Kyōwa scandal. To begin with, the Miyazawa administration altered its position slightly, at least publicly. Although the LDP's Head Office of Political Reform had planned to introduce its two-step plan for reform at the end of January, it delayed implementing it due to opposition from junior Diet members in the party who had formed the group *Wakate Kaikaku Ha* (the Group of Young Diet Members Committed to Reform).[3] Miyazawa continued to de-emphasize electoral system reform, but he did begin to point to the importance of increasing the transparency of political funds. He even considered introducing an independent political funding bill separate from electoral system reform, departing from the precedent established by the Kaifu administration. The opposition parties supported political funding reform and encouraged Miyazawa to take such steps (Taniguchi 1999: 103).

Members of the LDP, particularly members of *Wakate* and former Prime Minister Kaifu, were opposed to postponing action on electoral reform (Taniguchi 1999: 103). The members of *Wakate* tried to highlight the high costs of being a politician under the current electoral system by making their political expenses public on 29 May 1992 (Minkan Seiji Rincho 1993: 257). Their weak position in the party, however, prevented them from getting electoral reform back on the agenda even when the window of opportunity for reform was technically still open. The failed attempt by *Wakate* to pressure Miyazawa and the LDP to act on reform is considered in more detail in Chapter 6.

In May 1992, Miyazawa succeeded in shifting the focus back to the Peace-Keeping Operations (PKO) bill. This bill would allow the government to send Japanese Self-Defense Forces on UN operations. This bill had been stalled since it first made it to the floor of the Diet in December 1991. At the time Miyazawa was highly criticized for how he introduced the PKO bill. Specifically, he had pushed the bill through the Lower House committee without securing the opposition's approval. As a result, the opposition parties demanded that the bill be returned to committee. The situation in the Upper House was even worse. Since the LDP did not have a majority in this chamber it needed the support of both the Kōmeitō and the Democratic Socialist Party (DSP). While the Kōmeitō initially supported the PKO bill,[4] the DSP refused to support the Miyazawa administration in this effort in protest of the fact that Miyazawa had formed a cabinet so heavily stacked with members who had previously been implicated in scandals. The DSP actually was not ideologically opposed to the PKO bill; it was trying to use its swing position to force Miyazawa to answer questions concerning his involvement in Recruit ("Miyazawa Unravels": 33).

The situation was at a stalemate until a poll released in May 1992 revealed that the public actually, and somewhat surprisingly, supported sending Japanese troops on UN operations ("Japan: Cavalry to the Rescue": 34). In reaction to this and given the fact that the July Upper House election was approaching, the DSP and Kōmeitō became increasingly receptive to the PKO bill. All these parties were eager to claim credit for the passage of this now popular bill.

The successful passage of the PKO bill greatly boosted the LDP's support at the polls in the July Upper House elections, as did its action on the economic front. Just prior to the Upper House election, the LDP promised an economic stimulus package and hinted that the Bank of Japan was about to reduce the interest rate from 3.75 percent to 3.25 percent. The voters responded favorably to these promises and the LDP performed solidly in the Upper House election on 26 July 1992, winning 69 of the 127 seats contested ("Miyazawa's Moment": 29). It failed to reclaim its majority, but it nearly doubled the number of seats it won in the July 1989 Upper House election. As a result, the election was considered a victory, and the LDP felt renewed confidence in its mandate to lead and its ability to ignore political reform. The LDP also interpreted the election as an indication that the public had forgotten about the Kyōwa scandal, or at least decided not to punish the LDP for its involvement in yet another scandal. In short, the strong performance in the Upper House election closed this window of opportunity for reform. While the desire for political reform still existed for some, this issue had been overshadowed by other ones. Because the issue had lost salience, the LDP was able to take it off the agenda.

The window of opportunity did not remain closed long. The outbreak of the Sagawa Kyūbin scandal in August 1992 threw it open again. This scandal was much larger than Kyōwa, involving many more prominent politicians. The Tokyo Prosecutor's Office began investigating the Sagawa case in February 1992, but the full scale of the incident did not become apparent until late in the summer of 1992. The first major revelation came on 22 August 1992 when Kanemaru Shin, the acting head of the largest faction in the LDP, the Takeshita faction, was accused of accepting large sums of money from the Sagawa Kyūbin company, a parcel delivery company, in illegal campaign contributions. At first, Kanemaru denied these charges, but the following week he held a press conference and acknowledged accepting 500 million yen from Sagawa (Curtis 1999: 87).[5] He was accused of distributing these funds to at least 60 other politicians. In order to take responsibility for his involvement with Sagawa, Kanemaru resigned as vice-president of the LDP (Noble 1993: 3).[6]

One month later even more scathing allegations emerged. The former president of Sagawa's Tokyo subsidiary, Watanabe Hiroyasu, was accused of being enlisted by Kanemaru to pay members of the Inagawa gangster group, the second largest crime syndicate in Japan, to stop a negative campaign by the Japanese Imperial Subjects Party against Takeshita Noboru during the 1987 LDP presidential election (Noble 1993: 4). In addition, it was alleged that Watanabe used this crime syndicate to funnel money from Sagawa to over 100 politicians, as well as bully Sagawa's competitors in order to secure new delivery routes for the company ("Japan: Pass the Parcel": 28).

The connections among Sagawa, the crime syndicate, and the politicians remained ambiguous until the close of the investigations. Kanemaru, however, was indicted for violating the Political Funds Control Law's limit on contributions for the 500 million yen he admitted accepting (Minkan Seiji

Rincho 1993: 261).[7] A number of other prominent politicians also were implicated in Sagawa, including former prime ministers Nakasone, Takeshita and Uno, former LDP secretary general Ozawa, sitting foreign minister Watanabe Michio, sitting transport minister Okuda Keiwa, sitting telecommunications minister Watanabe Hideo, and faction head Mitsuzuka Hiroshi ("Japan: Dirty Dozen": 36). Both the number of politicians involved and the outrageous sums of money that passed hands upset the public. Indeed, the Kyōwa bribery scandal paled in comparison to Sagawa.[8]

As the Sagawa Kyūbin scandal unfolded, a window of opportunity for reform clearly re-opened by October 1992.[9] One indication of an open window of opportunity was the fact that Miyazawa's cabinet support ratings began descending immediately after the revelation of Kanemaru's involvement with Sagawa. By the end of October 1992 when the full extent of the scandal had been uncovered, Miyazawa's support ratings were hovering around 23 percent. As illustrated in Figure 4.1, after this point, Miyazawa's support ratings always remained below the 30 percent level (Minkan Seiji Rincho 1993; Sorifu 1993). The LDP candidate also lost in the Yamanashi gubernatorial race, the only major election held between the outbreak of the scandal in August 1992 and the end of the Miyazawa administration in June 1993. A candidate recommended by the JSP, Japan New Party and *Shaminren* crushed the LDP/DSP candidate on 14 February 1993, two weeks after the Tokyo Prosecutor's Office closed its investigation of Sagawa (Minkan Seiji Rincho 1993: 265).

The increasing salience of reform following the outbreak of Sagawa also indicates that a window of opportunity was open by October 1992. The increasing salience of reform is reflected in both the increasing calls for reform from the outside and the acceleration of LDP and Diet reform proposal activity. On 5 October 1992, less than two months after the disclosure of the Sagawa Kyūbin scandal, 100 assembly bodies from prefectures, cities, and villages demanded the establishment of political ethics standards. Two weeks later a *Mainichi Shinbun* investigation showed that 635 assembly bodies from prefectures, cities, and villages wanted to see the political ethics standards established (Minkan Seiji Rincho 1993: 261).

Politicians also increased their reform activities, indicating the increased salience of political reform. Miyazawa felt pressure to respond to the scandal both from within and outside his party, even though he did not support sweeping reform. On 16 September 1992, a little over three weeks after the outbreak of Sagawa, Miyazawa declared that he was determined to find a solution to political reform and promised a proposal for radical reform by mid-November 1992 (Minkan Seiji Rincho 1993: 261). Declaring one's determination and actually presenting a proposal to the Diet are two different things. Miyazawa did find it impossible simply to focus on reapportionment and political funding as he had tried to do at the beginning of his administration. Instead, the LDP's Head Office of Political Reform proposed an outline for the introduction of a pure single-member district electoral system on

2 October 1992 (Minkan Seiji Rincho 1993: 261). This outline became a fundamental part of Miyazawa's proposal for reform in November 1992.

In order to successfully realize reform while the window of opportunity was open, Miyazawa needed to build a coalition to support it. The LDP held the majority in the Lower House so at a bare minimum, Miyazawa needed to secure a consensus within his own party. In order to pass the bill in the Upper House, however, some opposition support would be necessary. Thus, the LDP needed to be willing to present a bill that met some of the opposition parties' demands or to amend a bill it proposed in order to reach a compromise with some of the opposition parties. Bending to the pressure of "reform fever" Miyazawa did try to get party consensus. Ultimately, however, he failed due to his unwillingness to challenge the constraints posed by internal party disagreement, as well as his lack of vision and commitment.

The party was divided along two different lines. The first was related to factional politics. Certain factions did not want Miyazawa to succeed for fear that such a success would be a win for Ozawa, a powerful behind-the-scenes player in the LDP (Curtis 1999: 93). The second division was policy-based, a division between pro- and anti-reformers that transcended factional lines. The willingness to take risks along with vision and commitment were all needed to overcome the constraints posed by these divisions. Miyazawa did not have these personal attributes and this deficiency largely contributed to his failure.

The constraints

Factional politics acted as one constraint on Miyazawa's ability to pass reform. The Sagawa Kyūbin scandal rocked the faction that placed Miyazawa in office, the Takeshita faction. The damage done by the scandal weakened the faction's overall position in the party and presented Miyazawa with new obstacles to reform. In particular, the power struggle that resulted after Kanemaru's resignation as faction head following the outbreak of the Sagawa Kyūbin scandal spread fear within the LDP of a party split (Curtis 1999: 91). In order to overcome these factional constraints effective leadership was important. Miyazawa did not provide such leadership.

The Sagawa Kyūbin scandal hit the Takeshita faction particularly hard and polarized the faction in a way that would affect the path of reform from October 1992 when the tensions within the faction first emerged to January 1994 when the Diet finally passed a reform bill. At the time the scandal broke, Kanemaru was the acting head of the Takeshita faction, and Ozawa was its second in command. Takeshita, while still in politics, had removed himself from an official position in the faction in response to the earlier negative outcry over his involvement in the Recruit stocks-for-favors scandal. All three power brokers were implicated in the Sagawa Kyūbin scandal, but the hardest evidence was against Kanemaru. Kanemaru reluctantly admitted that he accepted 500 million yen from Sagawa and finally resigned from his seat in the Diet on 14 October 1992 (Minkan Seiji Rincho 1993: 261).

Kanemaru's resignation from the Diet and thus from the Takeshita faction, set off a power struggle within the faction. At issue was who would take over the top leadership position. The two main contenders were Ozawa Ichirō and Obuchi Keizō. Both men had held top positions in the party, Ozawa serving as LDP secretary general from 1989 to 1991 and Obuchi taking Ozawa's place after he was forced to resign to take responsibility for the LDP's loss in the Tokyo gubernatorial race. Ozawa's main patron in the party was Kanemaru (Curtis 1999: 88–92). Until the outbreak of Sagawa, having the preeminent kingmaker in the party as his sponsor had been an advantage, but due to his involvement in the Sagawa Kyūbin scandal Kanemaru could not do anything to promote his protégé in the faction leadership struggle (Schlesinger 1997: 261). Moreover, members of the LDP who were eager to clean up the party's image were reluctant to support someone who had such close ties with the man at the center of the most recent scandal.

Ozawa had difficulties distancing himself from Kanemaru and the scandal. Partially because of this, he gave up personal aspirations to become faction head. Instead, he backed Hata Tsutomu for the position. Hata was more popular within the party because he was perceived as an earnest reformer. Still, all members of the LDP were aware that if Hata became faction head, Ozawa would be pulling the strings in the background (Curtis 1999: 90–91).

In the end, Obuchi won the battle with backing from Kajiyama Seiroku, the chairman of the LDP Diet Strategy Committee (*kokutai*) and one of the other strong forces in the faction. Kajiyama rallied the members of the LDP who wanted to distance themselves from the leaders who had been implicated in the scandal as well as those who feared Ozawa and his power and policy aspirations. Many members of the party were also wary of Ozawa's dictatorial leadership style (Curtis 1999: 90; Ōtake 1996: 290).

Outraged that he and then his candidate for faction head had been overlooked for the position, Ozawa left the faction the following December and took 36 faction members with him to form a new faction within the LDP that was formally dubbed Reform Forum 21, reflecting the group's support of political reform. Ozawa had advocated changing the electoral system since he was former Prime Minister Kaifu's secretary general. Ozawa's earnest pursuit of reform frightened many members of the Takeshita faction in particular and the LDP in general. This fear had prompted many to reject him as the next head of the Takeshita faction. Those who did support Ozawa and left the Takeshita faction did so for various reasons. Some of the 36 Takeshita faction members who split with Ozawa did so because they desired political reform. Most of the these, however, were junior Diet members who were personally indebted to Ozawa's financial patronage and left with him out of a sense of obligation (Ōtake 1996: 287).

The split in the Takeshita faction made many members of the LDP wary of an escalation of the disagreement over reform into an actual split in the party.

This fear combined with outside pressure for reform prompted Miyazawa to support a pure single-member district (SMD) system. Miyazawa officially announced his proposal on 10 December 1992. In addition to the introduction of an SMD electoral system, this "Outline for Political Reform" also included provisions concerning political funding transparency, party subsidies, and the abolition of factions. By 22 January 1993 the LDP's Head Office of Political Reform had the preliminary proposals of the four bills that would make up the Miyazawa administration's political reform package bill. This package included revisions to the Public Office Election Law, revisions to the Political Funds Control Law, reapportionment, and party subsidies (Minkan Seiji Rincho 1993: 265).

Miyazawa tried to formulate a proposal that would not exacerbate the split between the Takeshita faction under Obuchi, and Ozawa's new faction, Reform Forum 21. In the end though he chose a proposal that had little to no chance of gaining opposition party support. He ignored Ozawa's threat to leave the party if reform efforts failed in the Diet. As we shall see, this would prove to be a fatal miscalculation on his part.

Ideological divisions between anti- and pro-reformers within the LDP served as a second constraint on Miyazawa's ability to build support for his reform efforts. Many influential members within the LDP were in the anti-reform camp. While wary of being vocal anti-reformers given the public sentiment at the time, these politicians worked to ensure that Miyazawa's reform proposal did not pass. The lack of support for reform on the part of many senior leaders of the LDP became apparent between the time when the LDP's Head Office of Political Reform announced its outline and when the bill was actually brought before the Diet. Even though the leadership had come up with a proposal that was highly unlikely of ever receiving support from the opposition, many members of the LDP did not want any electoral reform proposal to be presented on the Diet floor. For example, on 8 March 1993 four up-and-coming members of the LDP (Yamazaki Taku, Katō Kōichi, Koizumi Junichirō, and Nakamura Kishirō) met with Mori who was the head of the Ministry of International Trade and Industry (MITI) at the time and pushed for tabling electoral system reform and instead implementing an anti-corruption law (Minkan Seiji Rincho 1993: 267). Obuchi, the new head of the Takeshita faction, also stated that political reform should be delayed and considered in a special session of the Diet that would be convened after the next election for party president (Minkan Seiji Rincho 1993: 265). This suggestion implied that realizing reform during the current session would be quite difficult.

The calls for a slower, more cautious approach to reform were countered by three groups of pro-reformers in the LDP – a group of junior Diet members referred to as *Wakate Kaikaku Ha* (the Group of Young Diet Members Committed to Reform), the League to Restore Trust in the Party, and Ozawa's Reform Forum 21. These groups formed at different times and had different motives and tactics. Because both *Wakate* and the League to Restore Trust in the Party had members across factional lines, some overlap among the three groups existed. In particular, some members of *Wakate* joined Ozawa's Reform Forum 21 when it formed two years after *Wakate's* inauguration. However, each group had a different type of influence on reform. The actions of these groups of junior politicians are analyzed in detail in Chapter 6. For now, it is important to note that these groups existed and exerted pressure on Miyazawa to come up with a plan that had a feasible chance of passing the Diet.

A survey of members of the LDP released on 2 June 1993 reveals the divisions within the party at the time. The survey focused on the preferred action on reform, offering politicians one of four options. From the pool of respondents, 35 percent said that according to party decision, a pure SMD system must be implemented. Twenty-five percent declared that it is necessary to make a small compromise with the opposition and create a system with 300 SMD seats and 150 PR seats. Thirty-four percent supported the 300 SMD/150 PR compromise but insisted that it be implemented during the current session of the Diet. The remaining 7 percent wanted to maintain the current multiple-member district system.[10] The only faction that presented a united stance on reform was Ozawa's Reform Forum 21. All 34 members who answered the survey declared that a compromise electoral reform bill must be passed during the current session. The rest of the factions had members supporting all four options in varying proportions (Taniguchi 1999: 142).

The survey reveals that by spring 1993 the LDP was split three ways with a third of the party in favor of Miyazawa's pure SMD system, a third wanting a small compromise with the opposition, and a third demanding that this compromise be realized during the current session. The divide between anti- and pro-reformers is not completely apparent from these survey results. In general, however, the anti-reformers supported Miyazawa's pure SMD proposal. The pure SMD proposal had little chance of being passed. Given the public sentiment at the time, anti-reformers were reluctant to come out directly against reform. Instead, many of those opposed to seeing reform passed supported Miyazawa's pure SMD system because it had little chance of receiving opposition support and passing the Diet (Sakamoto 1999: 109–10).

The old guard led by Kajiyama were not ardent supporters of reform. Kajiyama, however, did make some efforts to promote Miyazawa's SMD proposal, perhaps due to the unlikelihood of its passage. Between April and May 1993, Kajiyama tried to sell the pure SMD system by proposing electoral reform to both the Upper and Lower Houses of the Diet. Kajiyama argued that a pure SMD system in the Lower House and a PR system in the Upper House would constitute a combined system. Of course, this type of combined system was not the kind the opposition was reluctantly advocating. It did have the appearance of a combined system, though, and Kajiyama tried to exploit this fact. The opposition and even many members of the LDP did not buy Kajiyama's attempt to sell reform this way. In the end, Kajiyama reiter- ated the contention that more time was needed to develop electoral reform and pushed for postponing the decision on reform to a later date. Instead, he felt anti-corruption measures should be implemented during the current session (Taniguchi 1999: 140–41).

Frustrated with the direction that Kajiyama was taking the party, both *Wakate* (one of the groups of junior LDP politicians in favor of reform) and the Ozawa's Reform Forum 21 tried to influence Miyazawa in the opposite direction of Kajiyama. *Wakate* began a signature campaign in an attempt to pressure Miyazawa to realize reform during the current session (Taniguchi 1999: 140). Ozawa and his Reform Forum 21 continued to push for a com- promise with the opposition built around a combination SMD/PR system based on the German model, increasing its threats to leave the party if reform was not realized during the current session. Although the opposition's propo- sal of an SMD/PR system based on the German model differed significantly from the LDP's pure SMD proposal, it did have an SMD component (Saka- moto 1999: 110–11). This concession opened the door for compromise with the LDP. Realizing this, Miyazawa suggested at a press conference (two weeks prior to the opposition's official announcement of its proposal) that a compromise veering away from the LDP's original proposal was a possibility (Taniguchi 1999: 141).

Miyazawa actually asked Kajiyama to work on building LDP consensus behind such a proposal.[11] In the end, Kajiyama was not able to realize party consensus, in large part due to the fact that so many anti-reformers held positions on the LDP Executive Council. Given the divisions within the LDP over reform, Kajiyama argued that reform needed to be postponed until after the 1995 Upper House elections, reasoning that forcing a consensus would break apart the LDP. The fact that Kajiyama thought that he could postpone the reform debate clearly illustrated how he (and Miyazawa who deferred all domestic policy-making decisions to Kajiyama) misread the public mood, as well as Ozawa's conviction (Sakamoto 1999: 111; Taniguchi 1999: 140–43).

After Kajiyama made this declaration, the opposition parties submitted a no-confidence motion. Ozawa and his faction backed this motion in open protest of its party's inability to realize reform. With the support of 39 Ozawa followers and the abstention of 18 other members of the LDP, the no- confidence motion passed and the Miyazawa government fell with the LDP in a state of chaos (Sakamoto 1999: 112; Taniguchi 1999: 144).

The question we are left with is why Miyazawa failed. From the previous discussion, it is clear that he did not fail because of the political environment. As we have seen, with two successive scandals, a window of opportunity for reform remained open throughout most of his tenure as prime minister.[12] Miyazawa also did not fail due to insufficient resources. He was a senior politician with connections within and outside his party. Finally, he did not fail because the constraints he faced were insurmountable. The possibility to build a coalition for reform was there; he simply had to be willing to risk alienating the old guard in the LDP. In the end, he failed because he did not possess the personal attributes – vision, commitment, and the willingness to take risks – that favor the successful passage of reform. Without these personal attributes he was unable to use the resources he possessed in a way that would increase the chance of passing reform.

Miyazawa's resources

Miyazawa was a senior politician. He served two terms in the Upper House between 1953 and 1965 before being elected to the Lower House in 1967. Before becoming prime minister, he served in several cabinet posts including the head of the Ministry of Trade and Industry (1970–71), foreign minister (1974–76), finance minister (1986–88) and deputy prime minister (1987–88). In addition to these formal parliamentary positions, Miyazawa was the leader of the third largest faction within the LDP. All of these positions allowed him to build connections both within and outside the LDP. He was not in the most powerful faction in the LDP, but as faction head he was often at the table when internal party bargaining occurred (Schlesinger 1997: 212).

Once he became prime minister, the resources at Miyazawa's disposal increased. He not only had the formal powers to name his own cabinet and dissolve the Diet, but he also had the informal powers to set the policy agenda. In addition, prime ministers are the focus of a larger amount of media attention than other politicians. This increased media attention is a potential resource for advocates of reform to push their agenda (Shinoda 2000: 90). Miyazawa had all these resources. The way he chose to use (or not use) these resources differed from other advocates of reform and explains the ultimate fate of reform during his administration.

Miyazawa as a non-reformer

Miyazawa was not an advocate of reform. He was not committed to seeing reform passed, nor did he even attempt to present a vision of a reformed Japan. He proposed reform because he felt that the environment at the time demanded some action be taken. At best, he was indifferent to political reform (Curtis 1999: 94). He certainly was not going to take any risks to convince other politicians to support something he was not committed to. Gerald Curtis, a prominent political scientist who interviewed Miyazawa several years after the fall of his administration, explains,

> He [Miyazawa] readily admits that he submitted a bill to change the electoral system into a simple single-member district system not because he either thought that it was a particularly good idea or believed that it stood much chance of being passed by the Diet, but because the reform mood at the time required that he do something.

(1999: 94)

Miyazawa found himself in an environment that demanded reform. He, however, was not poised to challenge the constraints that stood in the way of passing reform.

When the first window of opportunity opened after the outbreak of the Kyōwa scandal, Miyazawa increased his reform rhetoric, but he did not actively pursue broad political reform. The Kyōwa scandal, like past scandals, centered on political finance abuses. Miyazawa considered introducing an independent funding bill, but he did not formulate a concrete proposal. Instead, the policy debate turned to the Peace-Keeping Operations bill. The Miyazawa administration's successful passage of the PKO bill boosted public support which translated into electoral success in the July 1992 Upper House elections, closing the window of opportunity for reform.

Miyazawa's failure to realize reform when the second window of opportunity for reform opened after the outbreak of the Sagawa Kyūbin scandal is more complex since this time Miyazawa eventually supported the passage of reform. While Miyazawa was not enthusiastic about seeing reform implemented, he was more sympathetic to the notion once it became clear that the fate of his administration rested on its passage. Lack of agreement on reform was breaking the LDP apart. Indeed, Miyazawa's failure to realize reform resulted in both his ouster as prime minister and the split of the LDP. The question is, why was Miyazawa not able to succeed? In contrast to Kaifu, it was not Miyazawa's slow approach that resulted in his failure. Miyazawa delivered a reform package while the window of opportunity for reform was still open. Part of the difference between Miyazawa and Kaifu was that Miyazawa faced a party that was much more divided, especially after Ozawa lost the power struggle in the Takeshita faction and it split. Still, effective leadership should be able to overcome such a constraint. Although Miyazawa chose a reform proposal that had no chance of receiving opposition support, he did not foresee that his proposal would also fail to get a consensus in his party and instead lead to its split. Miyazawa's unwillingness to challenge the constraints posed by the divisions within the LDP, as well as his lack of vision and commitment to reform, contributed to the failure of reform.

Even though Miyazawa had put forth a proposal that had little chance of receiving opposition support, a united LDP had a fairly good chance of realizing reform, especially if the LDP was willing to compromise with the opposition. The LDP might not have been able to convince the opposition to support a pure SMD system, but on 28 May 1993 the opposition put forth a counter-proposal that called for a combination SMD/PR system based on the German model. While this proposal differed significantly from the LDP's pure SMD proposal, it did have an SMD component. This concession opened the door for compromise with the LDP. Ozawa wanted to exploit this opportunity, but the party leadership refused to alter their proposal from a pure SMD system. In the end, Miyazawa was not able to get his own party to reach an agreement on reform – not his pure SMD or any of the counter-proposals coming from such groups as *Wakate* and Ozawa's Reform Forum 21.

Miyazawa's lack of commitment influenced his inability to build a coalition for reform in his own party. Unlike former Prime Ministers Miki and Kaifu, Miyazawa was not a life-long reformer. In fact, he actively opposed reform at points in his career (Sakamoto 1999: 106). As we saw in Chapter 3, Miyazawa was a vocal opponent of the Kaifu administration's reform proposal. He worked with two other factions to ensure that the Kaifu administration's proposal failed. These actions illustrate the fact that he was not committed to reform. In 1991, his true preferences rested with sabotaging Kaifu's reform. Given his position during the Kaifu administration, there was no reason to expect him earnestly to support reform when it became salient during his administration. Miyazawa agreed to support reform in order to gain Ozawa's support. However, he did not have a history of supporting reform. And once in office he did not actively pursue reform until he felt pressure from the Sagawa Kyūbin scandal. This scandal made it impossible to sweep the notion of reform under the carpet.

The content of his reform package provides further evidence of his lack of commitment. He put forth a reform proposal that had no chance of passing the Upper House since the opposition parties were firmly against a pure SMD system. Miyazawa most likely hoped a pure SMD would satisfy the demands of Ozawa and his group in the LDP and thereby restore calm to the party.

In the end, Ozawa would not sign on to Miyazawa's proposal because Miyazawa was not willing to alter his pure SMD stance. Even though the potential for passing reform existed due to the opposition's support of a combined system, it was not guaranteed. And, of course, compromise meant that the LDP would have to alter its call for a pure SMD system at some point, either before the party drafted its initial proposal or during its negotiations with the opposition. Ozawa felt that the likelihood of such a compromise being reached after the LDP had officially presented a pure SMD system proposal to the Diet was low; thus, he chose to pressure Miyazawa into altering his proposal prior to its release from the LDP. When Miyazawa refused, Ozawa defected, voting with the opposition in a no-confidence vote against Miyazawa (Sakamoto 1999: 111–12).

Only in the last weeks of his administration did Miyazawa appear willing to seek realistic reform, realizing late in the game that the fate of his administration rested on this issue. On 31 May 1993 Miyazawa announced in a television appearance that "We have to implement reform in this Diet session. We will do it. I am not telling a lie" (Taniguchi 1999: 141). At this time, Miyazawa did seem willing to consider a combined system instead of a pure SMD system. His changed position alone was not enough to convince other members of the Executive Council who were anti-reformers to change their minds. When reform failed, Miyazawa looked like a liar. Realizing this, Miyazawa made the following statement about his failure to realize reform at a press conference held after the passage of the no-confidence motion:

I really wanted to pass political reform. I had come to believe that reform had to be passed. It can be said that it is regrettable that it didn't pass and for this I must apologize. It wasn't that I wanted to lie and lied. There was a process I thought I could follow; however, in the end it was as difficult as I originally thought it would be.

(Taniguchi 1999: 146)

Miyazawa's commitment to reform, however, came too late.

Given Miyazawa's lack of commitment, it is not surprising that he was not willing to take risks to ensure that his reform proposal would be passed. Miyazawa did not act quickly. He took his proposal through the normal policy-making channels within the LDP. He bowed to the constraints posed by Kajiyama and the old guard. He was unwilling to defy his patrons.

Given that Miyazawa miscalculated Ozawa's determination to leave the party if it failed to act on reform, his proposal can be interpreted as a non-risky way of trying to appease Ozawa. Ozawa initially supported a pure SMD system when he was secretary general during the Kaifu administration. Miyazawa could have reasoned that Ozawa would look favorably upon his return to Ozawa's initial policy preference. Perhaps, Miyazawa thought that Ozawa would be placated by a pure SMD system proposal. In reality, Ozawa wanted a proposal that had a realistic chance of passing the Diet. Although an SMD system had been Ozawa's original preference, he changed his position once he lost the power struggle in the LDP. From this point on he began considering leaving the LDP and forming a coalition with the opposition parties. He also increased his visible attachment to reform. The fact that he called his new faction in the LDP Reform Forum 21 is evidence of this. Ozawa began staking his career on reform, making its successful passage all the more important.

Conclusion

Miyazawa had ample opportunity to pursue reform. As illustrated in Table 4.1, two separate windows of opportunity opened during Miyazawa's tenure in office. The Kyōwa scandal opened the first window of opportunity for reform. This window of opportunity remained open until the LDP's solid performance in the Upper House election in July 1992. The window did not remain closed long, though. The outbreak of the Sagawa Kyūbin scandal opened a second window of opportunity. This scandal was more severe than the Kyōwa scandal. The resulting window of opportunity was also open longer. In both instances, however, Miyazawa did not provide the leadership necessary to convince his fellow LDP party members to support reform. As we have seen in this chapter, although Miyazawa had sufficient resources to pursue reform, he was not a risk-taker with vision and commitment. In fact, until his final months in office he did not earnestly pursue reform. As a result, reform failed.

Many constraints did stand in the way of reform being passed during the

Table 4.1 A summary of Prime Minister Miyazawa's reform attempts

Length of the first window of opportunity while the leader is in government	6 months (Jan. 1992 to July 1992)
Magnitude of the scandal that opens the first window	Medium
Length of the second window of opportunity while the leader is in government	10 months (Oct. 1992 to Aug. 1993)
Magnitude of the scandal that opens the second window	High
Level of resources	High
Risk-taking	Low
Vision	Low
Commitment	Low
Outcome	No reform

Miyazawa administration. Perhaps the largest constraint was found in the divisions within the LDP between reformers and non-reformers. Miyazawa was not willing to use his position as prime minister to try to find some middle ground between these groups. If he had conceded to Ozawa's demands, he risked losing the support of the old guard in the LDP whom were adamantly opposed to reform. He chose to stand by the old guard; this decision in turn led to the defection of Ozawa and the downfall of his administration.

Ironically, though, the split in the Takeshita faction is also the main reason that reform succeeded in the end. The split put Ozawa in a position where he could realize reform. A coalition for reform within the LDP was not feasible given the intense opposition by many of the party elite. Ozawa had ties with the opposition that he had been building for years. Ozawa's first preference was to realize reform within his own party. When it became clear that this would not work, he then turned to an alternative plan – defecting from the LDP and building a coalition government with the opposition. As we will see in the next chapter, he had the personal attributes and resources to build this coalition and thus realize reform.

5 Ozawa Ichirō
Rebel with a cause

The most important thing to change in Japan is the consciousness of the Japanese people ... Interacting with the rest of the world in a Japanese way doesn't work. We need to be more effective. The Western World is a direct, agreement-oriented society. They discuss and debate things ... Japanese people need to become more logical and reasonable. We need to embrace debate and discussion. We have to change people's consciousness. It is consciousness reform. What I am talking about is a revolution.

Ozawa Ichirō, personal interview, 12 July 2003

Ozawa Ichirō has a radical vision of reform. And he has been unafraid to express it since he attained his first visible position of influence in 1989 as the Liberal Democratic Party's (LDP) secretary general. His book, *Blueprint for a New Japan*, exposed weaknesses in the Japanese political system and forcefully called for comprehensive reform. Changing the electoral system from a multiple-member district (MMD) system to a pure single-member district (SMD) system was but one step towards creating a country with strong leadership capable of influencing world politics. Ozawa argued that an SMD system would create a competitive two-party system in Japan. Instead of having an entrenched dominant conservative party, voters would have two options and be capable of throwing the rascals out when they were dissatisfied with the government. Party alternation would strengthen the legitimacy of the Japanese political system and allow Japan's leaders to speak with greater authority in the international arena.

As we will see in this chapter, Ozawa achieved electoral and campaign finance reform, but he failed to change politics as usual in Japan. What the case of Ozawa Ichirō reveals is that there is a fundamental conflict between the bold expression of new ideas and the maintenance of power, something that is necessary in order to enact comprehensive reform. Ozawa's propensity to take risks, his vision, and his commitment aided him in his quest to convince politicians to support electoral system and campaign finance reform. These very same characteristics, however, impeded his ability to govern. As a result, he has not seen his larger vision of reform come to fruition.

This chapter focuses on Ozawa's successful effort to pass electoral system and campaign finance reform. As we have seen in past chapters, leaders with adequate resources who lack vision, commitment, and the willingness to take risks fail to pass reform. While Prime Ministers Kaifu and Miyazawa were senior politicians with the resources to pursue reform, neither had the personal attributes that aid leaders in convincing politicians to pass reform. Kaifu's failure to pass reform was due in part to his unwillingness to dissolve the Diet after he threatened to do so following the Diet's rejection of his political reform bill. Kaifu could have forced his fellow party members to take responsibility for their rejection of reform by dissolving the Diet, but he backed down. Due to Kaifu's failure to take this risk, reform never regained salience. Miyazawa also played by the LDP's rules, refusing to take risks. Moreover, unlike Kaifu, he did not believe in reform. Miyazawa found himself in a political climate that demanded reform, yet he did not have the vision or commitment needed to convince other politicians that reform was in their best interest.

After the Miyazawa administration's failure to pass reform in 1993, Ozawa Ichirō, a disaffected leader within the LDP, broke away from the ruling party of 38 years in an attempt to build an anti-LDP coalition that could pass reform legislation. Ozawa's gamble paid off. The eight-party anti-LDP coalition he put together took over the government after the July 1993 Lower House election. Although the coalition was forced to compromise on several aspects of its original reform proposal, on 29 January 1994 it passed a reform package consisting of a new electoral system, stronger political funding regulations, government funded party subsidies and reapportionment.[1] Ozawa's connections both within and outside the LDP combined with his willingness to take risks, his vision, and his commitment were crucial factors in his successful quest to pass reform.

Ozawa's successful attempt to realize reform

The window of opportunity for reform

Ozawa was at the center of national attention after he and over forty of his fellow party members broke away from the LDP after the no-confidence motion against Prime Minister Miyazawa. After leaving the LDP, Ozawa immediately formed a new party, the *Shinseitō* (the New Renewal Party); however, it was not clear that Ozawa would be able to maintain any influence outside the LDP. What was clear was that reform was popular with both politicians and the public. In fact, the passage of the no-confidence motion confirmed the salience of reform.

Reform was the issue in the July 1993 Lower House election that followed the no-confidence vote. The investigation of politicians involved in the Sagawa Kyūbin scandal exposed additional scandals. Most of these scandals involved the construction industry giving bribes to political officials in return for government contracts. Since scandals kept being uncovered, political reform remained on the agenda.

Scandals were not the only thing keeping reform salient. The failure of the Miyazawa administration to pass reform prompted the no-confidence vote. The fact that this failure was the last item of business in the Diet before the election made the issue that much more prominent. Moreover, many politicians began staking their careers on reform, including Ozawa Ichirō.

New parties, reform, and voter confusion characterized this election. Three new parties emerged – *Sakigake* (the Harbinger Party), the *Shinseitō* (the New Renewal Party), and the Japan New Party (JNP). Both *Sakigake* and the *Shinseitō* were LDP breakaway parties. Under the leadership of Takemura Masayoshi, about a dozen predominantly second-generation former LDP Diet members formed *Sakigake*. The *Shinseitō*, Ozawa's party, consisted of 44 pro-reformers who had been part of the LDP, many of whom had only been elected to the Diet one or two times. The other new party of note was the Japan New Party (JNP) under the leadership of Hosokawa Morihiro. Unlike the two aforementioned parties, this party was predominately a grassroots party with a few ex-LDP politicians among its ranks. Hosokawa had a broad view of reform. He advocated deregulation of the bureaucracy and decentralization of the national government in addition to electoral reform. All these parties emphasized their newness, as well as their commitment to reform. In fact, due to the fact that these parties all supported some version of political reform, voters had a hard time distinguishing among parties in the election.

The new parties performed strongly in the 1993 election. Hosokawa's Japan New Party increased its number of seats in the Lower House from zero to thirty-five, mainly at the expense of the Japan Socialist Party (JSP). However, both LDP and JSP candidates lost votes in districts where new party candidates ran. Interestingly enough, LDP and JSP candidate vote totals were much less affected in districts where no new party candidate ran (Kabashima and Reed 2001: 631). In districts where new parties fielded candidates a trend towards voting for change and the alternation of power did emerge (Kabashima and Reed 2001: 637). The new parties were unable to field candidates in all districts, though.

The LDP did lose its majority in the Lower House for the first time in 38 years, but the public was not really "throwing the rascals out." Most LDP incumbents who remained in the party were re-elected in 1993. The LDP lost its majority because over fifty of its members broke away and joined new parties. Most of the members who broke away from the LDP and joined *Sakigake* and the *Shinseitō* were also re-elected. The big change in the relative strength of parties resulted from the split of the LDP, not the election of a large number of new politicians. No matter how the LDP lost its majority, though, the fact that it faced the new parliamentary session without a clear majority had a significant effect on the course of reform.

After the LDP lost its majority in the Lower House, the main question was whether the LDP could convince one or more of the opposition parties to join it in a coalition or whether all the opposition parties minus the Communists could overcome their differences and form an anti-LDP grand coalition. Prior to the election, Ozawa had secured agreements to form a coalition with four other opposition parties: the Socialists (JSP), the Kōmeitō, the Democratic Socialist Party (DSP), and the Social Democratic League (SDL) (Sakamoto 1999: 119). This five-party opposition group still lacked a clear majority; it had approximately the same strength as the LDP in numbers. Thus, the JNP and *Sakigake* became the swing parties in deciding whether the LDP or Ozawa's opposition group would compose the government. After being wooed from both sides, the JNP and *Sakigake* decided to join forces with the other opposition parties. Ozawa masterminded this deal by getting the other parties to agree to the combination electoral system desired by *Sakigake* and the JNP. Ozawa, who preferred to wield his influence from behind the scenes, also promised to make Hosokawa, the head of the JNP, prime minister (Curtis 1999: 111–14).

With the inauguration of the eight-party coalition government led by Hosokawa, the LDP found itself out of power for the first time in 38 years. This change of administrations played a significant role in keeping the window of opportunity for reform open. A change of administration can amplify the salience of reform if it places a pro-reform party/coalition in government. In the 1993 case, most parties that were members of the coalition had campaigned on the platform of reform. It is not a given that a new administration will actively pursue reform simply because it campaigned on reform, however. The new leaders could have emphasized reform because it resonated well with the public, not because they sincerely intended to implement reform. This was not the case with the Hosokawa administration backed by Ozawa, though. On 10 August 1993 Hosokawa publicly pledged to pass reform legislation by the end of the year, promising to take "political responsibility" if it failed (Sasaki 1999: 535). Hosokawa saw little choice but to pursue reform since all parties, including the LDP, saw the results of the Lower House election as a mandate for reform.

As the case of Prime Minister Kaifu in Chapter 3 illustrates, an open window of opportunity only sets the stage for reform; it does not guarantee the passage of reform. Kaifu did not act quickly. As a result, the window of opportunity was closed by the time his proposal was presented to the Diet. In contrast, Ozawa capitalized on his opportunity. His propensity to take risks, his vision, and his commitment influenced the way he used his connections within and outside the LDP to pursue reform while the conditions for reform were still ripe.

Ozawa's resources

Ozawa accumulated a variety of resources during his eight terms in office prior to breaking away from the LDP. Most of his resources came from his senior position. Two of the most critical resources were patron–client ties within the LDP and connections with opposition party leaders. Ozawa acquired these resources in his special role as political fixer Kanemaru's protégé in the influential Takeshita faction.

Patron–client ties are a resource that is common to senior LDP faction heads. Ozawa had not reached the status of faction head; however, given that he was Takeshita's and Kanemaru's pick to take over the faction, several of his responsibilities allowed him to build such patron–client ties. For example, Ozawa was responsible for distributing election money to many new Takeshita faction members. He also was involved in the selection of new LDP candidates, who viewed him as their patron. As a result, the candidates who were elected then felt a large sense of obligation to Ozawa for helping them gain office. In short, Ozawa's influential status in the Takeshita faction enabled him to create a loyal group of supporters in the LDP (Ōtake 1996: 287).

Ozawa's patron–client ties became an invaluable resource when Ozawa decided to break away from the LDP. Most of the junior members who followed Ozawa out of the Takeshita faction and then out of the party were elected when Ozawa was in charge of distributing funds. When asked how he was able to recruit members to follow him out of the LDP, Ozawa pointed to the importance of patron–client ties:

> One reason [I was able to recruit members to follow me] was that, in the Japanese way, I had looked after them. Also at that time creating a political reform administration was very popular ... I had the self-confidence that no matter what I would win the government. So even though many people were worried, they followed me out of the party.
>
> (personal interview, 12 July 2003)

Clearly, Ozawa's role as a patron helped him convince members of the LDP to follow him out of the party.[2]

At the time that Ozawa decided to leave the party he had a large enough following to actually put the LDP's majority in jeopardy. In fact, Ozawa and his new party, the *Shinseitō*, largely were responsible for depriving the LDP of its majority following the 1993 election. These followers also formed a support base that increased the legitimacy of his new party. This support base helped him as he tried to recruit new members.

Ozawa's ties to local politicians played an important role in the recruitment of new *Shinseitō* candidates to run in the 1993 election. Given his previous experience in recruiting candidates for the Takeshita faction, Ozawa knew the key players in every district. He functioned in a system of obligation and could capitalize on this. A journalist who covered Ozawa explained that Ozawa made direct appeals to local level politicians saying "Join my party and I will support you" (personal interview, 27 February 2001). A new recruit to the *Shinseitō* gave a very detailed account of Ozawa's recruitment of prefecture assembly members:

Many prefecture assembly members saw the *Shinseitō* as an opportunity. Before 1993, the LDP controlled the candidate slots and decided who could run where. The *Shinseitō* offered these politicians a way to run. Ozawa targeted these politicians. The prefecture level politicians were appealing to Ozawa because they had their own support base [*jiban*]. He saw them as a viable candidate base for a new party. He knew there were people in this group who wanted to become Diet members.

(personal interview, 23 February 2003)

Ozawa was able to use his connections at the local level to strengthen his new party. Recruiting party members was crucial for the *Shinseitō*'s survival as well as its push for political reform. The more candidates the party saw elected, the stronger its position vis-à-vis other small parties and the larger its voice in a potential anti-LDP coalition. Ozawa's recruitment strategy, which built on his connections at the local level, proved successful.

Ozawa's connections to opposition party leaders were another crucial resource. Ozawa established these connections with opposition party leaders through both formal and informal positions he held in the LDP. Ozawa's tenure as LDP secretary general during part of the Kaifu administration offered him access to LDP/opposition policy discussions and provided him with a deep knowledge of the policy-making process and the personalities involved in it. Ozawa continued his interaction with the opposition party leaders in his role as political don Kanemaru's right-hand man in the Takeshita faction. This position gave him even greater access to the informal policy-making process. Within the LDP, the politicians holding any of the top four party positions and the leaders of the most influential factions are included in the most important policy and personnel decisions. A smaller subset of these LDP actors is involved in negotiations with the opposition. Due to his close relationships with both Takeshita and Kanemaru, Ozawa was often privy to these exclusive meetings which gave him connections to opposition party leaders (Schlesinger 1997).

These connections to opposition party leaders facilitated his ability to build an anti-LDP coalition. By the time he decided to break away from the LDP, he had long-standing relationships with many of the opposition party leaders. Ozawa had built a certain level of trust and familiarity with these leaders. Such feelings played an indispensable role in the formation of the anti-LDP coalition. When Ozawa broke away from the LDP, he already had agreements with four other opposition parties to co-operate in the upcoming 1993 Lower House election with the goal of eventually creating an anti-LDP coalition that could take control of the government. These five parties did not have the combined numbers to take over the government. Still, together they could establish a strong presence (Sakamoto 1999: 119).

Ozawa's relationships with the opposition continued to benefit him once the anti-LDP coalition had been formed. Ozawa's relationship with Ichikawa Yūichi, the chairman of the Kōmeitō, was particularly strong. Ozawa's ties with Ichikawa came from years of nurturing, making it a rare resource, only available to a politician who had been privy to top-level backroom deals during his career. These two leaders often pooled their respective support bases in an attempt to control the direction of the eight-party coalition. This alliance, referred to as the *Ichi-Ichi* line, was a force that Ozawa's rivals in the coalition found hard to counter.[3]

The *Ichi-Ichi* line influenced the content of the coalition's reform bill. In particular, Ozawa and Ichikawa used their alliance to convince the other coalition members to adjust the details of its reform proposal in an attempt to receive LDP support even though the LDP was outside the coalition. The Socialists (JSP) opposed any amendments to the original coalition agreement. Despite this opposition, Ozawa and Ichikawa did get the coalition to amend its original proposal; however, they failed to get complete support from the coalition members. Several Upper House members of the JSP voted against the coalition's amended bill in protest of the changes. Ozawa and Ichikawa ignored the opposition from these Upper House coalition members, publicly discounting the role of the Upper House in the policy-making process (Sakamoto 1999: 122). In this case Ozawa's strong connections to Ichikawa had mixed results. Initially the relationship enabled him to influence the content of the coalition's proposal. The exclusive relationship, however, ultimately created dissention in the ranks of the coalition.

The importance of resources becomes clearer when comparing Ozawa's experience to that of Kōno Yōhei, a junior politician who broke away from the LDP in 1976 to create a new party, the New Liberal Club (NLC). Kōno failed to achieve any of his policy goals largely due to his lack of resources. Kōno did not have any connections to the opposition, so his party stood alone in its attempt to force change from the outside. He had only been elected three times when he decided to leave the LDP. In contrast, Ozawa had been elected eight times when he left the party. This level of seniority provided him with access to LDP/opposition negotiations and allowed him to establish connections to these parties. Ozawa had secured several deals with the opposition prior to his departure from the LDP. Kōno also did not have the long-standing patron–client ties within the LDP. As a result, he only convinced a handful of members to leave with him. The LDP still had enough members to stay in power, even with the exit of Kōno and his followers. Ozawa, on the other hand, took over 40 members with him when he left the party, denying the LDP a complete majority. Clearly resources matter in explaining the differences in these two cases.

A lack of resources hampered other reformers' efforts to realize reform. For example, two other groups of junior politicians, the Utopia Study Group and later *Wakate Kaikaku Ha*, had been pushing for reform since the outbreak of the Recruit stocks-for-favors scandal in 1989 (Ōtake 1996; Wolfe 1995). Their lack of resources, however, stymied their efforts. They did not have a voice within the party, nor did they have the connections outside the party to make their voices heard.

While resources are necessary, they are not sufficient to bring about reform. Ozawa also needed to be willing to take the risk of breaking away from the LDP in the first place. Although he could not have built the anti-LDP coalition without his connections to the opposition, he also needed vision and commitment to hold this coalition together. These characteristics played a large part in explaining Ozawa's success.

Ozawa as a risk-taker

Ozawa risked ostracism from the political elite with his decision to break away from the LDP. Even though Ozawa lost the battle for the top position in the Takeshita faction, he still had a loyal support base within the LDP. Ozawa could have used this support base to fortify his own independent faction within the LDP, one that could have challenged the old-guard politicians who were resisting change. Ozawa initially did this after he lost the Takeshita faction power struggle, setting up Reform Forum 21 inside the LDP.[4] However, Ozawa was not patient enough to work within the channels of the LDP, especially when it became apparent that passing reform was not a priority of the LDP old guard. Ozawa explained,

> [I decided I couldn't push reform inside the LDP] because Miyazawa lied ... Miyazawa said in a television interview that he would make people [in the LDP] reform. Miyazawa was for reform from what I could tell. But people around him were against it and destroyed it. After this, I decided that it was not possible for me to stay in the governing party. The no confidence motion then came up.
>
> (personal interview, 12 July 2003)

After the Miyazawa administration failed to pursue reform, Ozawa decided to leave the party and try to pass reform from outside the LDP.

Ozawa realized what a huge risk he was taking in leaving the party. The potential cost of breaking away is why he exhausted all his other options within the LDP first. There was no guarantee that he would succeed either at building an anti-LDP coalition or at passing political reform. Failure to build an anti-LDP coalition and get into government would leave Ozawa outside the dominant party facing the obstacles that the current opposition had struggled with for almost four decades. Put simply, Ozawa risked losing access to the decision-making power that comes from controlling the government. As we have seen, Ozawa was a senior politician who held considerable influence within the LDP. He did lose the battle for the head of the Takeshita faction, but he still could have wielded power as the head of his new faction, Reform Forum 21. Ozawa might not have been able to pass reform from within the LDP, but he would have had a position in a party that had successfully held on to power for 38 years.

The obstacles in the way of Ozawa building an anti-LDP coalition capable of passing reform were large. Ozawa's new party could not come close to approximating the financial resources that the LDP had at its disposal, making recruiting and supporting new candidates more difficult. Also, while the LDP's support had been declining, the public was wary of Ozawa's defection. Finally, if Ozawa were to achieve his ultimate goal of heading a party that could challenge the LDP, he would need to join forces with some of the existing opposition parties, something that would not be an easy or even a feasible task. Although many of the opposition parties were excited by the prospect of joining forces with Ozawa to form an anti-LDP coalition, reform and the desire to be in power were the only two things that these various parties had in common, and even their opinions on reform were not uniform. Overcoming their differences and creating a new party would be a difficult task. The fact that Ozawa had connections to leaders of the opposition helped. It did not, however, guarantee him success in building a cohesive, functional coalition.

The one previous example of a renegade politician breaking away from the LDP under the banner of reform provided Ozawa several reasons to think twice before leaving the LDP. The experience of Kōno Yōhei and his New Liberal Club illustrates the risks and challenges of political life outside the LDP.

In the aftermath of the Lockheed scandal in 1976, Kōno Yōhei, a junior politician frustrated with the inability of younger Diet members to influence internal policy making within the LDP, convinced six other junior politicians to leave the LDP and form the New Liberal Club (NLC). The party's main goal was to force change within the LDP by demanding internal party reform in exchange for their return to the party. Initially, the new party saw modest success with 17 of its 25 candidates elected in the 1976 Lower House election. By leaving the party, the NLC was able to deny the LDP a majority in the Lower House, forcing it to scramble for the support of independent candidates following the 1976 and 1979 elections and to officially ask the NLC for its support after the 1983 election. As we shall see in Chapter 6, however, the NLC could not agree on a clear vision for the party, something that would inhibit it from forming alliances with other political parties. In the end, the NLC failed to distinguish itself from the LDP, especially with its decision to join the LDP in government following the 1983 election (Curtis 1988: 32). Although the NLC started with the goal of changing politics as usual by increasing the voice of junior politicians, it was not able to direct its efforts into an effective political movement for reform, one that would attract more party members and a greater base of support. By 1986 the NLC's numbers had shrunk considerably and it had not achieved any of its major goals. Conceding defeat, the few remaining members of the party rejoined the LDP only having had a marginal influence on the party in their ten years outside the party. As we saw earlier, Ozawa held more resources than Kōno when he decided to leave the LDP. Parting from the party that had dominated Japanese politics for 38 years, however, was still a huge risk for him.

Ozawa's risk-taking behavior did not begin with his decision to break away from the LDP. His career has been full of examples of his going out on a limb to realize his policy goals. A case in point is his pursuit of the Peace-Keeping Operations (PKO) bill during the Kaifu administration. The PKO bill sought to make it legal for Japanese troops to participate in UN peace-keeping operations. This measure was quite controversial because if passed it would constitute a reinterpretation of article 9 of Japan's peace constitution that "renounces war as a sovereign right of the nation" and prohibits Japan from maintaining war capabilities (Hanrei Roppō Henshū Iinkai 1997: 45). Ozawa did not risk his political career, per se, by becoming this bill's most vocal supporter, but he did put his party's overall popularity in jeopardy.

Ozawa put his position as LDP secretary general in jeopardy as he sought opposition support for a financial aid package for the Gulf War. Specifically, Ozawa agreed to abandon the incumbent candidate whom the LDP had supported in the previous election and instead support a Kōmeitō/DSP candidate in the 1991 Tokyo gubernatorial race in return for the support of these two parties for the $9 billion contribution to the Gulf War coalition. The LDP/Kōmeitō/DSP candidate, Isomura Hisanori, lost to the incumbent, Suzuki Shinichi, whom the LDP had formerly backed. In order to take responsibility for this embarrassing defeat, Ozawa was forced to resign from his position as LDP secretary general ("Kaifu Loses his Minder": 33). This formal loss of power did not mean that Ozawa had lost his influence behind the scenes. Still, the public defeat was a slap in the face.

The above examples illustrate that Ozawa was willing to take chances in order to pursue his policy preferences at different points in his career. He pushed his party to support the controversial PKO bill even though the public's reaction was uncertain.[5] He openly criticized the decision-making process in his own party. He put his own position as secretary general on the line when he overlooked an incumbent who had previously been supported by the LDP and backed a Kōmeitō/DSP candidate in the Tokyo gubernatorial race to gain their support for Gulf War donations. He then took the biggest risk of all by leaving the party where he had sizeable influence in an attempt to pass political reform from the outside.

Ozawa's vision

Ozawa saw reform as a means to a larger end – increased international stature for Japan. Electoral reform would move Japan towards becoming a two-party system. This change would in turn push parties to become more policy-focused. An emphasis on policy would foster the development of leadership, and these leaders would be able to guide Japan to play a larger role in the international political arena, Ozawa's ultimate goal (Ozawa 1994). Ozawa explained,

I felt that electoral reform was the best way to change how both politicians and the public approach things. A multiple-member district system is a very good system for a consensus society. In a single-member district system you have to choose one person. You have to articulate your opinion directly in this kind of system. In a multiple-member district system you can be more fickle. In a single-member district system you have to choose between two people in a logical way. Directly stating an opinion is very difficult for Japan's consensus society. I was for a single-member district system because it seemed it would force both the people voting and the people running to directly state their opinions.

(personal interview, 12 July 2003)

According to Ozawa, once leaders can state their opinions directly, they will be able to guide Japan into taking a larger leadership role in the international arena.

Different aspects of Ozawa's vision appealed to the public and to politicians. The public supported change. The image of a Japan that commanded greater respect in the international arena, something Ozawa promised would occur if Japan adopted an electoral system that provided incentives for politicians to become more policy focused, certainly fits into this category. In contrast, politicians were drawn to Ozawa's assurances that a new electoral system would institutionalize party alternation. This idea appealed to junior politicians who hoped that party alternation would break down some of the rigidity in the LDP dominant system. Members of the opposition parties were enticed by the idea of being in government for the first time in 38 years, something that would become a possibility if they aligned themselves with Ozawa after he broke away from the LDP.

The most visible forum for Ozawa's ideas was his book, *Blueprint for a New Japan,* which outlined his vision for Japan's future. In this book, Ozawa argued that political reform was the first step towards increasing Japan's political leadership in the international arena. Drawing on the recent example of Japan's failure to contribute to the Gulf War effort beyond offering financial assistance, Ozawa claimed that Japan's domestic political institutions hamper its decision-making ability. In *Blueprint for a New Japan* he explained:

Today, those who object to the contribution of troops and other personnel to international peace-keeping efforts argue that Japan must adhere to its strict postwar refusal to send military personnel abroad. To do otherwise, the argument goes, would be to retread a familiar and tragic path. In truth, we do actually risk repeating history – but it is by our *lack* of leadership, by our *inability* to make political decisions that this is so ... The fundamental aim of political reform must therefore be to consolidate in both form and substance the democratic authority that has become so dispersed, so that we can give those nominally in charge both the responsibility and the power to make the necessary political decisions.

(1994: 25–26)

By connecting a recent policy failure to his larger vision, Ozawa attempted to increase the resonance of his vision of political reform.

Ozawa also argued that electoral system reform would clean up the political world. Immediately following the Sagawa Kyūbin scandal, the goals of many politicians and the public differed. As one current Diet member who was a member of the now defunct Japan New Party pointed out, "What the public and Ozawa wanted differed. Ozawa wanted a two-party system and the public wanted to regulate funds" (personal interview, 15 June 1999). Polls administered prior to the 1993 election support this contention. Specifically, these polls showed voter interest in strengthening penalties for corruption and implementing campaign finance reform to be much greater than support for electoral reform (Ōtake 1997: 3).[6] Ozawa worked hard to convince the public that a connection existed between electoral reform and the reduction of money politics. In his book Ozawa explains:

> Any change of rules on contributions or campaigns that is unaccompanied by electoral reform will be nothing more than a diversion designed to placate a public weary of political money scandals. Any reform that does not transform the electoral system itself will not have the backbone needed to change the nature of politics. I emphasize here that electoral reform is not itself the aim; it is merely the means to a broader political reform. We distinguish between our aims and our means.
>
> (1994: 63)

Ozawa worked hard to change the focus from political funding reform to electoral system reform because the latter would facilitate the realization of his grand vision for a new Japan.

In a personal interview, Ozawa made his position on political funding reform even clearer:

> I was against it [changing the Political Funds Control Law] at that time. I was the only one. I was saying let's not restrict corporate contributions. But at that time, the JSP kept saying, we have to do this, we have to do this. Since it was a coalition at that time, I had to give in.
>
> (personal interview, 12 July 2003)

Ozawa understood the necessity of compromising to realize change. However, in the end it is not clear the extent to which defining the debate in terms of political funding or electoral system change mattered. Studies indicate that the public simply was supporting change writ large (Kabashima 1998).[7] Ozawa's general vision certainly met this desire; the particulars of his vision might not have been that important to the public.

Different aspects of Ozawa's vision appealed to different politicians. The members of the Takeshita faction who left the party with Ozawa did so for a variety of reasons. These reasons included a sense of obligation, the fever for political reform, and a desire for government posts. Politicians were also attracted to Ozawa because he appeared to have money and to be more powerful than Obuchi, his opponent in the LDP factional battle (personal interview with journalist, 27 February 2001).

Four politicians I interviewed who left the LDP with Ozawa all pointed to policy reasons for following Ozawa. A then first-time member of the Diet and a now high-ranking office holder in the Democratic Party of Japan (DPJ) explained, "I believed in reform; this is why I followed Ozawa" (personal interview, 7 March 2001). Studies that explore why politicians broke with the Takeshita faction and with the LDP as a whole confirm that support of reform is the greatest predictor of defection (Reed and Scheiner 2003: 470).[8] Some defectors, however, were not simply drawn to reform. Another first-time Diet member who followed Ozawa out of the LDP pointed out that Ozawa's new party was not all about reform. This politician was more enticed by Ozawa's grand vision. He explained, "Ozawa had a clear vision on security issues. The LDP's position on security is fuzzy" (personal interview, 22 February 2001). The politicians who left the LDP with Ozawa definitely were attracted by Ozawa's position on reform. Within this group many were also attracted by the direction he wanted to push Japan.

Ozawa also recruited new members to run in the 1993 election that followed the dissolution of the Diet. These new recruits joined his party for one or more reasons. At the pragmatic level, Ozawa promised to support them in the election. At the ideological level, Ozawa's vision appealed to them. One new recruit explained, "I joined the *Shinseitō* because I wanted to have a system with party alternation with two conservative parties" (personal interview, 23 February 2001). Ozawa's vision of reform would bring Japan's political system closer to this ideal.

The rank-and-file members of the power-hungry opposition party latched on to the short-term consequences of Ozawa's vision, while the leaders of these parties were more enticed by the long-term consequences. The most appealing short-term consequence of Ozawa's vision was the prospect of participating in a governing coalition for the first time in their careers. The long-term consequence that resonated with opposition party leaders was the promise of influential positions in a new party that would emerge if the single-member district electoral system was adopted.

Several politicians I interviewed pointed to Ozawa's promise of kicking the LDP out of government as their reason for aligning with him. A first-term member of one of the opposition parties unabashedly admitted that the reason his party was willing to change its position on reform and join the coalition rested in its desire to form an anti-LDP administration (personal interview, 23 June 2001). The short-term benefits of being in government were too tempting to resist. The price for being part of the government was signing on to an electoral system proposal that had a single-member district component to it, something that could result in many members of smaller parties losing their seats. However, as a former LDP cabinet minister in the Upper House explained, short-term gain overshadowed the long-term consequences of reform (personal interview, 21 May 1999).

The long-term aspects of Ozawa's vision, however, did appeal to leaders of the opposition parties. If the SMD component of electoral reform pushed Japan to a two-party system, by itself Ozawa's new party, the *Shinseitō*, was too small to become the main party that would challenge the LDP. Ozawa hoped that many members of the coalition would eventually see it in their advantage to join forces with him and create a new party to challenge the LDP. While giving up their current party label was unpalatable to many of the rank-and-file members of the coalition, it was something many party leaders were willing to consider, especially if it would increase their chance to participate in government in the future.

A high-ranking member of the JSP at the time explained why his party decided to join the coalition:

> Bringing down the LDP was the decisive factor. The JSP didn't support the type of electoral reform Takemura and Hosokawa were supporting, but it believed that big change was important. For democracy, [Japan] needed a big change. [The JSP] had to be in government to bring about such a big change. Therefore, we decided to join the coalition.
>
> (personal interview, 8 March 2001)

"Big change" started with placing the LDP in the opposition and securing party alternation. In order to achieve this, Ozawa needed the co-operation of the JSP. The JSP was aware of its swing position and was persuaded to join the coalition because it saw being in government as the only way to actually realize parts of its own policy agenda.

Finally, many members of the opposition found it difficult to oppose Ozawa's two-party vision because this image resonated well with the public. A member of the Hosokawa cabinet characterized the situation in the following way:

> The people wanted to see [a system that supported] an alternation of power. Television programs that focused on the reform issue constantly emphasized the importance of the change in power. If non-LDP politicians said something against a system that would facilitate such an alternation in power, they would be attacked.
>
> (personal interview, 18 June 1999)

Pressure from the public to realize Ozawa's vision certainly factored into the opposition parties' support of reform.

Those members of the LDP who favored staying with the medium-sized district system were labeled as members of the *shukyu-ha,* a term that literally translates into "protectors of the past." The media frequently used this label. A member of the *shukyu-ha* detailed the negative effects this label had on his political career, explaining:

> Political reform got caught up with an image that was created by the media. If you supported reform, you were good; if you didn't, you were bad. Single member districts were good. Multiple member districts were bad. The *shukyu-ha* label was harsh. It is the reason I wasn't re-elected.
>
> (personal interview, 22 February 2001)

Whether this label was created by pro-reformers or the media, it did have a negative impact on some politicians who found themselves in this category (Curtis 1999: 91).

Overall, the image of a Japan with a two-party system was appealing to many. How realistic this image was, given that the only thing that the members of the anti-LDP coalition could agree on was reform, is a different issue. The important point for the purposes of this argument is that Ozawa's followers and political allies believed the image of reform he created. And they were willing to join forces with Ozawa based on this image.

Ozawa's commitment

Ozawa's record as a politician showed his long-standing commitment to reform. Ozawa is a second-generation Diet member. According to a journalist assigned to Ozawa during the Kaifu administration:

> From the beginning of his career Ozawa was in favor of changing to a single member district system. Ozawa saw the Recruit Cosmos stocks-for-favors scandal as an opportunity to push it. He used Recruit.
>
> (personal interview, 27 February 2001)

Ozawa began actively supporting a single-member district electoral system in 1989 following the Recruit Cosmos stocks-for-favors scandal and during his tenure as secretary general in the Kaifu administration. He convinced Kaifu to support a pure SMD system in October 1989. He felt that this type of electoral system would result in a two-party system that in turn would allow Japan to become more policy-focused. As we saw in Chapter 3, Prime Minister Kaifu eventually changed his preference from a pure SMD to a mixed SMD/PR system, a proposal that eventually failed.

Ozawa's determination to see some kind of reform passed did not falter. He formed a reform study group within the LDP and began considering various options to realize reform, including working with the opposition and leaving the party. By the time the Miyazawa administration submitted its reform package, Ozawa was making ultimatums about the type of reform that needed to be proposed and passed. He threatened to leave the party if the LDP did not pass a type of reform that would get opposition support. He was willing to veer from his initial position of a pure SMD system in order to see some kind of reform passed. The Miyazawa administration, however, stuck to its initial proposal of a pure SMD electoral system, a proposal that would never get the necessary opposition support. When Ozawa realized that reform within the LDP was an impossibility, Ozawa began considering forming a coalition with the opposition in earnest. Ozawa and his followers joined the opposition in a vote of no-confidence against Miyazawa and subsequently left the party (Curtis 1999: 92–97; Kohno 1997: 136–39; Sakamoto 1999: 108–12; Taniguchi 1999: 143–46).

A politician demonstrates his commitment by his willingness to pay a price for his cause. Ozawa clearly was willing to pay a personal price for reform. His decision to break away from the LDP and pursue reform from the outside illustrates his commitment. When Ozawa decided to leave the LDP, he gave up a considerable amount. He was a senior politician who had already held several important positions in the LDP. Granted, he lost the battle to take over the most powerful faction in the LDP, but this loss did not mean that his career in the LDP was over. Pursuing reform from outside the LDP was an arduous task. He did not have the same amount of resources to work with as he did in the LDP. The LDP did not do anything to keep Ozawa in the party because they thought he could not leave precisely because it would be his political death (personal interview with journalist, 27 February 2001). He, like Kōno Yōhei before him, would not be able to survive outside the LDP. Ozawa believed in his cause, though, and was willing to face these obstacles if it meant he had a chance of realizing his goal.

Ozawa's commitment, in turn, facilitated his ability to convince other politicians to tie their fortunes to his. Other politicians and political parties observed this high level of personal commitment to reform and found it reassuring. A then third-term Diet member who joined Ozawa's *Shinseitō* explained, "Ozawa took a chance even though [he knew] it might not work. ... People followed Ozawa because they believed that Ozawa would take responsibility" (personal interview, 20 February 2001). When comparing Ozawa to Katō Kōichi, another LDP leader who threatened to leave the party in 2000, this same politician pointed out that "Politicians did not have the same feeling about Katō. They were not certain he would take responsibility for them. Katō was indecisive" (personal interview, 20 February 2001). In contrast, Ozawa's position on reform was clear and his commitment was unwavering.

These examples illustrate how Ozawa's risk-taking, his vision, and his commitment facilitated his ability to gain support for reform. Ozawa clearly outlined his vision of how reform would fit into his larger plan for a new Japan in his *Blueprint for a New Japan*. He was committed to reform and saw it as the first step in creating a more policy-oriented political arena. Ozawa's predecessors, former Prime Ministers Kaifu and Miyazawa, both lacked these personal attributes. This fact partially accounts for their failure. Although Kaifu fostered the image of a career reformer, he did not have the necessary vision or commitment. Moreover, Kaifu worked through party channels instead of challenging these constraints in an attempt to convince politicians to go against their original preferences. He was not willing to take any risks to pursue his proclaimed goal. Miyazawa was not a reformer; thus, it is not surprising that he failed to secure support for reform. He found himself in a political climate that demanded reform, yet he did not have the characteristics that are needed to persuade other politicians that reform is indeed in their best interest.

The role of scandal and electoral competition

When looking at the 1994 case in isolation both the severity of scandal and increased electoral competition appear to be viable explanations for the passage of reform. These variables have less leverage when the 1994 case is put in comparative perspective, though. To begin with, while the Sagawa Kyūbin scandal played a critical role in keeping a window of opportunity for reform open, its overall severity did not guarantee the passage of reform, something that becomes clear by considering the Lockheed and Recruit scandals in comparison to the Sagawa Kyūbin scandal. The Sagawa Kyūbin scandal certainly was one of the largest scandals in Japan's postwar history. As we saw in Chapter 4, it broke in August 1992 when Kanemaru Shin, an influential LDP kingmaker and the acting head of the Takeshita faction in the LDP, was accused of accepting large sums of money from the Sagawa Kyūbin company, a parcel delivery company, in illegal campaign contributions. At first, Kanemaru denied these charges, but the following week he held a press conference and acknowledged accepting 500 million yen from Sagawa. He was accused of distributing these funds to at least sixty other politicians. Kanemaru was indicted, but he struck a deal with the Tokyo Prosecutor's office and pled guilty to a "summary indictment," a plea normally reserved for minor offenses. The fact that Kanemaru only received a minor fine for his offenses outraged the public. In order to take responsibility for his involvement with Sagawa, Kanemaru eventually resigned from his Diet seat (Curtis 1999: 87; Noble 1993: 3–4). Kanemaru was later charged with tax invasion and the subsequent investigation of his affairs opened up many doors to the world of bribery and influence buying in Japan's political world. Several smaller scandals emerged and kept political reform salient.

Kanemaru was the only politician indicted in connection with the Sagawa Kyūbin scandal. The scope of this scandal, like both the Lockheed and Recruit scandals before it, however, was broad. The media speculated that at least eleven other prominent politicians also were involved in the scandal, including three former prime ministers (Nakasone Yasuhiro, Takeshita Noboru, and Uno Sōsuke) and a former LDP secretary general (Ozawa Ichirō) ("Japan:

Dirty Dozen": 36). However, only one implicated politician, Fujinami Takeo, lost his seat in the election following the Sagawa Kyūbin scandal.

As we have seen, reform passed in the aftermath of the Sagawa scandal. In isolation this fact supports the contention that the more severe a scandal, the more likely the passage of reform. For this assertion to be correct, reform would need to follow all major scandals, though. As Table 5.1 illustrates, the Lockheed, Recruit, and Sagawa scandals were similar in severity when measured by the number and status of politicians arrested or implicated. In fact, based on these measures, if anything, the Sagawa Kyūbin scandal was slightly less severe than the Lockheed and Recruit scandals. More politicians were arrested and implicated in the earlier cases. Reform, however, only passed in the aftermath of the Sagawa scandal. Clearly, something else explains the passage of reform following Sagawa. The difference in the attempts to reform following the Lockheed, Recruit, and Sagawa scandals rests with leadership.

Electoral competition also intensified prior to the passage of reform in 1994. When looked at in comparative perspective, it is clear that this variable also is not decisive in the passage of reform. It might have aided leaders in the passage of reform, but it did not in and of itself lead to reform.

The LDP certainly faced greater electoral competition in 1993. As illustrated in Table 1.1, the LDP's vote share declined dramatically from 46.1 percent in the 1990 Lower House election to 36.6 percent in the 1993 Lower House election. Not unrelated, three new parties contested this election. All three new parties – the Japan New Party, the *Shinseitō*, and *Sakigake* – stood for change. As mentioned earlier, in districts where new party candidates ran, both the LDP and JSP lost votes (Kabashima and Reed 2001: 631).

The question is, did this increased electoral competition result in reform? When comparing political reform attempts in Japan, Italy, New Zealand,

Table 5.1 A comparison of the severity of postwar scandals in Japan

Scandal	Number of politicians arrested	Status of arrested politicians	Number of implicated politicians
Lockheed	3	Former prime minister, LDP secretary general, parliamentary vice-minister of transportation	14 gray politicians (only five names released)
Recruit	2	Chief cabinet secretary and a member of the Kōmeitō	43 politicians, bureaucrats, journalists, and business people forced to resign from positions
Sagawa	1	LDP vice-president and kingmaker	At least 12, including the LDP vice-president

Sources: Several sources were consulted in the compilation of this table, including Allen 1991a, 1991b; Asahi Shinbunsha 1977; "Japan: Dirty Dozen": 36; Johnson 1986.

Germany, and the Netherlands in the 1990s, Reed argues that electoral pressure leads to a similar dynamic in all the countries. He explains,

> A party sees a short-term gain to be made in promising a reform which, if implemented, would work against its long-term interests. The party makes the promise in the hope that it will not have to be kept and parties can often, but not always, ignore their promises once in office. In each of these cases of political reform, parties got caught in bidding wars, competing to be the true reformers, and sooner or later found they had painted themselves into a corner. They could not avoid keeping their promises, because the electoral costs of breaking the promise had un-expectedly outgrown the costs of enacting the reform.
>
> (Reed 1999a: 190)

This explanation, however, fails to explain why parties were able to ignore promises to reform after the 1976 and 1990 elections which followed the Lockheed and Recruit scandals respectively. Why was the pressure too great to ignore in 1993? One possible explanation is that in the 1990s for the first time in the postwar period the LDP faced two elections in a row where scandal was a major issue (Reed 1997: 267). Here, the argument would be that the momentum from the close succession of the Recruit and Sagawa scandals was too difficult to ignore. This contention, however, begs the questions of why Miyazawa failed to enact reform after the outbreak of the Sagawa Kyūbin scandal and prior to the 1993 election. The Sagawa Kyūbin scandal played out for nearly one year before the Miyazawa government fell in the vote of no confidence. The split of the LDP, following the no-confidence motion, arguably increased the pressure on the LDP to reform, but this split was initiated by the agency of individual leaders willing to risk being margin-alized outside the LDP. Agency was the decisive factor, not the severity of the scandal or the increased electoral competition the LDP faced following the creation of new parties.

Conclusion

The analysis of the events presented in this chapter clearly illustrates that leadership matters in the process of reform. Table 5.2 summarizes Ozawa's successful reform attempt. Ozawa provides evidence that leaders can over-come the structural constraints in place and bring about change. Ozawa played a significant role in the passage of the first revision to the electoral system in the postwar period and the first major revision to the political funding system in almost twenty years. His decision to break away from the LDP and form a new party significantly altered the political landscape. The LDP lost its majority in the Lower House, opening up the possibility for an anti-LDP coalition to take control of government. Ozawa played a large role in securing the deals among the eight parties that eventually succeeded in

Table 5.2 A summary of Ozawa Ichirō's reform attempt

Overall length of the window of opportunity	15 months (Oct. 1992 to Jan. 1994)
Length of the window of opportunity while the leader is in government	5 months (Aug. 1993 to Jan. 1994)
Magnitude of the scandal that opens the window	High
Level of resources	High
Risk-taking	High
Vision	High
Commitment	High
Outcome	Revisions to the Public Office Election Law and the Political Funds Control Law

building this anti-LDP coalition. And, even though Ozawa was not the prime minister leading the coalition government, he was the driving force behind the coalition's quest to fulfill its inaugural promise to pass reform. He was involved in determining the content of the original coalition bill and played an integral role in the negotiations with the LDP in November 1993 that produced an amended coalition bill and the behind-the-scenes deals that produced the bill approved by the joint conference and both houses of the Diet.[9]

The Sagawa Kyūbin scandal was a necessary condition for opening the window of opportunity for reform in 1992. As we have seen in this chapter, it was a severe scandal in terms of the number and status of politicians arrested or implicated in the scandal. The string of mini-scandals that followed Sagawa in 1993 maintained the salience of reform. As the earlier cases of failed reform under Kaifu and Miyazawa illustrate, though, the outbreak of scandal alone, even a very severe one, is not sufficient for explaining why reform is enacted. Leadership is also critical.

Resources and personal attributes matter when leaders initiate reform. Ozawa was a leader with the resources and personal attributes particularly suited to convincing other legislators to pass regulations that would adversely affect their own behavior. Indeed, none of the politicians interviewed denied the important role Ozawa played in the passage of reform. His experience as a political fixer created a loyal following within the LDP, provided him with connections to the opposition, and increased his ability to negotiate and build alliances. Ozawa's willingness to take risks, his vision, and his commitment influenced the way he used these resources. Convincing his followers to leave the LDP with him and pursue change from outside the party was risky, but it was an important step towards actually passing reform. The cumbersome policy channels within the LDP inhibited the passage of reform. Supporting reform from outside the LDP allowed Ozawa to challenge these constraints. Meanwhile, Ozawa's vision provided reluctant politicians with a clear image of what reform entailed and what the likely consequences would be, causing these politicians to re-evaluate the costs and benefits involved in passing reform. Finally, Ozawa's commitment to reform was clear. Such commitment helped him recruit supporters. Clearly, Ozawa's leadership was critical in the passage of reform in Japan in 1994.

Ozawa's successful quest for political reform illuminates several characteristics of an effective leader in Japan. In the area of political reform, connections within and outside one's party are significant resources. The ability to mobilize blocks of support is important and facilitated by a leader's willingness and ability to take risks, his vision, and his commitment. Ozawa had these resources and personal attributes and thus was successful in his quest for reform.

What conclusions then can be drawn concerning what it takes to be an effective leader in Japan? Here, a distinction needs to be made between the type of leadership that is effective in securing the passage of reform and the type of leadership that is effective in everyday policy making in Japan. The characteristics of an effective leader in these two categories diverge. Ozawa's fate after the passage of reform illustrates this point.

Ozawa only remained in a position of influence for a short period after the passage of reform.[10] The fact that he did not continue in power, however, does not mean that the conclusions concerning political reform put forth thus far are incorrect. Ozawa had the resources and personal attributes best suited for pushing the passage of reform. Interestingly enough, though, these personal attributes did not facilitate his long-term tenure in power. One journalist explained:

> Ozawa was skilled at coming up with a grand design, but he couldn't hold his followers. His vision attracted people and encouraged them to go into battle. But his leadership style made it impossible for people to follow him for a long period of time.
>
> (personal interview, 27 February 2001)

An effective leadership strategy for political reform is one that challenges the constraints in place. This strategy is less effective for the everyday management of government, at least in Japan where consensus building is the norm. As one of Ozawa's new recruits pointed out:

> Ozawa had some leadership qualities. He had a strong will, especially in the area of reform. The problem is that Ozawa is quite clear about what he likes and what he doesn't like. He is not about compromise. This style doesn't fit with the type of daily decision making in Japanese politics.
>
> (personal interview, 23 February 2001)

Indeed, the qualities that are important to bring about dramatic change are not necessarily the qualities that lend themselves to the everyday decision-making process.

Ozawa's unwillingness to seek compromise after reform passed caused many of his followers and coalition partners to leave his political camp. A high-ranking JSP politician who participated in the anti-LDP coalition in 1993–94 blamed Ozawa for the eventual break-up of the coalition, explaining:

> Ozawa is not very good at protecting things once he has built them. He played an important role in the passage of reform and the formation of the coalition, but his inability to seek compromises with the coalition parties caused problems – it led to the downfall of the Hata adminis-tration.
>
> (personal interview, 8 March 2001)

Ozawa failed to consult the Socialists (JSP) on key policies in the anti-LDP coalition. The JSP resented being left out of the decision-making process and left the coalition, an action that resulted in the eventual downfall of the anti-LDP government.

Ozawa's top-down leadership style ran counter to the consensus decision-making norm where fostering personal relationships is quite important. While Ozawa had many connections to opposition leaders and local politicians, these connections were based on obligation created from the dispensation of favors more than the nurturing of personal relationships. One politician who left the LDP with Ozawa explained that while Ozawa was good at making deals, he was not good at relating to other people (personal interview, 20 February 2001). A former member of the *Shinshintō*, Ozawa's second political party, described Ozawa's leadership style in the following way: "You have to say yes to Ozawa if you follow him and that is why so many people have left him" (personal interview, 22 February 2001). Politicians associated with Ozawa were often frustrated by the fact that they always remained on the same level beneath him. This distance proved detrimental to Ozawa over time.

Ozawa was openly hostile to the consensual decision-making style characteristic of the Japanese Diet. In his book Ozawa claims, "'unanimous consensus' turns out to mean the tyranny of the minority" (1994: 28). Here, Ozawa is pointing to the fact that the JSP or the media can put pressure on the majority, the LDP in this case, to make concessions since consensual decision-making is the norm. Ozawa argued that if Japan wanted to increase its role in the international arena, then it needed to change this decision-making style.

Ozawa is aware of the limitations of his own leadership style in the Japanese context. When reflecting on the political funding system in 2003, Ozawa explained,

> [The idea of] the current system is that we have to do everything possible to restrict contributions. But [in reality] there are a lot of scandals

breaking out. This is because politicians can't function with such small sums of money; therefore, everyone receives dirty money. Companies give it and politicians receive it and scandals occur. Politicians can't talk about this state of affairs to the public. The people who say things like this, like me, get cut out from society. Even though they think what we say is true, they cut us out.

(personal interview, 12 July 2003)

Ozawa went on to explain the relation between direct communication and Japanese society:

In Japan, if you have a difference of opinion, people believe it will turn into a fight. Therefore everyone works hard to avoid disputes. This is how we are different. We have this different culture.

(personal interview, 12 July 2003)

Given this, Ozawa believes the only solution is to produce a change in the Japanese consciousness, something he realizes constitutes revolutionary change:

Japanese people need to become more logical and reasonable. We need to embrace differences of opinion. We have to change people's consciousness. It is consciousness reform. What I am talking about is a revolution.

(personal interview, 12 July 2003)

Until such consciousness reform occurs, however, chances are that Ozawa's leadership style will be rejected, or at least roundly criticized, in the everyday policy-making process in Japan.

Thus, while Ozawa's propensity to take risks, his vision, and his commitment aided him in his pursuit of reform in the short-term, these personal attributes actually hampered his ability to lead over the long term. If a politician is trying to change the system, vision is important. However, when this same leader attempts to run the system, then vision can impede the process. Similarly, while taking risks and challenging constraints like consensus-based decision making can help one overcome the obstacles in the way of reform, such actions cannot be sustained over the long term. The personal attributes that Ozawa had aided him in securing the passage of reform; these attributes were antagonistic to the day-to-day operation of government. The passage of reform is no small feat, but it is a rare event and different from everyday policy making.

6 Junior politicians
Ideas and action without access

The four leaders examined in the previous chapters – Miki Takeo, Kaifu Toshiki, Miyazawa Kiichi, and Ozawa Ichirō – all share at least one common characteristic – seniority. Miki, Kaifu, and Miyazawa had all served as politicians long enough to attain the prime ministership. Although Ozawa never became head of state, he was a senior politician and had held numerous influential party positions. All these politicians had the same basic level of resources. They had connections within and outside the LDP. They also had access to the formal and informal policy-making process and had been privy to this process before achieving their positions of influence. The difference between successful and failed reform in these cases rested with the personal attributes of the leaders.

Senior politicians, however, are not the only advocates of reform. Many junior politicians also favor changing the rules of the game. In fact, in Japan where the rules often benefit those higher up in the political hierarchy, one would expect junior politicians to be more open to reform. Indeed, the history of the political reform debate in postwar Japan provides several examples of junior proponents of reform. The one thing all these groups share is that they failed to realize their agenda, something I argue is due to the dearth of resources at their disposal. This chapter illustrates this point by looking at four cases of junior politicians pursuing reform between 1976 and 1994 – the New Liberal Club, the Utopia Study Group, *Wakate Kaikaku Ha*, and the League to Restore Trust. The leaders of these groups had varying degrees of vision, commitment, and risk-taking. Their efforts, however, were all thwarted by their lack of resources. All these groups failed to realize reform. Success only came in 1994 when Ozawa, a senior politician, mobilized these junior politicians as a support base and broke away from the LDP. An exploration of these groups of junior politicians illustrates the importance of political resources in securing the passage of reform.

Junior politicians and reform

The New Liberal Club

Kōno Yōhei and his breakaway New Liberal Club (NLC) present a very persuasive case for the importance of political resources in the political reform process. Kōno had many of the personal attributes that facilitate a leader's pursuit of reform. He had a history of taking risks. He was committed to reform. He also had several ideas about party reform and to a lesser extent anti-corruption. Despite these characteristics, though, he was not able to push through his desired reforms. This inability was due to the small number of resources his junior status afforded him.

Kōno pursued political reform in the wake of the Lockheed scandal, a time when the environment was ripe for such reform. As we saw in Chapter 2, several indicators suggest that the Lockheed scandal opened a window of opportunity for reform. Following the revelation of the Lockheed scandal at the US Senate subcommittee hearing in February, Miki's cabinet support ratings dropped eight percentage points from the previous November to 26 percent support (Sorifu 1976). This drop arguably reflects the public's decreased support of the LDP government, even with a reformer at the helm. The following December the LDP performed poorly in the 1976 Lower House election barely maintaining its majority, securing 263 of the 511 seats after convincing several independents to join the LDP (Masumi 1995: 186).

While the public's support of the government was declining, the salience of reform was increasing. Specifically, Kōno's decision to break away from the LDP and form the New Liberal Club in June 1976 placed the issue of reform center stage. Kōno formed his party on the issue of reform. The publicity the new party received served to keep reform in the forefront of the public's mind. In addition, Prime Minister Miki also used the Lockheed scandal to illustrate the continuing plight of money politics in Japan. For example, in his written resignation after the LDP pushed him out of office in December 1976, Miki emphasized the need to reform the seniority and faction dominated money politics of the LDP. He also called for the creation of a primary system in the selection of the party president (Masumi 1995: 186).

Despite this favorable environment for reform, Kōno failed to realize reform due to an insufficient amount of political resources. Kōno was a second generation politician. His seat was secure because he inherited a strong support group from his father. Since he had a secure seat he did not need an LDP faction's monetary support or political endorsement. Aside from monetary support and political endorsement, the greatest benefit that could come from factional membership is access to party posts. According to the LDP's informal institutional rules, however, these positions are reserved for senior politicians. As a result, Kōno would be forced to wait his turn before he could reap this benefit from factional membership, a waiting game that would last around 10 more years, since influential cabinet positions only come after five to six terms in office. As a junior Diet member, Kōno was expected to vote the party line and essentially be seen but not heard. Kōno was not pleased with this constraint and challenged it throughout the early years of his career. He was a risk-taker and had both vision and commitment concerning reform.

Kōno's most significant risk in relation to political reform was his decision to break away from the LDP in 1976 in the aftermath of the Lockheed scandal. Kōno's goal was to weaken the LDP so that it would be willing to listen to his demands for reforming the party. Kōno and his followers hoped that the LDP would be put in the position to listen to their demands and that they would be asked to rejoin the party on their own terms. By leaving the party, Kōno and his followers were able to deny the LDP a majority in the Lower House, forcing it to scramble for the support of independent candidates following the 1976 and 1979 elections and to officially ask the NLC for its support after the 1983 election. While the NLC received a cabinet position as part of its agreement with the LDP in 1983, by this point the window of opportunity for reform was closed (Curtis 1988: 33–34).

The risks involved in leaving the LDP were huge, especially for junior politicians.[1] Kōno's group was the first to leave the LDP in its 20-year history; thus, the consequences of cutting ties with the LDP were not clear. The fact that forming an opposition party capable of challenging the LDP was risky, however, was clear.

At a minimum the party had to find 25 candidates to stand for election in order for it to be officially recognized. Exactly 25 candidates ran in the 1976 Lower House election and 17 of them won. This number fell short of the 20 needed to get official representation on Diet committees but was still considered a victory for the renegade party.

Kōno's actions should not be interpreted as reckless simply because the chances of forming a viable opposition party were slim. Not all of the members of the NLC saw becoming an opposition party as the primary goal of the party. One strategy advocated by some of the NLC members was to draw in new members in hopes of denying the LDP a clear majority. These members hoped such a situation would force the LDP to ask the NLC and its members to rejoin the LDP on their own terms (Curtis 1988: 33).[2] This strategy too was quite risky because it assumed that no substitutes for the junior members of the NLC existed. If the LDP found itself short of a majority following the Lower House election, several coalition options were available, although some were more palatable and realistic than others. The LDP had cooperated with certain opposition parties rather successfully prior to the NLC's formation and could have conceivably cooperated with some of these parties more formally as governing partners. When the LDP did in fact find itself short of a majority after the 1976 election, it was able to recruit enough politicians who had run as independents to avoid bringing in other opposition parties. Substitutes for the six NLC members existed and were used. The members of the NLC had no way of predicting the LDP's response, though, given that no other cases of defection existed.

The costs of leaving the LDP were high and the probability of success was low. Yet, the other option – forcing change within the party – presented even less chance for success for these junior members who sought party reform. While the chances of Kōno's strategy of pushing change within the LDP from the outside were low, they were higher than his chances of realizing change inside the LDP. The fact that Kōno was willing to take this enormous risk to pursue his political agenda certainly suggests that he had one of the critical personal attributes that facilitate a leader's pursuit of reform.

While Kōno Yōhei was only a third-term Diet member when he decided to leave the LDP, his activities prior to the break illustrate his high propensity to take risks.

His frustration with the seniority rule became apparent in the debate surrounding a no-confidence vote proposed against sitting foreign minister Fukuda Takeo in 1971. The Satō government had supported a counter-proposal to defeat a UN resolution that demanded the admission of the PRC to the UN and the simultaneous expulsion of Taiwan. The counter-proposal was roundly defeated and the resolution to admit the PRC and expel Taiwan passed, causing Japan much embarrassment. The no-confidence motion against Fukuda proposed by the opposition was aimed to rebuke the government for this embarrassment. The LDP asked its members to vote against the no-confidence motion and support the Satō government and its foreign policy. Kōno held a pro-PRC position and disagreed with the government's position. Unable to wield any influence within the party, Kōno chose to abstain from the no-confidence vote on the Diet floor (Pharr 1982: 41–42; Pharr 1990: 112–13).

Abstention is not unheard of in the LDP. In fact, it is the only way for LDP members to voice their disapproval of the party line, but most members do not choose this path because it is a risky one. It is a form of protest only to be used on select items particularly unpalatable to the politician. Abstaining from a vote sends a message to the party and could result in future costs to the politician in the form of positions or money withheld. Abstaining is a particularly risky move for junior politicians given their reliance on the party leadership for funds and future appointments. Failure to support the party's position definitely can harm a junior politician's political future in the party.

Another example of Kōno's propensity to take risks by challenging the LDP leadership came following Tanaka's resignation from the prime ministership when Kōno and his junior followers tried to force an open election for party president. A large part of Kōno's frustration with the LDP centered on the party's closed decision-making process. Most decisions were made by senior leaders behind closed doors. The selection of party president was no exception. Formal provisions for an open election of the party president existed; however, an open election for party president had not been held since the LDP's formation in 1955. The unprecedented nature of Kōno's attempt to force an open election made it that much more bold and risky.

Kōno hoped to use the LDP's formal provisions for the election of a party president to derail the standard closed process of party president selection. According to these provisions, if more than one candidate emerged and each candidate had the support of a certain number of supporters, then the president was to be chosen in an open election in which all party members had the chance to vote. Kōno recognized that the best chance he and his junior followers had was to find a middle-generation politician sympathetic to their cause to run for president and challenge the candidate proposed by the senior leadership. The three politicians Kōno approached, however, turned him down. As a result, Kōno decided to run for office himself (Pharr 1982: 43–46; Pharr 1990: 106–7).

Kōno's decision to run for office was quite bold. Kōno knew that his chances of winning an election against a senior-level opponent were slim. He had a reason for taking the risk of standing for office, though. Running for office allowed Kōno to draw attention to the closed nature of the party president selection process. Such an open display of criticism of the LDP's norms infuriated the senior leadership.

Kōno's attempts to secure the support of junior members across factional lines failed, as did his effort to garner mid- and senior-level support. In the end, he only had about forty supporters in his bid for the party presidency. In the meantime, the senior leadership prevented this open contest by getting the faction leaders together and coming to an agreement on the party's next candidate. They presented the candidate as a *fait accompli*. Given the small number of supporters he rounded up, Kōno had no choice but to accept the decision negotiated by Shiina, a senior political fixer. Kōno's attempt to organize horizontal and vertical alliances without any regard for factional affiliation was daring. It produced a definite response in how the party dealt with Kōno and his followers in the future as well. The senior leadership used go-betweens to communicate with Kōno and his followers and attempted to attach the image of "spoiled brats" to these young turks who seemed intent to challenge the established way of doing things (Pharr 1982: 43–46; Pharr 1990: 113–14).

Kōno had a vision for reform, although it changed over time. Kōno's original vision of reform focused on internal party reform within the LDP. In particular, he wanted to rid the party of its strict seniority rule, or at the very least relax the seniority rule, which prevented junior politicians from participating in the most important aspects of the decision-making process. According to the seniority rule, politicians were not even eligible for cabinet posts until their fifth or sixth term in office. As the party aged, the number of senior politicians increased, making fewer and fewer important party posts available to junior members. Most of these posts were monopolized by a handful of powerful senior politicians by the time that Kōno was elected to the Diet. Kōno argued that such a monopolization of power was not healthy for the party and felt that increasing the participation of junior members was one way to modernize the party (Pharr 1982: 40).

With the real-estate scandals that forced prime minister Tanaka to resign from office in 1974 and the outbreak of the larger Lockheed bribery scandal in 1976, Kōno expanded his vision of reform to include the strengthening of anti-corruption measures and political finance regulations. He linked these scandals to the closed decision-making process within the LDP and posited that the internal party reform he had been advocating for many years also would help clean up the political world.

Kōno also was committed to reform. He began his formal pursuit of reform with the formation of a study group, the Political Engineering Institute, inside the LDP. He used this as a forum for his ideas about internal party reform. Kōno extended his push for party reform when he tried to force an open election for party president in 1974. Then, he used the outbreak of the Lockheed scandal in 1976 as the impetus for his break with the LDP and the formation of the New Liberal Club. This move was largely in protest of the Tanaka-type of money politics that fostered the Lockheed scandal and an attempt to push party reform that would increase the voice of junior politicians within the LDP (Curtis 1988: 31).

Kōno's commitment to his vision of political reform did not falter until a decade after he formed the NLC, when he and the remaining NLC members finally rejoined the LDP.

Kōno's readmission to the LDP was a relatively low-key affair, but this circumstance was not something that Kōno could have predicted ten years earlier when he left the LDP. Moreover, while the LDP "let" Kōno and his followers back into the party, they had all paid a price for leaving the LDP and pursuing their vision.

Kōno clearly was willing to suffer politically in an attempt to see his beliefs realized. Kōno came from a politically elite family. He took over his father's seat in the Lower House, and his uncle was the speaker of the Upper House. As a second-generation politician his seat was secure. Moreover, given that his father had been the head of an LDP faction and his uncle's prominent position in the Upper House, Kōno was set for an elite career in the LDP; he simply had to be patient and accept the party the way it was (Pharr 1982: 38).

By choosing to leave the LDP, Kōno put his political future in jeopardy in order to pursue reform from the outside. To begin with, there was no guarantee that his party would survive. Since no precedent of defection existed, there was no way for Kōno to assess the costs and benefits of leaving the party. If the party did not survive, then it also was not clear that the LDP would ever let Kōno and his followers back into the party. Given that the LDP was based on seniority, even if Kōno and his followers were let back into the party, they would have to wait even longer for government appointments. Kōno's willingness to make political sacrifices for his cause illustrates his "passionate devotion to a 'cause'" (Weber 1946: 115).

Despite the fact that Kōno had the personal attributes that facilitate a leader who wishes to implement reform, he did not see his vision of reform realized. This failure is largely due to the fact that he had limited resources at his disposal as a junior politician. He did not have patron–client ties within the LDP, nor did he have connections to opposition leaders. Most significantly, he did not have access to the policy-making process. The only resources he had were media exposure and public opinion. His actions did maximize these resources, but these resources proved insufficient in the end.

Due to his famous family, Kōno commanded much more media attention than most other politicians at such an early stage in their career. Kōno's election to the Diet and his entry into his father's former faction, which had been taken over by the relatively young Nakasone, received a large amount of media coverage. Kōno's defection and the creation the NLC also created much interest on the part of the media (Pharr 1990: 54).

His decision to break away from the LDP only fueled the media's interest in his activities. The media gave Kōno's new party a good deal of attention, and this attention in turned helped the party in its first election. Seventeen of its 25 candidates won their race. The initial success of the candidates was related in part to the media's attention to the breakaway party and its critique of rule by senior officials in the LDP. Public and media support, however, did not prove sufficient to pressure the LDP's senior leaders to actively pursue reform.

Kōno's personal connections and loyalties were not that developed when he broke away from the LDP as a third-term Diet member. These two resources are important in securing deals with other politicians. The deficiency in Kōno's bargaining skills were apparent in the organization and activities of the NLC. Kōno never was able to resolve the internal conflicts in the NLC over the party's primary goal. Moreover, Kōno was not able to negotiate a return to the LDP on his terms (Curtis 1988: 30–35). Kōno had several ideas about reform, but these proposals never made it to the agenda. In order to influence policy, a politician must be privy to the behind-the-scenes dealings within the LDP or between the LDP and the opposition. Once Kōno left the LDP he either needed to ally with several opposition parties in an attempt to form an anti-LDP coalition capable of challenging the LDP's control of parliament or he needed to form an alliance with the LDP so that he could be treated as an equal partner. Because the LDP was able to maintain its majority without allying with the NLC, Kōno was not able to secure a place at the bargaining table. He did not have the connections with the opposition to build an anti-LDP coalition. As a result, his risk of leaving the party did not pay off.

An alternative explanation for reform suggests that politicians are more likely to pass reform in the wake of increased electoral competition (Scarrow 1997). Electoral competition increased following the Lockheed scandal and the creation of the New Liberal Club in 1976. This increased competition did not result in the passage of reform, providing more evidence that increased electoral competition alone does not predict the passage of reform. One indicator of this increased electoral competition is the decline of the LDP's vote share in the 1976 election. When comparing the LDP vote share in the 1972 and 1976 Lower House elections we see it fell 5.1 percentage points in

1976, as illustrated in Table 1.1. The corruption-mired LDP lost both seats and votes in the 1976 election (Reed 1999b: 145). The New Liberal Club with its reform platform experienced an electoral bonus, which Reed refers to as a "new party boom" when it ran in the aftermath of the Lockheed scandal (1996b). This bonus was limited by the fact that the New Liberal Club only ran candidates in a very small number of districts. The party failed to predict that support for change was so great in this election (Kabashima and Reed 2001: 637). Unfortunately for the NLC, a new party boom only occurs in the first election a newly formed party contests (Reed 1999a: 188). Perhaps because the New Liberal Club did not run enough candidates to fully illustrate this demand for change, the LDP did not seriously consider reform following the 1976 election. More likely, as discussed above, Kōno's insufficient resources inhibited his ability to capitalize on the public environment that favored reform.

Of all the junior politicians considered in this chapter, Kōno has the most personal attributes that favor reform. In this sense, he provides the best test case for the argument that resources matter. He clearly had a high propensity to take risks for causes he believed in. Such activities did not begin with his push for party reform and his subsequent break with the LDP, but date back to debates on the PRC's admission to the UN. His vision for a "new" LDP was clear and his commitment was strong enough that he was willing to incur potentially large costs by breaking away from the LDP. As a junior politician, though, the only resources that he had at his disposal were media exposure and public opinion. These resources were insufficient to realize reform. In order to push policy through, a politician needs to be at the policy-making table. Kōno did not have access to the policy-making process, either as a junior politician in the LDP or as the leader of a small new conservative alternative to the LDP. He chose not to ally with more senior leaders within the LDP. He also did not pursue alliances with opposition parties. These decisions were at least partially related to the fact he did not have the connections necessary to do this.

Kōno's bid to see party reform enacted did not fail because he was not a leader with vision and commitment who was willing to take risks; it failed due to his lack of resources, something that was directly related to his junior status in the political world. While Kōno, as a second-generation politician, had enough personal resources to secure his own re-election independently of the LDP, he did not have the financial backing or elite connections necessary to create a viable opposition party. Bolting from the party did increase his voice to a certain degree, but Kōno was unable to sustain this new party and finally returned to the LDP without receiving concessions on the issues that he left the party over.

As we shall see below, the leaders of the other groups of junior politicians do not stand out in terms of personal attributes to the same extent that Kōno Yōhei does. While these junior politicians took risks, they were more limited in scale and scope. They all had ideas on reform and were committed enough to speak out publicly on these issues. Again, however, their ultimate failure rests with their lack of resources. In a sense, it did not matter the extent to which their personal attributes were developed as their limited resources would always prevent them from realizing change.

The Utopia Study Group

In 1988, a group of first-term Diet members formed the Utopia Study Group under the leadership of Takemura Masayoshi. Although Takemura was a first-term Diet member, he had a considerable amount of political experience. He moved onto the national scene after serving as a prefectural governor (Curtis 1999: 121–22). Takemura organized this group in response to the outbreak of the Recruit stocks-for-favors scandal. Not surprisingly, one of the main messages of the members of Utopia was the need for political reform. Although the Recruit scandal directed the focus of much of the group's activity on publicizing the role of money in politics, these junior politicians had a larger agenda. In addition to seeing political funding reform enacted, the members of Utopia also wished to lower the barriers of entry for new politicians. This goal is not surprising given Takemura's career history. Having served as a prefectural governor, he was an experienced politician. Due to the strict seniority system within the LDP, however, he would not be able to hold a leadership position within the party until he had served at least five or six terms. In the end this group made little progress towards realizing its agenda of political funding reform and internal party reform. The fact that the members of the Utopia Study group had few political resources at their disposal given their position as junior politicians is important in explaining this outcome.

Since these first-term Diet members did not hold any influential party or parliamentary positions, the most significant resource they had at their disposal was publicity. The Recruit scandal outraged the public. The members of the Utopia Study Group tried to capitalize on this outrage by mobilizing public opinion behind their reform agenda in hopes of using it as leverage to influence the decision-making process within the LDP. One strategy these members used was to publicize their annual expenditures in an attempt to illustrate how costly a politician's life can be and to emphasize the need for reform. While this public disclosure of political finances did have an impact, it did not prove to be enough to get the LDP to act quickly on reform.

The LDP had been faced with scandal numerous times during its history, and it had many counter-tactics to diffuse the public outrage over scandal. One strategy it employed was to make Kaifu, a known supporter of reform with a clean image, prime minister. A second strategy the LDP leadership used was to establish several investigative committees to explore the issue of reform but to refrain from taking any quick action on reform. As explained in earlier chapters, the window of opportunity for reform is only open for a short period of time. Failure to act quickly reduces the chances that reform will be implemented. After the LDP did well in the 1990 election, politicians no longer felt the pressure to change the rules of the game. In short, the dilatory tactics of the LDP worked to diffuse the initial outrage over the Recruit scandal.

The Utopia Study Group's outsider strategy of using the media to gain publicity for reform was not sufficient in pressuring other LDP politicians to go against their self-interest and pass reform. A more effective strategy would have been to exert pressure for the speedy formulation of a reform bill, like Miki had done in 1975. These first-term Diet members, however, did not hold influential positions in the LDP. In fact, junior politicians in the LDP are practically shut out from the policy-making process. Mobilizing media attention can influence what is on the agenda. The LDP did debate reform at the time Utopia was implementing its financial disclosure scheme. The formation of advisory councils and extended debate and discussion within the party allowed the party to appear to be seriously addressing the issue. The appearance of action was enough to calm the public's anger over Recruit. By the 1990 election, attention had shifted to other issues, such as the Gulf War and the Peace-Keeping Operations Bill. The LDP no longer felt pressure to reform. The members of the Utopia Study Group did not have the resources to speed up the policy-making process; therefore, they failed to realize reform.

Wakate Kaikaku Ha

The window of opportunity for reform opened again in the early 1990s with the outbreak of the Sagawa Kyūbin scandal in 1992. Miyazawa was the prime minister, and as discussed in Chapter 4 he was uninterested in pursuing reform. At this time, several advocates of reform were on the scene, the largest number of whom were junior politicians. After the outbreak of the Sagawa Kyūbin scandal, the LDP was almost evenly split between anti- and pro-reformers. The calls for a slower, more cautious approach to reform predominantly made by the elite members of the party were countered by three groups of junior politicians in the LDP – *Wakate Kaikaku Ha* (literally translated as the Group of Young Diet Members Committed to Reform), the League to Restore Trust in the Party, and Ozawa's Reform Forum 21. These groups formed at different times and had different motives and tactics. Because both *Wakate* and the League to Restore Trust in the Party had members across factional lines some overlap in membership among the three groups existed. In particular, some members of *Wakate* joined Ozawa's Reform Forum 21 when it formed two years after *Wakate*'s inauguration. Each group, however, had a different type of influence on reform. The relative success of each group in realizing its agenda is related to the resources each group's leader had to pursue reform.

Wakate formed in December 1991 under the leadership of Ishiba Shigeru. At this time Ishiba was a second-term Diet member, very low on the LDP's hierarchical totem pole. Part of his motivation for organizing *Wakate* was to give junior members of the LDP a voice on the issue of reform. *Wakate* had 56 junior members, many of whom formerly had been members of the Utopia Study Group. *Wakate* adopted similar tactics to its predecessor. Building on the example set by Utopia, 29 members of *Wakate* made their expenses for political activities public in May 1992, a few months prior to when the full scale of the Sagawa Kyūbin scandal became apparent (Minkan Seiji Rincho 1993: 257). The goal of this tactic was to expose the money pressures junior politicians faced and to bolster the case for the need for reform.

Many of the activities of *Wakate* aimed to increase the salience of reform. For example, in November 1992, *Wakate* opened a forum on political reform where a combined proportional representation/single-member district electoral system similar to the one proposed under Kaifu was discussed (Minkan Seiji Rincho 1993: 263). A year later when Miyazawa's reform proposal was in danger, *Wakate* experimented with a different strategy in its attempt to exert pressure on the powers that be within the LDP. Specifically, it started a signature-gathering campaign to realize political reform during that session of the Diet. They turned in 204 names of reform supporters to three representatives of the party (Taniguchi 1999: 140). In the end, their support was of no avail as the party failed to reach a consensus on reform.

Wakate chose a non-confrontational approach as it tried to persuade the party to earnestly pursue reform (Wolfe 1995: 1067). This group worked within the party using the accepted methods and going through the regular channels. Due to their junior status, though, while their voice was heard in the public and within the party, the senior members still could choose not to support their position. And indeed, ultimately, the senior officials were unsympathetic to their cause.

The senior leadership in the LDP dealt with this opposition from within from *Wakate* using similar methods to the ones it used to diffuse the opposition parties throughout its 38 years of dominance. Specifically, the senior leadership co-opted the issue of reform, accepting its broad tenets but devising a plan that had no possibility of receiving opposition support. The senior leadership formulated a proposal for a pure single-member district (SMD) electoral system. This proposal had no chance of receiving opposition support. The LDP did not have a majority in the Upper House so without opposition support the bill had no possibility of passing. Once the senior leadership devised its proposal for a pure SMD electoral system, however, *Wakate* had much less room to push its more specific agenda. A pure SMD system was not *Wakate*'s preference, but the public was less interested in the details of reform than it was in the passage of some kind of reform (Wolfe 1995: 1067). By coming up with its own proposal for reform the senior leadership within the LDP took away the only resource that Ishiba and his fellow junior politicians had – public support. These junior politicians were not high enough in the LDP's political hierarchy to hold positions on the influential policy-making bodies within the party, such as the Policy Affairs

Research Council (PARC) and the Executive Council. More significantly, these junior members did not have access to the behind-the-scenes dealings where a large portion of the LDP's policy making took place. While their tactics did bring some attention to the issue of reform, these tactics were not sufficient to produce change.

The League to Restore Trust in the Party

Another group of junior politicians that advocated reform during the early 1990s was the League to Restore Trust in the Party. It formed in October 1992 under the leadership of Ōta Seiichi in response to the outbreak of the Sagawa Kyūbin scandal. Ōta was a fourth-term member of the LDP and still relatively low within the LDP's hierarchy. This group's tactics were more confrontational than *Wakate*'s. For example, the group's first action was to call for Kanemaru's resignation from the LDP. Kanemaru was the political don of the powerful Takeshita faction. Not surprisingly, members of the Takeshita faction did not join the League to Restore Trust. In the end, Kanemaru was forced out of the party, but it is unclear whether the actions of the League to Restore Trust were decisive. The next move by the group was to call for Takeshita's and Kanemaru's testimony in front of the Diet. This too occurred. Its last push was for Takeshita's resignation from the LDP, something that did not happen (Wolfe 1995: 1068).

Although the pressure from the League to Restore Trust certainly contributed to Kanemaru's resignation and Takeshita's testimony, this group was unable to formulate a concrete proposal for reform, not to mention see it passed. As illustrated below the members of this group did have some of the personal attributes that favor the passage of reform, especially the willingness to take risks and challenge the constraints in place. They did not, however, have the access and influence within the party to realize reform.

The League to Restore Trust in the Party was much more vocal and defiant than *Wakate*. This group used non-traditional methods in an attempt to force the senior leadership to take notice of its demands. The members of this group took risks and challenged the constraints posed by the rules established by the party leadership. Like other groups of junior politicians before them, the League to Restore Trust saw the media, especially the talk show circuit, as its best resource to influence the party leadership. Members from this group publicly called for Takeshita's resignation the day before he was supposed to testify in the Diet (Wolfe 1995: 1068). In reaction to such tactics, the LDP leadership tried to quiet the rank-and-file's vocal opinions on reform by declaring in late November 1992 that all party members must get permission before appearing on Japanese television. Ōta Seiichi protested this decree by appearing on television the following evening. He further defied the leadership by demanding such things as banning the transfer of funds from one Diet member to another, something that many members of the LDP opposed ("Japan: Young Turks": 37).

Ōta's defiance of the LDP decree with his television appearance was clearly a risky move. He was challenging the constraints posed by the rules established by the senior leadership, and he risked being punished. This punishment could have come in the form of the denial of future party or political appointments or the withholding of political funding. The LDP leadership certainly had many retaliation mechanisms under its control. What Ōta hoped to gain from this public defiance was greater exposure of the plight of the junior politicians within the LDP. Although the risk might have achieved the proximate goal of publicizing the new party restrictions on speech, little forward progress was made on reform. Risk-taking is a personal attribute that facilitates a leader's pursuit of reform. The possession of this attribute alone, however, is insufficient. As Ōta's case illustrates, advocates of reform also need access to the policy-making process. This access only comes with seniority in the Japanese case.

Reform Forum 21 and the importance of seniority

The third group of junior politicians that formed during the early 1990s was Reform Forum 21. Unlike *Wakate* and the League to Restore Trust, this group had a senior politician, Ozawa Ichirō, at its helm. Reform Forum 21 was composed of 36 former members of the Takeshita faction who left with Ozawa along with eight other members of the LDP whom Ozawa recruited. Many of these politicians had been active in the non-factional Utopia and *Wakate* groups. Ozawa's new faction was a moderate force in the LDP but certainly one to be reckoned with.

Aware that his own name had been tarnished in the Sagawa Kyūbin scandal, Ozawa named Hata Tsutomu to serve as the head of this group. Hata, a former foreign minister, had long been a public advocate of political reform and even served as the chairman of the LDP's Electoral System Investigative Committee. He, too, was a senior politician with connections within and outside the LDP. He also had a more positive image with the public than Ozawa had. After assuming the top position in Reform Forum 21, Hata started touring the country in an attempt to mobilize public support for reform and this new group within the LDP. Despite Hata's active public role, he did not have control over the faction; ultimate decision-making power rested with Ozawa (Curtis 1999: 91).

Ozawa eventually defected from the LDP, frustrated by its insincere effort to reform. The members of Reform Forum 21 followed him out of the LDP to form the base for his new party, the *Shinseitō*. Ozawa was only the second politician to leave the powerful LDP. The first was Kōno Yōhei, the junior politician explored at the beginning of this chapter. Ozawa, unlike Kōno, had several resources to aid him in his attempt to realize reform from the outside.

As illustrated in Chapter 5, Ozawa, unlike Kōno, had strong patron–client ties within the LDP. Ozawa had supported many of the 36 former members of the Takeshita faction who left the party with him. These members left at least partially out of sense of obligation. In addition to patron–client ties, Ozawa also had connections to the opposition. His relationships with the leaders of the opposition parties helped him build an anti-LDP coalition. Kōno never successfully secured opposition support. Finally, Ozawa exuded power. Several of the members of the LDP who tied their fortunes to Ozawa did so because he seemed more powerful than Obuchi, the member of the LDP who was chosen to take over the Takeshita faction. As a third-term member who broke away with Ozawa explained, "people left with Ozawa because they thought he would take responsibility [for them]" (personal interview, 20 February 2001). The junior politicians who left with Ozawa had seen what he had accomplished in the LDP and did not doubt that Ozawa could do well outside the party. At the very least, these junior politicians trusted that their patron would continue to take care of them outside the party. Ozawa needed the support from these junior politicians to gain legitimacy as a force outside the LDP and the junior politicians trusted that Ozawa had the resources and political clout to ensure their continued success outside the party. As we have seen, Ozawa's resources, combined with his propensity to take risks, his vision, and his commitment, contributed to his successful bid to see the passage of reform.

Conclusion

This chapter illustrates that resources matter in the pursuit of reform. Insufficient resources can prevent advocates of reforms from successfully realizing reform, even if these advocates possess some of the personal attributes that favor the successful pursuit of reform.

The amount of resources at a politician's disposal is linked to the leadership positions he has held, which in turn are determined by seniority. The politicians explored in this book can be distinguished by level of seniority. Miki, Kaifu, Miyazawa, and Ozawa were all senior politicians having served well over six terms in office by the time each was involved in the political reform debates considered here.[3] Both Ozawa and Miyazawa had served nine terms at the time they were in positions to push the passage of political reform. Kaifu had served eleven terms at the time he was prime minister and Miki had been a politician over twenty years. In contrast, Kōno (NLC), Takemura (Utopia), Ishiba (*Wakate*), and Ōta (The League to Restore Trust) had all served four or fewer terms and thus never held important party and/or Diet posts.

Because Miki, Kaifu, Miyazawa, and Ozawa had all served comparable number of terms, they had the same set of basic resources available to them, resources that the leaders of the groups of junior politicians had not acquired yet. They had all held cabinet-level positions and important faction and/or party-level posts. As a result, they had had access to the policy-making process in the past and continued to be in position where they had access when they were pursuing reform. In contrast, the junior politicians were on the outside and remained on the outside as they tried to push reform.

As evidenced in this chapter, all junior politicians have a limited amount of influence in the reform process due to their lack of resources in comparison to senior politicians. Junior politicians do not have the resources necessary either to build LDP consensus or to build a coalition with the opposition. Most junior politicians who support political reform also support internal LDP party reform. Their frustration rests with their inability to gain positions of influence based on merit. But in this sense junior politicians are faced with a dilemma. The only politicians with the resources and positions needed to change the seniority system are senior politicians. Without seniority, these junior politicians cannot force change. Certain junior politicians, like Kōno Yōhei, might have some personal attributes that favor reform, like the willingness to take risks, but these attributes minus access and connections are not sufficient to force change. One solution for these junior politicians is to align themselves with at least one senior politician. If this senior politician assumes the main leadership position, then something might be accomplished using the junior politicians as a vital support base.

Finally, although differences in resources are important, these differences only explain part of the reason why some advocates of reform succeed while others fail. The ability and willingness to use these resources in ways that challenge the constraints in place is important in realizing policy success. The fact that the senior politicians considered in this book all had a similar amount of basic resources reinforces the point that resources alone do not determine success. Of the four senior politicians considered, only two – Ozawa and Miki – succeeded in seeing a reform package passed. These politicians had connections within and outside their party and were willing to use these resources in a risky way that underlined their commitment to reform and that promoted their vision.

7 Koizumi Junichirō
A new kind of leadership?

Since his inauguration as prime minister in April 2001, Koizumi Junichirō and his leadership style have drawn a considerable amount of attention in the media as well as in scholarly work. Many have labeled Koizumi a maverick and see his leadership style as quite unique in the Japanese context. From a historical perspective, however, is this really the case? Has Koizumi's leadership style significantly differed from other leaders considered in this book? In this chapter I explore this question and argue that when looking at Koizumi and his campaign for postal reform we can find many parallels to past leaders with legislative successes in political reform. In fact, an exploration of the case of Prime Minister Koizumi illustrates the more general applicability of the theory of leadership and reform developed in this book.

Koizumi's quest for postal reform demonstrates that risk-taking, vision, and commitment are key personal attributes that aid leaders when facing the institutional constraints of LDP party politics in the post-1994 system. Even though the institutional environment that Koizumi faces differs from other leaders considered in this book due to electoral reform in 1994, cabinet reforms in 1999, and administrative reform implemented in 2001, radical reform still requires a leader who is willing to challenge the self-interest of his fellow party members. Koizumi has not achieved his entire reformist agenda. He has, however, taken risks to push many of his policies. These risks, along with his vision and commitment, have aided him in challenging the various constraints presented by his own party, the LDP. Given the constraints he has overcome and the policies he successfully has advanced, Koizumi represents the case of a successful reformer.

The extent of Koizumi's success as a prime minister is a contested notion. Koizumi successfully has passed reform measures in the areas of highway construction, the postal saving system, public works, and health insurance, but he has failed to achieve his overarching goal of comprehensive economic reform. The reforms passed have been marked by compromise between reformers and anti-reformers in the LDP. These reforms, however, represent a gradual chipping away at old-style LDP pork barrel politics. The reforms target key LDP constituents and challenge, to varying degrees, the influence these groups will be able to exert in the future. Moreover, in many ways

Koizumi's agenda is a progressive one, each reform building toward larger change. For example, while his first postal reform bill opened the postal system to competition in a very limited way, his second proposal was more substantive, giving the initial changes more meaning. Koizumi has not pursued symbolic reform. The compromises he has made with LDP anti-reformers represent political necessities for Koizumi to maintain party support and remain in power so as to continue pursuing his reformist agenda.

Even though postal reform differs in some respects from the type of reform in the earlier chapters of this book, we can use the analytical framework developed here to assess Koizumi's success. As we have seen, a shared aspect of campaign finance and electoral system reform is the fact that such regulations directly affect the future behavior of politicians. Self-interest is a formidable constraint in these cases, but it is not absent from other types of reform. In fact, self-interest is involved in the calculus to pass any legislation. Politicians are always asking themselves how their position on issues will influence their re-election and fund-raising abilities.

Clearly, the types of reform Koizumi has pursued have gone against the self-interest of many of his fellow LDP members and their core constituents. The postmasters, for example, have always been a core backer of the LDP. The passage of the first postal reform bill in 2002 was particularly difficult due to this fact (Maclachlan 2004: 310). Because the reforms Koizumi has supported have been antagonistic to the party and its supporters, he has faced difficulties in getting them passed.

Many scholars who have addressed Koizumi's inability to achieve his entire reformist agenda point to the rigidities remaining from the 1955 system. The iron triangle relationships among bureaucratic agencies, LDP *zoku* politicians,[1] and business interests have proven to be an ongoing constraint (Pempel 2006; Lam 2002: 73–75). Although electoral reform has influenced the Policy Affairs Research Council (PARC) in various ways, incentives still exist for LDP party members to become specialized in policy areas through the PARC. This specialization aids them in party advancement and iron triangle relations (Krauss and Pekkanen 2004: 20). The LDP has stayed in power, albeit in coalition with other parties, and it has been reluctant to pass policies that will harm the various inefficient sectors of the economy that provide its members with votes and/or political funding (R. Katz 1998; Pempel 2006).[2]

This structural explanation presents part of the picture by illuminating one of the largest constraints facing Prime Minister Koizumi – the entrenched ties among bureaucratic agencies, LDP politicians, and special business interests. This study, however, suggests an alternative explanation for Koizumi's record in achieving his reformist goals. As we have seen from previous cases, institutional constraints are present in the passage of legislation in general, especially legislation that goes against the self-interest of the party in power. The results from this study suggest that risk-taking, vision, and commitment are essential in passing policies that challenge the interests of the dominant

LDP and its member politicians. Koizumi has achieved more in areas where he has presented a clear vision of change and taken risks such as bypassing the LDP's policy-making process to pursue his policies.

I would like to investigate some of Koizumi's policy pursuits to assess his effectiveness as a leader. In particular, the two postal reform bills are telling cases because these pieces of legislation, like electoral system reform and campaign finance reform, clearly cut at the self-interest of the LDP and its member politicians. In these cases Koizumi has succeeded in overcoming significant structural constraints due to his willingness to take risks, vision, and commitment.

Koizumi and postal reform

The changing constraints facing Koizumi

While many of the constraints Koizumi faces are similar to the ones in the cases explored in this book, the institutional environment he is working in is different from that of Miki, Kaifu, Miyazawa, and Ozawa. With the passage of electoral reform in 1994, the institutional changes to the Cabinet Law in 1999, and administrative reforms in 2001, Koizumi is functioning in an altered 1955 system where some constraints are the same, some have lessened, and some new ones have emerged. These changes to the institutional environment are significant in that they have reduced the necessity of some resources and increased the importance of others. This section evaluates the way constraints have changed since 1994.

The most enduring constraints are the iron triangle relations between special interests, bureaucrats, and *zoku* politicians within the LDP. Many politicians asserted that the changes to Political Funds Control Law in 1994 followed by the ban on corporate contributions in 1999 would weaken the incentives for pork barrel politics that have driven the iron triangle relations between special interests, bureaucrats, and *zoku* politicians.

This prediction, however, has not been fully met. For one, special interests not only provide money; these groups also provide votes. The postmasters are a good example of this type of electoral influence. The 20,000 postmasters throughout the country are valued for their vote-getting abilities. With the larger single-member districts the ability to recruit votes is a highly valued asset.[3] In addition, money is still being channeled to the LDP (Taniguchi 2002: 81). Although the power of bureaucrats has been reduced and the power of politicians has increased through administrative reform and the revisions to the Cabinet Law, the bureaucracy remains a key actor in the policy-making process (Amyx and Drysdale 2003). As we will see in the case of Koizumi, challenging the interests backed by various iron triangles produces great resistance within the party. Koizumi has met this resistance by using his popularity and media coverage to exert pressure on his fellow politicians. Ties within and outside the LDP have been less important.

While the LDP has had divided interests since its inception, the nature of this division has changed. The mainstream/anti-mainstream division within the party that characterized the Miki administration began to change to a division between the reformers and anti-reformers with the outbreak of the Recruit scandal in 1989.[4] The consideration of electoral reform solidified this division. Even after Ozawa and his group split from the LDP, though, reformers and anti-reformers remained.[5] Today the main anti-reformers are the old-guard politicians who seek to protect the iron triangle relations that they have fostered for decades. Many of the new young turks in the party, however, support Koizumi and his vision of a new LDP and a new way of politics.

While the policy-making process within the LDP has always posed constraints to prime ministers, coalition government, which has characterized the new electoral system, has added to the barriers that stand in the way of getting policies passed in some respects, but also lessened some of the previously prominent constraints. Strong pressure from party elites exists to respect the LDP policy-making process that requires bills to be considered by the PARC and the Executive Council before being submitted to the cabinet. Since the LDP regained control of government in 1994, however, it has ruled in coalition with at least one other smaller opposition party. This circumstance has added another dimension to this constraint. Now reaching agreements among coalition partners is also important, increasing the instances when compromise becomes necessary. Aside from making the LDP a lame-duck government, though, their coalition partners have few resources to influence the policy agenda. In fact, the calculus of coalition partners to date suggests that they put more weight on staying part of the government and supporting the LDP than in bringing the government down. Coalition partners are more willing to use their leverage to have some influence on the legislation than to completely risk participation in government in order to see their own policies passed (Mulgan 2003: 41). Nevertheless, the existence of coalition partners has added to the venues in which policies must be vetted, thereby increasing the constraints prime ministers face.

While in general, coalition government is a new constraint prime ministers face when trying to pass their policy agendas, this new decision-making process has lessened the PARC's overall role in the policy-making process. Many times the discussion begins among party leaders in the coalition. In this sense, coalitions have become a potential tool for prime ministers, providing them with a way to bypass the LDP. One possible strategy is to get coalition support first and propose legislation to the LDP elite as a *fait accompli*. Koizumi used this tool in the case of healthcare premiums for salarymen. In this case, Koizumi got the support of the Kōmeitō first and then used this as leverage against the LDP *zoku* in the party (Krauss and Pekkanen 2004: 23).

Factions within the LDP are a constraint that have lessened but far from disappeared. Factions have become less powerful for several reasons (Krauss and Pekkanen 2004: 13–17). For one, the new electoral system has taken away one of the main prongs in the multifaceted bargain between faction heads and faction members. Specifically, the multiple-member district system forced members of the LDP to compete against each other in the same district. This competition provided incentives for the formation of factions. Faction leaders provided support for members in return for their support in the LDP presidential election if successfully elected. Now with party subsidies and single-member districts this exchange is no longer necessary. A change in the selection process for prime ministers has also weakened factions. Koizumi's election to the prime ministership came with the participation of party members at the prefectural level. This grassroots involvement was decisive in his selection and has made him less beholden to the bosses of the most powerful factions.

Finally, many scholars have pointed to the limited formal powers of the prime minister as a constraint on his ability to realize his policy agenda. Recent government reforms in 1999 and 2001, including changes to the Cabinet Law, have given the prime minister some new powers, reducing this constraint to a considerable extent. In 1999, the LDP in coalition with Ozawa's Liberal Party initiated reforms that increased the power of politicians vis-à-vis bureaucrats as well as enhanced the centralization of the cabinet. This reform decreased the size of the cabinet in hopes of facilitating the ease of unified decision-making. It also reduced the role of bureaucrats by limiting their role to act as witnesses on technical matters during Diet deliberations. Now politicians are responsible for responding to Diet member concerns (Shinoda 2003: 24–25). This reform reduces the influence of one of the prongs of the iron triangle – the bureaucrats – on the policy-making process. Finally, among other things, the revisions to the Cabinet Law gave the prime minister the power to initiate his own policies at cabinet meetings (Shinoda 2003: 26). This change also enhances the prime minister and cabinet's independence vis-à-vis the bureaucracy.

Koizumi's resources

One could interpret the government and Diet reforms of 1999 and 2001 as a lessening of constraints. These reforms also represent an increase in the resources available to prime ministers to pursue policy. In addition to these new resources, Koizumi also has used public support, media coverage, the Internet, and advisory councils to increase his leverage in the policy-making process and hedge against the smaller support base within his own party. Patron–client ties and ties to other parties have been less important.

Initially, overwhelming public support was Koizumi's greatest resource. As we have seen, grassroots support brought Koizumi into office. While this has made Koizumi less beholden to LDP faction heads, it also has meant that he has fewer ties within his own party. Koizumi comes from the Mori faction, but at least initially his main support in the party came from his reformist allies Yamasaki Taku and Katō Kōichi. Yamasaki, however, heads one of the smallest factions in the LDP and Katō Kōichi was forced to resign from the party in 2002 after his implication in a scandal (Lam 2002: 70). Even though a significant portion of the LDP elite opposes Koizumi's policy goals, they have not been willing to risk sacking Koizumi for fear of retribution at the polls. When Koizumi first came to office his support ratings were at an unprecedented level, hovering around 80 percent (Lam 2002: 78). In his fifth year in office this percentage dipped down to the high thirties (Asahi Shinbun 2005). Comparatively speaking, though, this percentage remains high for a sitting LDP prime minister.

Koizumi has often used his popularity to threaten the LDP in hopes of achieving his policy goals. For example, in the lead up to Koizumi's second postal privatization bill Koizumi directed the following threat at the largest LDP faction:

> The privatization of postal services has been a taboo in the LDP and the people in the Hashimoto faction are against it ... But if they don't want me, they should try to elect someone else as prime minister.
>
> (Takahashi 2003)

Koizumi's message is clear – in this era of coalition governments and declining LDP support, stage new elections without me at the helm to your own peril.

Koizumi has used the media to pressure his fellow LDP members. This coverage has helped him hedge against his weak position in the party. Koizumi, like Miki, has often chosen to "go public" with his message in hopes that the public support for his initiatives would increase the pressure on the LDP lawmakers to pass his reforms. When first elected Koizumi held town meetings across Japan to introduce his reform agenda. He has also mobilized support through the Internet, establishing an Internet magazine. Shortly after his inauguration, his Internet magazine had 2.2 million subscribers (Lam 2002: 70).

Koizumi has formed various advisory councils to develop policy. Although prime ministers formed several advisory councils to consider electoral reform during the postwar period, none of the leaders considered in the previous chapters effectively used these advisory councils as a tool to pressure their party to adopt policy independent from the bureaucracy. If anything, the electoral reform advisory councils served as a symbolic response to public outcry over various scandals. Koizumi, however, has followed Prime Ministers Nakasone and Hashimoto's leads in using these advisory councils as a means to develop policy independent of both the bureaucracy and the LDP's PARC.

Prime Minister Nakasone can be credited with institutionalizing advisory councils as a resource for prime ministers during his tenure in office (1982–87) (Samuels 2003a). His *Rincho* advisory councils for railroad and telecommunication privatization provided him with a mechanism to consider policy free from the factional politics and power wielding within the LDP.

Rincho reported directly to the prime minister and the prime minister was then obligated to act on its recommendations. Nakasone chose political allies to participate on the *Rincho* as well as created links between *Rincho* and the LDP elite by setting up an LDP committee that reported to the Executive Council. Nakasone also threatened to punish any bureaucrat that hindered the process (Samuels 2003a: 12–13). Using *Rincho* and its connections with the LDP, Nakasone was able to push through these controversial privatiza-tions. In these cases the main loser was the JSP; however, many conservative politicians within the LDP were at least initially opposed to the privatization of pan National Railways (JNR) due to the pork the railway system had availed them over the years (Samuels 2003a: 20).

Given the changes to the Cabinet Law discussed earlier, Koizumi has been able to establish advisory councils both outside and within the government. Nakasone's *Rincho* functioned outside the government. Koizumi continues to use this resource to gain legitimacy, support, and outside expertise. For example, Koizumi established an outside advisory council on the three postal services to develop his postal reform proposal. In addition, the new Cabinet Law allows for the prime minister to develop policies within the cabi-net through Cabinet Office Councils. These advisory councils within the cabinet have added legitimacy and authority over policy due to their legal foundations (Mulgan 2002: 76–77). The composition of these councils also differs from the *Rincho*-type advisory councils. Specifically, instead of rely-ing on outside experts, the majority of participants are ministers. The fact that the cabinet ministers are participating in the policy-making process ensures the ultimate ease of cabinet approval (Mulgan 2002: 77).

While all these resources are significant, they do not guarantee success. Other prime ministers such as Prime Minister Kaifu have had high public support but been unable to achieve their policy goals. Personal attributes are also significant because they determine how prime ministers use the resources available to them. Koizumi's risk-taking, vision, and commitment allowed him to effectively use the resources outlined above to pursue postal privatization.

Koizumi as a risk-taker

Koizumi has taken numerous risks during his tenure as prime minister. Some risks have had a greater payoff than others. All risks illustrate his willingness to challenge the constraints posed by his party and reach for the impossible – the destruction of the LDP political machine. Here, I would like to explore the risks he has taken in his pursuit of postal privatization. With the first postal privatization bill, he bypassed the PARC to push forward the legis-lation. This risk was only marginally effective. Koizumi, however, did not give up with the watered-down postal privatization bill that passed in 2002. Instead, he made postal privatization one of the central goals of his second term in office, continuing to challenge the interests of his own party. As we shall see, he risked losing what leverage he had in his party in 2005 by dissolving the Lower House of the Diet when the Upper House rejected his postal reform bill. In the end, however, this risk opened up new possibilities for the passage of Koizumi's second postal reform bill by changing both the composition of the Lower House and the willingness of LDP anti-reformers to challenge Koizumi. The second postal reform package passed the Diet in October 2005.

In 2002 Koizumi bypassed the PARC and submitted a postal reform bill to the 154th session of the Diet. With the cabinet's new explicit power to initiate legislation, it has received more freedom from the LDP and its policy organs. By bypassing both the PARC and the LDP Executive Council, Koizumi risked angering other factions. In order to remain party head, Koizumi needed to avoid completely alienating the strongest faction in the party, the Hashimoto faction. Prior to changes in the institutional environment outlined earlier, the PARC and the Executive Council were the main venues through which policies were vetted. Members of the most powerful factions often dominate the top positions in these party decision-making bodies. Koizumi's grass-roots support and overall popularity has protected him to a large extent from factional politics, but bypassing the PARC and the Executive Council angered the old guard that still wielded influence in these bodies. The ultimate expression of this anger could have been a push to oust Koizumi from office. Koizumi, however, was betting that his popularity with the public would temper the anti-reformers' desires to sack him. Moreover, Koizumi had the power to dissolve the Diet and force the members of his party to face re-election in the face of going against a campaign promise if they crossed him.

Before Koizumi, few prime ministers directly challenged the LDP's PARC and Executive Council. Much of this is related to the more limited powers of the prime minister and the cabinet prior to the 1999 and 2001 reforms. Miki tried to force the LDP's hand with anti-monopoly legislation by gaining the support of opposition parties first. This attempt failed (Masumi 1995: 168–71). With the Political Funds Control Act, Miki took his revisions through the LDP policy apparatus. This process proceeded quickly because he had his own draft of the bill prepared. Still, he was forced to back down from a complete ban on political contributions.

With his first postal privatization bill, Koizumi too was forced to accept compromises. However, since the members of the PARC and the Executive Council were not able to influence the legislation before it was sent to the Diet, these compromises occurred once the postal reform bill reached committee negotiations in the Diet. The main opponents to postal reform came from the postal reform policy *zoku* headed by Nonaka Hiromu. Koizumi reportedly secured an unofficial agreement with Nonaka before directly submitting the cabinet bill to the Diet bypassing the PARC. Nonaka's support, however, only came due to his belief that this reform was limited and would mark an end to Koizumi's quest to privatize postal services (Mulgan 2002: 223). Koizumi challenged Nonaka's understanding when he declared,

I deem the bills to be the first milestone on the road toward the privatization of postal services ... I don't regard the establishment of the Postal Public Corporation as my eventual goal.

(Mulgan 2002: 223)

This direct challenge to Nonaka's expectations revealed Koizumi's long-term intentions and fueled the LDP's opposition in the Diet committee deliberations. Perhaps realizing that all could be lost from this point, Koizumi backed down from the statement above, claiming it was too soon to look that far into the future (Mulgan 2002: 223–24). In order to secure the passage of the bill in the Diet, Koizumi was forced to negotiate with the chairman of the PARC, the chief cabinet secretary and the LDP secretary general, along with the secretary generals of the LDP's coalition partners, the New Kōmeitō and the New Conservative Party. The end result was a watered-down postal reform bill with all the signs of compromise that would have been part of securing LDP party approval beforehand (Mulgan 2002: 224).

Given these compromises the postal reform bill has been classified as a failure (Maclachlan 2004; Mulgan 2002). Later events, however, illustrate that Koizumi made his pledge to continue to pursue further measures to privatize the postal system in earnest. Taking risks does not guarantee success. It opens up possibilities. Constraints prevailed in the first case of postal reform. Koizumi, however, was not deterred. The risk he took with the second postal reform bill is even more significant and served to greatly strengthen Koizumi's overall position.

Illustrating both his commitment to postal reform and his continued willingness to challenge the LDP, Koizumi put postal reform back on the agenda in 2003, pledging to present new legislation to the Diet during FY2005 (Koizumi 2003). The reform package ultimately devised was much more comprehensive than the weak postal reform bill that passed in 2002. In essence, Koizumi was following the initial promise he made when submitting the first bill. His second postal reform bill, which came before the Diet in summer 2005, called for the division of Japan Post into four different operational units, each focusing on a different service – banking and savings, insurance, branch network management, and courier services (Hiwatari 2005: 48). This proposal emerged from the cabinet-based Economic Financial Policy Council (EFPC). As explained above, this new resource allows the prime minister to formulate policy independent of the bureaucracy and the various special interests tied to it. While the cabinet approved the EFPC's proposal, the LDP as a whole did not. Koizumi's response was to reshuffle his cabinet, only appointing pro-reform politicians as his ministers. This strategy was a risky one as a possible consequence was concretizing Koizumi's opposition within the LDP (Hiwatari 2005: 47).

Koizumi took an even larger risk when he dissolved the Lower House of the Diet after the bill failed in the Upper House. The bill met fierce opposition from fellow LDP members when it was introduced to the Lower House. In fact, when the bill was put to a vote, 37 LDP Diet members opposed it, an act of open rebellion. As a result, the bill only narrowly passed the Lower House. The coalition's position was even weaker in the Upper House. Koizumi threatened to dissolve the Lower House if the Upper House failed to pass his bill. While this is a legitimate power of the prime minister, it is hardly ever used to hurt the party in power. Kaifu made a similar threat when his electoral reform bill did not pass, but as we saw in Chapter 3 he backed down after receiving strong pressure from the power wielders in the LDP. Many anti-reformers within the LDP did not believe that Koizumi would actually dissolve the Diet. Kaifu's earlier experience sheds light on the legitimacy of these expectations. In the past, prime ministers have been unwilling to challenge the party that has placed them in office.

Koizumi, unlike Kaifu, however, was willing to push the institutional constraints to the limit, even if the eventual consequence was his own loss of power. From the beginning Koizumi threatened to bring the LDP down if it stood in the way of reform. While Koizumi suffered many defeats within the party, resulting in a series of reforms marked by compromise, in the end when Koizumi perhaps felt like his back was completely against the wall he took this ultimate risk – dissolving the Diet against the will of his fellow LDP politicians.

This risk paid off. During the 2005 Lower House campaign the public backlash fell on LDP defectors and the Democratic Party of Japan (DPJ), the largest opposition party, not on Koizumi. Koizumi effectively used the media to portray those who voted against his legislation as traitors. Many analysts doubted whether postal reform would resonate with the public and be a decisive issue at the polls. Koizumi successfully made the Lower House election a referendum on postal reform. He withdrew support from the 37 LDP members who voted against the bill and ran new LDP candidates against them (Yoshida 2005a). Only 18 of the rebels were re-elected. Meanwhile the LDP secured an outright majority in the Lower House, winning 296 seats (Glosserman 2005).[6] To the surprise of many politicians and political pundits, Koizumi began the special session of the Diet following the election with renewed strength due to his decision to take the risk and challenge the anti-reformers in the party. His public support ratings increased dramatically during the course of the election. Moreover, his bold actions which led to the landside victory for the LDP in the Lower House squelched any remaining opposition from LDP members in the Upper House who had previously voted against electoral reform (Yoshida 2005b). Koizumi faced the rigidities of factional politics head on, took a decisive risk, and changed the political landscape in a way that has increased the possibilities for him to achieve his policy goals.

Koizumi's vision

Earlier cases of reform illustrated that vision aids a leader in his pursuit of reform. The definition of vision that has guided this study suggests that a leader with vision presents a clear picture of how reform will affect interested parties if implemented. Such vision reassures self-interested politicians reluctant to support reform. It helps these politicians to look at the world differently by allowing them to imagine new possibilities. Koizumi is certainly an effective speaker. The crucial question is how much substance resides behind Koizumi's catchy rhetoric. An examination of his policy speeches to the Diet illustrates an unmistakable vision for change. Koizumi's vision is clear, but it has resonated with the public more than it has reassured his fellow party members mainly because his vision attacks the status quo in the LDP. Koizumi has the support of the reform contingent in the LDP, but many anti-reformers reject his vision completely.

Koizumi's vision of postal privatization is best understood in the context of his larger vision of the political economy. Specifically, Koizumi is an advocate of small government, free and open markets and individual responsibility in the marketplace (Maclachlan 2006: 1). Koizumi clearly outlined his goals in relation to the political economy upon becoming prime minister in April 2001. In his first substantive speech to the Lower House of the Diet he highlighted the following three goals related to economic reform: (1) the elimination of non-performing loans in the next two to three years, as well the minimization of the shareholdings of banks; (2) the creation of a competitive economic system; and (3) the implementation of fiscal structural reform (Koizumi 2001: 8–9). Creating a competitive economy included the controversial notion of moving away from public-works spending to stimulate the economy. Deregulation and privatization of inefficient public corporations, such as the postal system, represented key pillars of fiscal structural reform (Lam 2002: 70–71). In relation to reform of the LDP, Koizumi called for the popular election of the prime minister, a reform that would require amending the constitution for the first time (Japan Times 2001).

Koizumi has been able to convert his reformist goals into strong slogans meant to antagonize LDP anti-reformers. These slogans make excellent media sound bites, capturing the public's attention. Examples of these catchphrases include "structural reform without sanctuaries," "change the LDP, change Japan," and "rely on the private sector to do what the private sector does best." These slogans effectively transmit a clear message to the LDP and the public. These slogans also seem to be more than mere rhetoric. For example, Koizumi has taken action to achieve structural reform without sanctuaries. He has reduced spending on public works, and he has sought privatization of the postal system as well as highway reform. Both postal reform and highway reform bills passed the Diet. His dissolution of the Diet was a significant step he took to change the LDP. By forcing the party to face election following the rejection of his second postal reform bill, he opened a debate on the party and its rigidities. Earlier in his tenure, Koizumi defied party norms by rejecting the notion of factional balancing when making cabinet appointments.

Koizumi's general reformist stance appealed to the public. Prior to the 2005 Lower House election, however, evidence suggests that Koizumi's specific vision of postal privatization did not have widespread public support.

For example, in spring 2005 less than 10 percent of the public indicated that they thought postal privatization warranted immediate government action.[7] This limited support for postal reform suggests that Koizumi was not effectively selling his vision to the public before the 2005 Lower House election (Maclachlan 2006: 13).

Politicians in the opposition and the LDP have been even less enthusiastic about Koizumi's reformist vision. Bringing politicians on board to his vision has proven difficult since his reforms cut at the heart of many politicians' support bases. In many ways, like Miki before him, Koizumi's vision resonates better with the opposition. He has co-opted the DPJ's platform. For obvious reasons, however, this new opposition party is unwilling to lend Koizumi support while he is a member of the LDP. In contrast, the public is weary after weathering over a decade of recession and relishes Koizumi's attempts to change politics as usual. The LDP's overwhelming success in the 2005 Lower House election that centered on postal reform suggests that his vision has majority support. This vision combined with risk-taking and commitment has helped him overcome obstacles to reform.

Koizumi's commitment

Koizumi's commitment to reform has aided him in his pursuit of his policy goals. Commitment is reflected in the persistent pursuit of one's vision and one's willingness to pay a price to see this vision realized. Leaders are committed if they pursue their ideals throughout their careers with little regard of the negative consequences to them personally. Commitment ensures that a politician will be ready to act when the environment is conducive to reform.

Koizumi's reformist roots are deep. He was Fukuda Takeo's political secretary before his first election to the Lower House in 1972. Fukuda, Koizumi's mentor, was known for opposing LDP money politics, especially after he lost the battle for the prime ministership to Tanaka Kakuei (Curtis 1988: 101–2). Following in Fukuda's footsteps, Koizumi has been a long-time opponent to the pork barrel politics that fuel the LDP. One of Koizumi's main rivals in the LDP is former Prime Minister Hashimoto. Not surprisingly, Hashimoto heads the faction from the Tanaka faction line (Takahashi 2003).

Koizumi made a name for himself as a reformer in the early 1990s as one of the three members of the YKK trio in the LDP, which sought to challenge the most powerful factions in the LDP. Yamasaki Taku (Y), Katō Kōichi (K), and Koizumi Junichirō (K) formed this group in 1991. Similar to Ozawa and his reformist study groups within the LDP, this leadership trio recruited younger, reformist-minded party members across factional lines to form the *Shinseki* (New Century) study group within the LDP. Bolstered by these cross-factional ties and his increasing name recognition, Koizumi ran for party president in 1995.[8] He only received a very small amount of support in this election. Koizumi used his increased name recognition, however, to bring attention to his call for postal reform.

Koizumi's commitment to postal reform dates back to when he served as minister of posts and telecommunications in the Miyazawa cabinet in 1992. In 1999, Koizumi and Matsuzawa Shigefumi of the DPJ formed a non-partisan Postal Privatization Study Group. The 17 politicians who made up this group produced a draft proposal for postal privatization. The proposal called for the separation and privatization of the three postal system services (postal services, savings, and insurance) and drew lessons and ideas from the past experience of privatizing Nippon Telegraph and Telephone Corp. (NTT) and Japan National Railways (JNR) (Maclachlan 2006: 8).

Koizumi's reformist positions prior to gaining the prime ministership never put his membership in the LDP in jeopardy. Instead, Koizumi was able to use these positions as a way to make a name for himself and his issues with the public. His challenges of the LDP from within as a member of YKK helped build his legitimacy with the public. It enhanced his popularity. His consistent push for postal reform helped him enter the prime ministership with a clearer vision of reform. This vision was concretized in his books on the need for postal reform (Koizumi and Kajiwara 1994). Koizumi did not make progress on realizing this vision until he became prime minister and even then, as we have seen, he faced great obstacles. The key point concerning his commitment is that it allowed his ideas to develop and prepared him to pursue his goals once the environment was more in his favor.

Conclusion

Many claim that Koizumi's leadership represents a new kind of leadership in Japan. Unlike past prime ministers, Koizumi has ignored the dictates of factional balancing and chosen his own cabinet ministers independent of factional influence (Kitaoka 2004: 8). He also has shown the importance of effective public speaking and media savvy under the new electoral system (Blechinger-Talcott 2004: 23). What this analysis illustrates, however, is that Koizumi has personal attributes that have aided other leaders in their pursuits of political reform in postwar Japan. Koizumi challenged his party by placing a greater emphasis on the cabinet as a policy-making body. He came to office with a vision of radical change, and his actions both prior to becoming prime minister and as prime minister illustrate his commitment to his vision. As with Miki and Ozawa, Koizumi's risk-taking, vision, and commitment facilitated his pursuit of reform.

Koizumi too has faced a party that is staunchly opposed to radical change. Miki used the media and speed of action to pass reform. Ozawa left the LDP. In contrast, during the first four plus years as prime minister, Koizumi used anti-party rhetoric while essentially pursuing reform inside the LDP. The result of this approach was the passage of less comprehensive reform with the mark of compromise with the anti-reform LDP contingent. As we have seen, however, in August 2005 Koizumi took a strong stand against the anti-reformers in the LDP regarding his second postal reform package, threatening to dissolve the Lower House if the bill did not pass the Upper House. Unlike Kaifu, Koizumi did not back down from this threat. He dissolved the Lower House. This risk paid off. Koizumi reintroduced his postal reform package to the Diet with his party's full support. The Diet passed reform in little over a month after the Lower House election.[9]

Koizumi faced weaker constraints than Kaifu. Koizumi was less beholden to factions given the changes in the selection of the LDP president. He also held greater formal powers due to the changes in the Cabinet Law. Still, as we have seen, the obstacles to reform within the LDP were significant. Dissolving the Diet weakened these constraints and increased the possibility for reform. Leaders who take risks in pursuit of their policy goals have a better chance of seeing their policy agenda passed. While a leadership style reliant on risk-taking has been rare in the postwar period, it has not been absent. Here, Koizumi joins Miki and Ozawa as leaders who have successfully used this strategy to see their vision of reform enacted.[10]

8 Conclusion
Political leadership in Japan

The major finding in this investigation can be summed up in two words – leadership matters. The puzzle guiding this study asked why politicians enact laws against their self-interest. The conventional explanation claims that politicians pass reform in response to the outbreak of scandal. By examining in detail two successful and two failed cases of reform, all of which involve scandal, I show that scandal is a necessary but insufficient part of the explanation. In these cases the difference between success and failure is leadership.

The examination in Chapters 2–5 of four proposals for electoral system and political funding reform between 1975 and 1994 in postwar Japan reveals that while scandal increases the salience of political reform, leaders with a certain set of political resources and personal attributes are necessary to secure the passage of reform. Important political resources include patron–client ties and connections with other parties. Significant personal attributes are the willingness to take risks, vision. and commitment. These resources and personal attributes contribute to effective leadership with regard to the passage of political reform in Japan.

In my exploration of political reform, leaders who lacked either the necessary resources or personal attributes did not pass reform. As we saw in Chapter 6, members of the New Liberal Club, the Utopia Study Group, *Wakate Kaikaku Ha*, and the League to Restore Trust did not have the seniority and connections needed to successfully build a coalition for reform inside or outside the LDP. The clearest case of the importance of political resources is the case of Kōno Yōhei, the head of the New Liberal Club. Kōno took significant risks in pursuit of reform, such as his exodus from the LDP, a risk comparable to the one taken by Ozawa Ichirō almost two decades later. Kōno had a vision for clean politics and pursued this vision outside the LDP for ten years, illustrating his commitment to reform. However, Kōno lacked adequate resources. He was not a senior politician, only having been elected three times at the time he left the party; therefore, he did not have the patron–client ties necessary to recruit a large number of LDP politicians to leave the LDP with him. He only convinced five members to break away with him, whereas Ozawa, a senior politician with considerable patron–client ties, recruited over forty members to leave with him. Kōno also lacked ties to opposition parties. As a result, he was unable to build an anti-LDP coalition, something Ozawa was able to do since he had been privy to backroom deals as a senior LDP member. Table 8.1 summarizes the level of resources and personal attributes for the politicians considered in previous chapters. As Table 8.1 indicates, the only difference between Kōno and Ozawa was the amount of resources each possessed. Kōno's low level of resources inhibited his pursuit of reform.

Leaders who lacked necessary personal attributes also failed to pass political reform. As illustrated in Table 8.1, in contrast to Kōno, Prime Ministers Kaifu and Miyazawa had the resources to pursue electoral system and political funding reform, but they lacked the personal attributes. Kaifu and Miyazawa were both senior politicians when they assumed the prime ministership, having been elected ten and nine terms respectively. They were from smaller factions, but they had the minimum set of resources to pursue reform, as the successful case of Miki, another senior politician and prime minister who was from a small faction, illustrates. While having adequate resources, Kaifu and Miyazawa were not willing to take risks to pursue their proclaimed goal. Instead, they sought reform through the normal policy channels within the LDP and were stymied by the desire of most politicians to maintain the status quo. Kaifu had the image of a clean politician but his rhetoric was more symbolic than substantive. His failure to dissolve the Diet when it shelved his political reform bill ultimately showed his unwillingness to pay a price for reform, unlike Koizumi and his quest for postal reform. Koizumi followed through on his threat to dissolve the Lower House of the Diet if the Upper House rejected postal reform. This risk paid off, eventually leading to the passage of postal reform. Miyazawa had no signs of vision or commitment to political reform. He simply found himself in office when reform was impossible to ignore. In both these cases, scandal occurred but did not lead to reform. The failure to realize reform was due to the absence of the right kind of leader.

Successful reformers, Miki and Ozawa, however, had the necessary resources and personal attributes to pass reform. Both were senior politicians with connections within and outside the LDP. Furthermore, they also had clear visions of reform and were willing to take risks to pursue these visions. Miki

Table 8.1 The level of resources and personal attributes of advocates of reform

	Resources	Risk-taking	Vision	Commitment	Policy outcome
Miki	High	High	High	High	Success
Kōno	Low	High	High	High	Failure
Kaifu	High	Low	Low	Low	Failure
Miyazawa	High	Low	Low	Low	Failure
Ozawa	High	High	High	High	Success
Koizumi	High	High	High	High	Success

used the media to mobilize public support and pressure his fellow party members to pass revisions to the Political Funds Control Act in 1975. Ozawa broke away from the LDP and built an anti-LDP coalition that passed a political reform package in 1994. In these two cases effective leadership led to successful reform.

Koizumi's actions in the case of postal reform illustrate the more general applicability of the theory of leadership and political reform developed in this book. Postal reform does not fall into the category of political reform that directly affects the behavior of politicians in the future. Such reform, however, does go against the self-interest of politicians who get support from groups that oppose postal reform. We saw in Chapter 7 that similar personal attributes aided Koizumi in his pursuit of reform. Significant institutional changes, such as electoral system reform and changes to the Cabinet Law changed the set of resources available to prime ministers, as well as the set of resources necessary for those seeking reform. This shift is reflected in the choices available to Koizumi. However, the necessary personal attributes – risk-taking, vision, and commitment – were still decisive in the passage of postal reform. In particular, Koizumi's decision to dissolve the Lower House increased the possibility of the passage of reform after it had been rejected by the Upper House of the Diet. By forcing members of the Lower House to face election based on their stance on postal reform, Koizumi created a public mandate for reform. His vision of reform added to the effectiveness of this electoral campaign, and his commitment to reform ensured that he was willing to pay a price to see reform enacted if need be. As shown in Table 8.1, Miki, Ozawa, and Koizumi's high level of resources, risk-taking, vision, and commitment led to the successful passage of reform in all cases.

Evidence considered in the preceding chapters also refuted several alternative explanations for the passage of reform, including the severity of scandal, the length of the window of opportunity, and increased party competition. Unlike political leadership these variables fail to explain the major successful and unsuccessful cases of reform in the postwar period. The Lockheed, Recruit, and Sagawa Kyūbin scandals arguably are the three most severe scandals in the postwar period. Political reform only followed the Sagawa Kyūbin scandal, and even in this case Miyazawa, the leader in office when the scandal broke, was unable to capitalize on the environment and pass reform. Reform only came with Ozawa's risk of breaking away from the LDP with the goal of forming an anti-LDP coalition government in support of reform. Similarly, the lengths of the windows of opportunity in the Recruit and Sagawa Kyūbin scandals were almost the same; however, once again reform only passed in the aftermath of the Sagawa Kyūbin scandal due to the leadership of Ozawa Ichirō. Longer windows of opportunity do not guarantee the passage of reform. Leaders with certain resources and personal attributes are needed to exploit these windows. Finally, the postwar period has seen several instances of increased party competition measured by the entrance of new parties into the political arena. The Democratic Socialist Party and the

Kōmeitō did not choose to make political reform a major issue in the 1960s. The New Liberal Club broke away from the LDP on the issue of political reform, but Kōno Yōhei, the party leader, did not have enough resources to build a coalition against the LDP and force the issue of reform. Reform did pass in 1994 following the creation of the Japan New Party and the two LDP break-away parties (the *Shinseitō* and *Sakigake*). This sole success in the wake of increased party competition, however, suggests that other variables were at play. As we have seen, the leadership of Ozawa Ichirō was decisive in this case. Leaders with sufficient political resources along with a propensity to take risks, vision, and commitment are best poised to exploit windows of opportunity for reform created by decreasing government approval and increasing salience of reform in the wake of scandal.

In the remainder of this conclusion, I would like to consider the implications of the findings in earlier chapters by addressing under what circumstances leadership matters, what kind of leadership matters, and why leadership matters. This chapter will speak to these points by exploring both the general and the Japan-specific implications of the conclusion that leadership matters. The first section explores how insights about leadership gleaned in this study affect political science theorizing more generally. Political science has tended to ignore the role of leadership, a factor in policy making that is admittedly difficult to measure. Yet labeling leadership irrelevant does not reflect reality, as has been shown in this study. After briefly reviewing how the current schools of thought in political science have dealt with leadership, I then illustrate how the literature on policy making and leadership in Japan follows these more general trends in political science. Both the more general literature and the Japan-specific literature emphasize the constraints that inhibit effective leadership. Evidence from this research exposes the problems in these approaches. Having discussed the inadequacies of the current state of the literature, the second section in this chapter addresses when, how, and why leadership matters. I conclude by outlining the implications of the conclusion that leadership matters for Japanese politics.

Treatments of leadership in political science

Leaders are rarely completely absent from discussions of politics. Political science scholarship, however, looks for generalizable causal relationships. This endeavor is an important one, but it often results in political scientists giving too much weight to causal determinants (constraints) and too little import to individual leaders and their ability to circumvent those constraints. Leaders are usually part of the story, but how their actions and the effect of their actions are explained differs. Two approaches currently dominate most political science research – rational choice and institution-based approaches. Both approaches minimize the role of individual political leadership.

The unit of analysis in rational choice is often, although not always, the individual and the constraints that the individual faces. In this school, the choices of actors are derived from their preferences and therefore are predict-able. The choice of actors is by definition determined by the leaders' maxi-mizing behavior in which they weigh the costs and benefits they anticipate encountering given a particular decision (Bawn 1993; Brady and Mo 1992; Geddes 1991).[1] Although some more rigorous works deduce the costs and benefits from theory, more frequently the costs and benefits actors face are measured ex post facto. That is, the actors' preferences are induced from the choices made.[2]

This approach has been used to explain the events surrounding the passage of reform in 1994. For example, some scholars have classified Ozawa's deci-sion to leave the LDP as rational. This classification is based on an analysis of the costs and benefits that Ozawa faced at the time he decided to leave the LDP. In his analysis of Ozawa's decision to leave the party, Kohno Masaru claims that when senior reformer, Gōtoda Masaharu, refused to run for party president following Miyazawa's failure to support a reform package that had a chance of gaining opposition support, Ozawa had no other option than to exit the LDP. Kohno explains,

> Gōtoda's endorsement of (or his lack of opposition to) a general election, however, left Ozawa and Hata no option but to dissociate themselves from the LDP. In other words, they were finally forced to pay the price of portraying themselves as reformers, build a new party, and start an electoral campaign from scratch.
>
> (1997: 149)

Kohno argues that because these actors were constrained by their preferences only one course of action was available to them.

The empirical evidence presented in the preceding chapters challenges this interpretation of Ozawa's actions. Without the benefits of hindsight, Ozawa's actions seem less rational given the environment at the time he chose to leave the party in order to pursue political reform from the outside. His short-term goal was to secure the passage of political reform, hopefully by forming a coalition with several of the opposition parties and creating a non-LDP government. The fact that he did this, however, does not mean that it was clear from the beginning that he would succeed, or even that he had a high probability of succeeding. In fact, the past failure of Kōno Yōhei and his breakaway party in the 1970s (the New Liberal Club) should have given Ozawa pause and provided him with many reasons not to leave the LDP.

Even without the historical example to draw lessons from, the costs of leaving the LDP were high – less funding and high uncertainty surrounding both re-election and the formation of an anti-LDP coalition. The benefits of leaving the LDP only came if (1) Ozawa and his followers secured a place in government and (2) the group actually passed reform. Neither one of these occurrences was a foregone conclusion.

Moreover, what Ozawa was trying to maximize at the time was unclear.

Some explanations suggest that he was trying to maximize the benefits of being a reformer (Kohno 1997: 149). Other accounts claim that Ozawa and the other defectors were attempting to maximize "voice" (Kato 1998). The empirical evidence does not support either assertion. It was not clear what Ozawa was trying to maximize at the time or even what the "best" course of action was, regardless of what he was trying to maximize. If we accept the assumption that Ozawa was trying to maximize voice, then it still was not clear ahead of time that his actions at the time would have achieved this goal. His actions actually put his influence on policy making in great jeopardy. By leaving the LDP he was giving up a secure position in government, gambling that he would be able to form an anti-LDP coalition. Although Ozawa lost the power struggle to take over the largest, most powerful faction in the LDP, he could have made his presence felt in the breakaway faction that he initially created. Taking over as the head of the Takeshita faction was not his only chance to wield power in the future in the LDP. Power struggles are a constant within the LDP. He certainly could have tried to reorganize the internal alliances in his favor despite his initial defeat. His chances for influence within the party were not exhausted when he chose to leave. Given the strength of the LDP when Ozawa decided to break away, leaving the party in which he had secured a position of high seniority, arguably was not the most "rational" decision if he was trying to maximize his voice in the policy-making process.

The case of Kaifu provides further evidence of the flaw in the rational choice interpretation of the events in 1993. Kaifu spent an enormous amount of time and energy developing his image as a clean reformer. He had invested more than Ozawa in developing this persona. Kaifu highlighted his connection to Miki and even wore a polka-dotted tie, Miki's trademark, to symbolically remind the public of his commitment to reform. Given his high-profile image as a reformer, according to the rational choice logic presented above, one would also expect Kaifu's only option once his proposal failed in 1991 to be to dissolve the parliament. That is, if Kaifu, like Ozawa, was maximizing his image as a reformer, then according to rational choice logic Kaifu would have had no option other than dissolving the parliament in an attempt to pressure his party members to actually pass reform. Kaifu did not take this risk. Unlike Ozawa, Kaifu was unwilling to challenge the constraints in place. The difference between these two leaders did not rest in their preferences – they both desired reform. The difference rested in what they were willing to do to realize this goal. Ozawa was a risk-taker; Kaifu was not. These personal attributes influenced each leader's pursuit of reform and ultimately the fate of reform.

These empirical examples from Chapters 3 and 5 illustrate that leaders face looser constraints and have more agency than are assumed in the rational choice approach. The costs and benefits of a decision are not always clear ahead of time. Moreover, what a leader is trying to maximize also is not always apparent. Only the actors know what their ultimate goals are and what they are willing to risk to achieve these goals. Kaifu and Miyazawa were not willing to antagonize LDP power brokers to realize reform; Miki and Ozawa were. Rational choice is correct in its emphasis on choice. It fails to recognize that preferences are not fixed over time. Leaders can and do change their own preferences as well as the preferences of followers. In addition, leaders recognize a broader array of choices than often imagined. As the cases in this research indicate, the key is how able leaders are to see available choices and how willing they are to take risks, when necessary, to realize change.

In contrast to rational choice explanations, institutional explanations focus on how rules and institutions constrain the options available to leaders. Leaders are not constrained by their preferences, but by the institutional environment in which they function. Drastic change only occurs when some exogenous shock shakes up the system. Smaller change occurs within the constraints of existing rules and institutions. Leaders cannot act independently from these rules and institutions (Immergut 1992; Steinmo 1993; Weaver and Rockman 1993).

Institutional explanations of leadership in Japan emphasize the constraints posed both by the environment in which leaders operate and, in the case of prime ministers, the constraints posed by the formal and informal powers of the office. For example, in his study of prime ministers in Japan, Kenji Hayao points out:

> ... the prime minister is subject to severe limitations. The selection process makes his position highly vulnerable to challenges from his own party. The political system is extremely inertial: the party, the National Assembly, and subgovernments are all significant constraints. His staff is small and its loyalties are at best mixed ... All these factors limit the number of issues in which the prime minister is involved, as well as his ability to initiate change in policy and influence the development of alternatives.
>
> (1993: 202)

According to Hayao, these constraints lead to reactive policy making on the part of prime ministers. Prime ministers tend to consider items already on the agenda, instead of adding their own items to the agenda. If a new item is placed on the agenda, then this is because some international or domestic crisis has made it salient. In this conception of politics, these leaders do not have a political vision; they simply react to circumstances (Hayao 1993).[3]

Like Hayao, Tomohito Shinoda emphasizes the institutional constraints on power. He also points to some of the informal sources of power at a prime minister's disposal, however. These sources include the prime minister's support base in the party, popularity, influence over the bureaucracy, ties to the opposition, and experience (2000: 89–90). The extent to which prime ministers are effectively able to use these informal sources of power varies. Shinoda recognizes this and asserts,

> Because prime ministers must rely on informal sources of power to effec-
> tively utilize institutional sources of power, their effectiveness varies
> depending on their background, experience, political skills and person-
> ality.
>
> (2000: 201)

The types of background, experience, political skills, and personality that are
most effective in utilizing these informal sources of power are not clearly
outlined. Instead, Shinoda focuses on the informal sources of power of each
prime minister without elaborating on what allowed the prime minister to
use the resources effectively.

Constraints always exist. Constraints, however, do not always stand in the
way of change. As examples in this research illustrate, leaders can and do
ignore these constraints, even when it is not *rational* to do so. Ignoring some
existing constraints constitutes taking a risk. Risk-taking is one of the defining
characteristics of a successful advocate of reform. For example, prior to 1993
most members of the LDP could not fathom a political existence outside the
party. Ozawa, by leaving the LDP and successfully forming an anti-LDP
governing coalition, proved that this constraint was subjective, thereby
changing the perception of the possible. In Weber's terms he reached for the
impossible. This type of action is consequential and cannot be ignored.

Most institution-based arguments do not allow for the possibility that
actors can challenge the constraints in place. Constraints exist and do exactly
what their name suggests – constrain leaders from making certain choices.
The LDP's thirty-eight year dominance should have kept Ozawa from leaving
the party, especially given his high level of seniority. Ozawa was not deterred
and instead strove to create a better environment, despite this constraint.
Leaders, like Ozawa, sometimes take risks and successfully weaken the constraints. What this research illustrates is that leaders do sometimes act autono-
mously. This autonomous action has real consequences for policy change.

The importance of leadership

In the remaining pages, I would like to push this assertion that leadership
matters by addressing the following questions: Under what circumstances
does leadership matter? What kind of leadership matters? And, why does
leadership matter? The findings in previous chapters speak to each of these
questions. I will highlight the implications of these findings below.

When leadership matters

In the cases of electoral reform and campaign finance reform considered in
this book, leadership matters most when a window of opportunity for reform
is open. Such a window opens when public support in government decreases
and the salience of reform increases, a circumstance that most often emerges
when a political scandal occurs.

More generally, the relationship between the leader and the political environment plays a critical role in the leader's overall success. Leaders can overcome institutional constraints, but this is easier when the political environment the leader is working in favors the policy change the leader is advocating. The causal arrows between the environment and the leader, however, run both ways. That is, the environment influences how successful leaders can be in pursuing their policy agendas, but leaders also are capable of influencing the environments they operate in (James 1961).

Koizumi and postal reform is a case in point. At the time Koizumi dissolved the Diet, the public was not demanding postal privatization. Koizumi, however, made this issue the centerpiece of the LDP's campaign by kicking LDP members who had voted against postal reform out of the party and running new candidates against them in their districts. In a very real way, the election then became a referendum on postal reform. With the LDP's decisive victory interpreted as being a vote for reform, it became very difficult for the remaining members of the LDP to oppose Koizumi's bill. Koizumi made the environment more favorable through his own agency.

Certainly leaders are not successful at achieving all their political goals. Miki failed to oversee the passage of anti-monopoly legislation, Ozawa's coalition quickly dissolved, and Koizumi did not pass comprehensive economic reform. The key to the successes these leaders had is related to the environment each was operating in as well as the personal attributes and resources the leaders used to exploit this environment.

What kind of leadership matters

Different leaders are effective in different situations. From a comparative perspective, one can expect that the personal attributes needed for effective leadership are policy-specific, while the resources that aid advocates of reform are country-specific. Leadership scholars have long recognized that different personal attributes facilitate different pursuits by leaders, the first portion of the hypothesis above. For example, Max Weber maintains that charisma is the defining characteristic of a leader seeking dramatic social change (1947). Charisma, however, does not aid a leader in day-to-day governing. Burns also acknowledges that while some overlap exists, the characteristics of successful reformers, revolutionaries, bureaucrats, and party leaders differ (1978).

The results from this study suggest that the personal attributes that are important in the realm of political reform are vision, commitment, and the propensity to take risks. Charisma is not necessary. Non-revolutionary reform does not require others to change their own identities. It simply requires them to be open to new rules of the game, rules that could potentially impose future costs on them. Vision facilitates this by providing others with a picture of what the reformed system will look like. Commitment reassures others that the pursuit of reform is a worthwhile one and also increases the chances of reform by lengthening the possible time frame during which an advocate of reform pursues this policy. Finally, risk-taking allows leaders to challenge constraints. These insights should be valid cross-nationally for similar types of reform.

In contrast to personal attributes, resources that facilitate reform are country-specific and related to the institutional environment in which the advocate of reform is operating in. Policy-making processes differ by country, as do the larger institutional environments where policies are made. Comparing the battle for campaign finance reform in the United States and Japan illustrates this point. Varying institutional rigidities exist in the policy-making process in the United States and Japan. In the United States, for example, many relevant institutional constraints are found in the rules and procedures of the House and Senate. In the particular case of campaign finance reform, poison-pill amendments, the House leadership's control over the agenda, and the filibuster in the Senate hampered the progress of reform from 1996 to 2001. Senator John McCain (Rep-AZ), arguably the most influential sponsor of the Bipartisan Campaign Reform Act, used several resources to aid him in his pursuit of reform. These resources included ties to outside groups such as Common Cause and the League of Women Voters, "going public" through his presidential campaign, and editorial boards and town meetings to combat these institutional constraints. As we saw earlier in this book, in the Japanese case, factional politics and the limited powers granted to the prime minister are particularly prominent constraints to reform. Personal ties inside and outside one's party are more useful in combating these constraints. Interestingly enough both McCain and Ozawa exhibited the willingness to take risks, vision, and commitment as they mobilized these varying resources to push for similar reforms (Gaunder 2005). Similar pursuits require similar kinds of leaders even if the resources necessary to navigate varying institutional environments differ.

Why leadership matters

Leadership matters because it provides a way for actors to challenge and sometimes overcome constraints posed by the institutional environment or the self-interest of other actors. While leadership can act as an intervening variable influencing the character of change, it also can act as an independent variable which results in significant change. The scope of this change varies. Some types of leaders bring about dramatic social change, while others influence policy.[4]

Studies of leadership are important because they expose the interaction between actors and the constraints they face. Such studies open the door to comparisons among actors within countries, such as this study, as well as future studies of actors across countries facing varying constraints, as suggested above when considering what kind of leadership matters.

The idea of challenging or "stretching" constraints is not a new one. Samuels emphasizes how bricoleurs, leaders who use symbols from the past to push for change in the present, have been particularly adept at institution building in Japan and Italy (2003b: 7–8). Similarly, Breslauer investigates the ability of leaders to build authority to assess the extent to which leaders have been able to stretch constraints and exercise transformational leadership in both the Soviet and post-Soviet eras (2002). These studies are significant because they expose the ways in which leaders build legitimacy in varying institutional settings.

This study of leadership and political reform complements the approaches above by exploring leadership in the realm of policy change. It adds to the current debates on leadership in Japan by exploring leadership in terms of reform, rather than nation building (Samuels 2003b) or clientelism (Schlesinger 1997). It also provides a corrective to previous works on Japanese leadership that focus on the institutional constraints leaders face, not how leaders can overcome the constraints (Hayao 1993; Shinoda 2000)

In his classic study *Leadership*, James MacGregor Burns asserts that "leadership is one of the most observed and least understood phenomena on earth" (1978: 2). The goal of his study is to form a generalizable theory of leadership that can be applied across time and borders (ibid.: 3). Many studies since Burns have aspired to this goal and moved us to a greater understanding of the kinds of leadership both within and across countries. This study falls into this category. Leadership is the decisive factor in the passage or failure of political reform legislation that could negatively affect the future behavior of politicians in Japan.

Implications for Japanese politics

The conclusion that leadership matters is a surprising one in the Japanese context where leaders have long been ignored as unimportant. Several explanations for the policy-making process in Japan exist, but none of these approaches allows for the possibility that individual leaders, acting alone, can play a critical role in the final outcome.

The most common image of the policy-making process in Japan under the 1955 system of LDP dominance is captured in the catch phrase "Japan Inc." Proponents of this view claim that a triad of bureaucrats, conservative party (LDP) politicians, and big business runs Japan. The bureaucrats create policy acceptable to big business that is ratified by the conservative politicians. The bureaucrats rule while the politicians reign (Johnson 1982). In this bureaucratic-dominant model, individual politicians have no role in policy change. The main drive for policy comes from the bureaucracy.

A different image of policy making in Japan sees policy being formed by iron triangles. These iron triangles form around certain issue areas and draw members from the relevant bureaucratic ministry, LDP policy tribe (*zoku*), and special interest group. This school does not deny the institutional capacity of the bureaucracy. Instead, the notion of subgovernments disaggregates the bureaucracy and political parties. The conflict is not between the bureaucracy and politicians but across subgovernments (Campbell 1977). Individual leaders do not lead these subgovernments. Agency does not have a role.

The most extreme image of policy making in Japan claims that the Japanese government is best represented by a truncated triangle where no head exists at all (van Wolferen 1989). This explanation claims that other countries have problems interacting with Japan because it is completely unclear to the outsider where power lies.

These analyses are correct in identifying significant constraints, but limited because they do not provide for the possibility of overcoming the constraints. In contrast to these images of policy making in Japan, the results from this research suggest that leaders are just as important in Japan as in other countries. When and how leadership expresses itself in Japan simply differs from how it is expressed elsewhere. Japan's system of seniority is a rigid one.[5] Politicians do have to serve several terms before they are able to exert any real influence on the policy-making process. The only hope for junior politicians who desire change is to tie their fortunes to an established, well-connected senior politician. Senior politicians need not be from the largest, most powerful factions or parties; however, these politicians do need to be willing to challenge the constraints of the formal policy-making process in order to realize reform. The cases of Miki, Ozawa, and Koizumi illustrate that non-traditional approaches to policy making – such as Miki formulating his own policy and mobilizing public support behind it, Ozawa creating a new political party, or Koizumi dissolving the Lower House of the Diet – can open, soften, or even bypass some of the normal constraints that stand in the way of political reform.

Political science often relegates leadership to a residual variable. The results from this research, however, suggest that leaders matter and thus deserve more attention in future studies of the policy-making process. Specifically, leadership should be treated more systematically as an explanatory variable. Leadership can usefully be broken up into institutional resources and personal attributes. Effective resources vary by country due to differing institutional environments; significant personal attributes vary by policy area and should be similar cross-nationally. Certain combinations of resources and personal attributes allow leaders to overcome rigidities in the system.

Outside observers have puzzled over where political power rests in Japan. My research suggests that leaders with certain resources and personal attributes can devise effective policy-making strategies. Miki, Ozawa, and Koizumi all exercised leadership that resulted in the passage of reform. Policy makers from other countries would be able to deal more effectively with Japan if they realized that at least some of the time, Japan is a "normal" country, meaning that what high-level politicians say and do influences policy outcomes.

Notes

1 The puzzle of political reform

1 Political reform in the context of this study refers to legislation that directly affects the future behavior of politicians. Examples of political reform include electoral system reform, political funding regulations, and political ethics laws.

2 The names of Japanese subjects will be referred to following the Japanese convention of family name first.

3 Matsuda defected from the LDP in 1993 and joined the pro-reform party started by Ozawa Ichirō, a rebel inside the LDP. After losing his re-election bid in 1996, he became an independent and successfully ran for a seat in the Upper House of the Diet in 1998. His status as an independent, as well as his new bid for the Upper House, could also account for the high costs of running for office. Matsuda did not mention these factors in our interview.

4 Reed and Scheiner argue that the members who followed Ozawa out of the party had varying motives. The politicians elected while Ozawa was secretary general of the party followed Ozawa out of the LDP based on loyalty to the patron who got them elected. In contrast, the other members who followed him out of the party did so more out of a conviction for reform (2003: 474).

5 The Sagawa Kyūbin scandal was one of the largest scandals in Japan's postwar history. It broke in August 1992 when Kanemaru Shin, a prominent LDP kingmaker, was accused of accepting large sums of money from the Sagawa Kyūbin company, a parcel delivery company, in illegal campaign contributions. At first, Kanemaru denied these charges, but the following week he held a press conference and acknowledged accepting 500 million yen from Sagawa. In order to take responsibility for his involvement with Sagawa, Kanemaru resigned as vice-president of the LDP but initially retained his seat in the Diet. The scandal continued to get bigger as connections among politicians, Sagawa, and the Inagawa gangster group were revealed (Curtis 1999: 87; Noble 1993: 3–4).

6 Richard Samuels's work is an exception. In *Machiavelli's Children*, Samuels argues that leaders can "stretch" constraints posed by personality, culture, structure, power, and utility (2003b: 2–5).

7 Richard S. Katz is an exception. He addresses a puzzle similar to one explored here using parties as the unit of analysis. He proposes several circumstances when a party might consider changing the rules of the game when it is winning. For example, he suggests a party might consider electoral reform when its future chances of winning under the current rules are assessed to be low or if the party places a premium on long-term versus short-term gains. In addition, outside forces might be able to exert control on the process via such mechanisms as referendum. A party also may be maximizing something other than seat share or rightly or wrongly assess that it will do better under new rules. Finally, interests within the

party may not be uniform. Such division opens the door for reform (R.S. Katz 2005: 63).

8 For example in her study of Sweden, France, and Switzerland, Immergut (1992) compares and contrasts successful and failed cases of health care reform. She argues that if the country had numerous institutional veto points, the groups who were against health care reform were better able to block the legislation. Immergut concludes that the differing health care regimes in Sweden, France, and Switzerland can be explained by the various institutions that set the "rules of the game" for the policy debate in each country. Institutional arguments have been used in exploring other policies areas as well. See Steinmo (1993) and Weaver and Rockman (1993).

9 Rational choice explanations of political reform also recognize the role that institutions play in structuring the bargaining process among actors attempting to maximize their preferences (Bawn 1993). The main emphasis, however, is placed on actors' preferences in determining choice.

10 This discussion of windows of opportunity for reform directly builds on John Kingdon's discussion of policy windows (1984). Kingdon defines a policy window as "an opportunity for advocates of proposals to push their pet solutions, or to push attention to their special problems" (1984: 173). According to Kingdon, "a window opens because of change in the political stream (e.g., a change of administration, a shift in the partisan or ideological distribution of seats in Congress, or a shift in the national mood); or it opens because a new problem captures the attention of governmental officials and those close to them" (1984: 176).

11 Kingdon points out that policy windows are not open for a long period of time (1984: 177).

12 Once a window of opportunity opens, a few additional developments can open the window of opportunity even wider. These factors include a change in administrations as well as economic downturns. A scandal is needed initially to open the window of opportunity for political reform, but once open a change of administration can amplify the salience of reform and economic downturns can increase the lack of government support. Kingdon emphasizes the effect of a change of administration as well (1984: 176).

13 In his exploration of the passage of reform in 1994, Reed makes a connection among scandals, windows of opportunity, and something he refers to as "electoral booms" which are defined as opportunities for changes in government. Specifically, Reed argues that scandals open a window of opportunity for opposition to the ruling government. If an alternative to the governing party exists in the presence of the public outrage over corruption, then a change in government is possible if the alternative can mobilize this outrage into electoral support (Reed 1999a: 186–87). If the alternative party supports reform, as was the case in 1994, the probability of the passage of reform is great (Reed 1999a: 180, 189). The role of individual leadership is absent from this explanation.

14 Kingdon gives the following explanation for when a policy window closes. He explains, "First participants may feel they have addressed the problem through decision or enactment. Even if they have not, the fact that some action has been taken brings down the curtain on the subject for the time being. Second, and closely related, participants may fail to get action. If they fail, they are unwilling to invest further time, energy, political capital, or other resources in the endeavor ... Third, the events that prompted the window to open may pass from the scene ... Fourth, if a change in personnel opens a window, the personnel may change again ... Finally, the window sometimes closes because there is no available alternative" (1984: 177–78).

15 Max Weber does link motive to success. In "Politics as Vocation", Weber argues the greatest danger that all leaders face is letting the quest for power become a

means of personal fulfillment instead of a way of realizing the goals of the "cause". Weber elaborates, "The sin against the lofty spirit of his vocation, however, begins where this striving for power ceases to be *objective* and becomes purely personal self-intoxication, instead of exclusively entering the service of 'the cause'" (1946: 116).

16 The resources that are most effective vary depending on the type of government (parliamentary or presidential), the institutions associated with this type of government, and the type of coalition for reform (intra- or inter-party) that a leader is trying to build.

17 Richard Neustadt (1990) makes a similar argument about the importance of resources. In his exploration of a president's power to persuade, Neustadt points to several indirect ways that a president can influence the agenda of Congress, such as vetoing a critical appointment or adding publicity to a controversial policy. Both formal and informal powers of the presidency give the president a set of resources to use in bargaining with Congress (1990: 31).

18 Although it is impossible to quantify the exact amount of resources that are necessary to prevent a reformer's failure, it is possible to indicate a particular set of resources that are important if a leader is to succeed. Resources alone do not guarantee success, but the lack of certain resources can guarantee failure.

19 One's position in the political hierarchy is represented by the number of times a politician has been elected to office. Junior politicians are those elected three times or less. Mid-level politicians refer to those who have been elected four to six times. Politicians elected seven or more times are considered to be senior (Curtis 1988: 88–98).

20 Samuel Kernell (1986) investigates this media/public support strategy. Here, Kernell argues that the president can bypass bargaining with Congress by directly appealing to the public for support. If the public responds positively, then the president can pressure Congress to act without having to give members any benefits in return for their support.

21 Vision does not necessarily require a charismatic leader for its transmission, especially when the goal is more incremental political reform, not revolutionary social change. Charisma enables a leader to get others to change their identities and adopt that of the leader. Vision in and of itself, however, has more modest effects. Vision aids a leader in persuasion. Vision provides a longer-term perspective that can help potential supporters re-evaluate the costs and benefits associated with implementing reform.

22 This type of commitment is shown in what Weber terms "value rational action." Here, Weber elaborates, "Examples of pure rational orientation to absolute values would be the action of persons who, regardless of possible cost to themselves, act to put into practice their convictions of what seems to them to be required by duty, honour, the pursuit of beauty, a religious call, personal loyalty, or the importance of some 'cause' no matter in what it consists" (1947: 116).

23 The personal attributes discussed above are not exclusive to politicians pursuing political reform. Other politicians can have varying levels of these attributes and bring them to bear on other policy areas. The argument here is that given the nature of political reform these attributes are particularly useful in building a coalition for this type of reform.

24 Scarrow makes a similar argument when exploring the circumstances that favor the passage of political finance regulations in Germany. Specifically, she argues that prevailing patterns of competition, as well as how a party defines its interests, influence whether political finance reform is considered. With cartel parties that seek to maximize revenue more than compete on political finance reform, as in Germany, the likelihood of reform is very small even in the wake of scandal (2004: 659).

25 The support of at least some opposition parties was necessary to secure passage of the bill in the Upper House since the LDP had lost its majority.
26 The evidence to support this conclusion comes from in-depth interviews with Japanese politicians, a survey distributed to Diet members, and secondary accounts of the policy-making process. I conducted in-depth interviews with over 20 politicians involved in the process of political reform. Two politicians participated in the 1975 reform process. The remaining politicians were involved in the reform movements in 1991, 1993, and 1994. Several of these interviewees volunteered to talk with me after filling out a survey about the passage of reform in 1994. Over 200 members of the Lower House participated in this survey. For the most part, the interviewees are referred to using a general description of their position in government. Interviewees are referred to in this way to protect their anonymity.

2 Miki Takeo: an outsider stands firm inside the LDP

1 The shipbuilding scandal was very similar in nature to the earlier Shōwa Denkō scandal in 1948 where this company was accused of giving bribes to government officials in order to get favorable interest rates on loans from the government (Curtis 1988: 160).
2 The actual bill allowed for 457 single-member districts and 20 two-member districts. The two-member districts were included in the proposal to accommodate LDP politicians who feared losing their support bases in their districts due to the redrawing of district lines (Reed and Thies 2001a: 158, fn. 5).
3 The electoral system was in great flux after the end of the World War II. Changes were made to the Public Office Election Law twice prior to the discussions in the 1950s. The law was revised in 1945 and 1947 (Kusunoki 1997: 50–51).
4 According to Masumi, factional politics also influenced Miki's decision to resign from the cabinet. Specifically, the Tanaka faction ran a candidate against a Miki faction incumbent in Miki's home prefecture of Tokushima in the 1974 Upper House election. The Miki faction candidate won as an independent, but the incident caused added tension between Tanaka and Miki (1995: 149).
5 The factions put Shiina in charge of selecting the next prime minister and agreed to abide by his final decision a priori (Curtis 1988: 162). Shiina chose Miki Takeo from among the four politicians (Ōhira, Fukuda, Nakasone, and Miki) contending for the position for two reasons. First, Shiina was afraid that choosing between Ōhira Masayoshi and Fukuda Takeo, long-time political rivals backed by the two largest factions in the LDP, would split the party. Second, he felt that choosing a reformer with a clean image would help restore the LDP's legitimacy (Johnson 1976: 31).
6 The leaders of larger, more powerful factions within the LDP were reluctant to give the top position to Miki; however, the circumstances at the time made them sympathetic to Shiina Etsusaburō's recommendation. Ultimately, these senior leaders decided to back Miki, despite their reservations, as they felt that Miki could be manipulated given his weak base of support within the party (Curtis 1988: 162–63). Later events would prove that the party leaders had underestimated Prime Minister Miki's ability to use the public disgust over money politics to push his agenda for reform.
7 The fact that Miki had proposals ready when coming to office is significant. In his discussion of policy windows Kingdon points to the importance of timing in the success or failure of an advocate of reform. Policy windows are open for a short period of time. A leader must have a proposal ready when the window opens (Kingdon 1984: 190). If he takes the time to formulate a new proposal, then the sense of urgency created by the scandal probably will have passed. Indeed, some politicians have incentives to close the policy window. These politicians will work

to create a perception that the problem has been handled. An advocate of reform must take advantage of the policy window/window of opportunity quickly or another politician may succeed in turning the focus elsewhere.

8 The revisions to the Public Office Election Law passed in the Upper House with the Socialists (JSP) and Democratic Socialists (DSP) joining the LDP in supporting these revisions that focused primarily on limiting publicity and increasing the public supervision of elections. The JSP and DSP were in favor of the portion of this bill that would increase the number of seats. The religious-affiliated Kōmeitō and the Communists (JCP) were opposed to strengthening the regulation of the distribution of political leaflets and therefore voted against the bill (Nakamura 1981: 72).

9 Miki was the most vocal supporter of Kōno Kenzō's successful bid for speaker of the Upper House in 1971. Kōno surprisingly decided to challenge Shigemune Yūzō, the sitting speaker for nine years, calling for reform of the Upper House (Masumi 1995: 119). This personal tie might have influenced his decision to support Miki's revisions to the Political Funds Control Law.

10 In his book, Kōno reflects that he was surprised when the Upper House clerk passed him a memo saying the vote was tied since the LDP had a majority in the Upper House. He then explains that the revisions to the Political Funds Control Law were paired with the revisions to the Public Office Election Law. Given that that the revisions to the Public Office Election Law passed, Kōno voted for the revisions to the Political Funds Control Law (Kōno 1978: 74–75).

11 The revisions to the Political Funds Control Law and Public Office Election Law passed the Upper House on the last day of the plenary session. These bills were two of six bills to hit the Upper House floor for approval by the closing day, July 5, 1975. This type of Diet management led to the first Diet session of the Miki administration to be labeled the "Wandering Diet." The Miki administration was highly criticized for its mismanagement of the legislative agenda. Other bills on the floor included the anti-monopoly bill, the alcohol and tobacco bill, a bill to raise postal rates and a bill ratifying the Nuclear Nonproliferation Treaty. The only thing these bills had in common was the division between the positions of the ruling party and the opposition. More significantly, the LDP's priorities were not clear. That is, there was great disagreement within the LDP as to the relative importance of each of these pieces of legislation (Satō et al.1990: 350). While there was disagreement within the LDP over priorities, Miki clearly placed a great deal of energy and effort on securing the passage of the revisions to the Political Funds Control Law.

12 The Executive Council was not created until after Miki served as prime minister.

13 Kent Calder describes Miki as an "issue-oriented outsider" and characterizes his faction as being closer to an "externally mobilized" party within the LDP given the faction's propensity to question the bureaucracy and pursue policies counter to the status quo (1988: 189). Reflecting on Miki's prime ministership, a former administrative assistant of Miki's notes that Miki was more like a prime minister from the opposition party because he pushed so many policies that ran counter to the party's mainstream positions (Nakamura 1981: 52–53). Masumi provides a similar characterization of Miki, explaining, "his [Miki's] policies were more likely to win support in the opposition parties than within his own party. In this way, the anti-Miki majority in the government party became the de facto opposition [during the Miki administration]" (1995: 168).

14 Following his resignation from the cabinet, Miki abstained from the vote on the security treaty (Masumi 1995: 166). Abstaining from a party vote is another somewhat risky way to register one's disagreement with the party line.

15 Several indicators suggest that the Lockheed scandal opened a window of opportunity for reform. Following the revelation at the US Senate subcommittee hearing

in February, Miki's cabinet support ratings dropped eight percentage points from the previous November to 26 percent support (Sorifu 1976). This drop arguably reflects the public's decreased support of the LDP government, even with a reformer at the helm. The following December the LDP performed poorly in the 1976 Lower House election, barely maintaining its majority, securing 263 of the 511 seats after convincing several independents to join the LDP (Masumi 1995: 186). Two developments indicate the increasing salience of reform following the outbreak of the Lockheed scandal. First, in June 1976 six members of the LDP left the party on the issue of reform to form the New Liberal Club (NLC). Chapter 6 explores the New Liberal Club's failed attempt to exploit the window of opportunity for reform in 1976. Second, in his written resignation after the LDP pushed him out of office in December 1976, Miki emphasized the need to reform the seniority- and faction-dominated money politics of the LDP. He also called for the creation of a primary system in the selection of the party president (Masumi 1995: 186).

16 Miki tried to use the media to diffuse this second campaign. He appeared on an NHK program and proclaimed, "I will not bow to a forced resignation. I cannot consent to a withdrawal before the extraordinary Diet session. I will not enter into compromises that bend principles" (Masumi 1995: 183). He was unable to produce enough public outrage to prevent the power brokers from removing him from office this time.

17 Miki's strategy of resigning as cabinet minister, abstaining from votes when he disagreed with the LDP mainstream, and shifting alliances in order to gain support for his policies earned him the title of "Balkan politician." According to Masumi, Miki did not like this label and retorted that he wanted to be "a Balkan politician with ideals" (Masumi 1995: 166). This quote gets at the fact that he was willing to challenge constraints and had a vision.

18 Ikeda became ill shortly after the committee submitted its report. According to Kujiraoka, a former member of the Miki faction, Miki later reflected that if Ikeda had not become sick, then the quest to abolish factions might have succeeded (Kujiraoka 1993: 7).

19 Masumi claims that the platform of the Miki cabinet was threefold: "politics stressing public opinion," "overcoming social inequity," and "metamorphosis into a national party" (1995: 167).

20 The five "gray officials" included LDP secretary general Nikaidō Susumu, former minister of transportation Sasaki Hideyo, former chairman of the Aviation Committee Kikunaga Kazunori, former parliamentary vice-minister of transportation Katō Mitsuki, and former Prime Minister Tanaka (Allen 1991a: 157). Given his subsequent indictment Tanaka arguably was more than a "gray official" in this matter.

21 Masumi also characterizes Miki as not being skilled at negotiating consensus ahead of time. He did not like it and he was not good at it. Instead of feeling the waters and finding common ground, he would talk with specialists, adopt a position, and then try to prevail it upon others. Masumi describes it as a method of "personal and intellectual persuasion." He called on people individually and either talked with them on the phone or invited them to his office to try to convince them of his position (1995: 167–68).

22 With the anti-monopoly legislation his failure to seek consensus proved detrimental. In this case Miki did get support of certain actors, such as the chairperson of the relevant committee, but he did not target faction leaders. *Nemawashi* is a time-consuming process that involves making sure that everyone's voice is heard. Convincing faction leaders is important because they have influence over their followers. In the case of his anti-monopoly legislation, Miki did not diffuse the opposition to the bill by LDP members of the Upper House. As a result, these

members killed the legislation. Many pointed to Miki's unwillingness to seek consensus as the cause of this policy failure (Shinoda 2000: 92).

3 Kaifu Toshiki: Mr. Clean plays it safe

1 While Takeshita was forced to resign from his formal position of prime minister, at this time he still remained the "owner" of the largest faction in the LDP and was one of the major kingmakers in the party (Curtis 1999: 85).

2 The vice-minister of labor, Katō Takashi, was accused of helping Recruit's job placement subsidiaries by working to block any attempts by the government to place controls on the job placement sector in return for the shares he received from Recruit. The vice-minister of education, Takaishi Kunio, also received shares from Recruit. In return for these contributions Takaishi allegedly appointed the chairman of Recruit, Ezoe, to two of the education ministry's committees (Kearns 1990: 66; Yayama 1990: 101)

3 Stocks are technically not illegal contributions. Recruit's manipulation of this fact caused great controversy. The company also bought a large number of tickets to politicians' fundraising events, a common way of getting around the limit on contributions to politicians (Hirose 1989: 74–77; Kearns 1990: 64).

4 It is difficult to determine the exact date a window of opportunity opens. In this case, two indicators suggest that the window was open by November 1988. First, Prime Minister Takeshita's cabinet support ratings began to decline during November, with the percentage opposing his cabinet exceeding the percentage supporting it for the first time. This development demonstrates declining public support of government. Second, the Electoral Systems Committee was charged with exploring reform proposals in November, illustrating the increased salience of reform.

5 His Justice Minister, Hasegawa Takashi, resigned on 30 December 1988, three days after the cabinet was formed. The deputy prime minister and director-general of the economic planning agency then resigned on 24 January 1989 (Minkan Seiji Rincho 1993: 233).

6 According to the Electoral System Advisory Council Law passed in 1961, the Diet could establish an advisory council to investigate issues related to the electoral system or political funding, when deemed appropriate. Historically, this council was composed of members of the community and politicians; however, when the council was reconvened for the first time in 17 years in 1989, politicians were excluded as these representatives were credited for inhibiting the decision-making process in the 1960s and 1970s. Instead, the council was composed of academics, journalists and former bureaucrats and overseen by the Ministry of Home Affairs. The proposals of the council are in no way binding but are recommendations to be considered by the ruling party/coalition. The council is a way to secure community involvement and take advantage of outside expertise. It should be noted, however, that none of the members of the Eighth Electoral System Advisory Council had any special knowledge of electoral systems (Curtis 1999: 148–52).

7 These proposals were resubmitted by both the Uno and Kaifu administrations. The final bill making the minor revisions outlined above passed on 13 December 1989 and was implemented on 1 February 1990 (Minkan Seiji Rincho 1993: 239). These revisions are an example of cosmetic reform.

8 Three days after Uno became prime minister the fact that he had been keeping a Geisha was revealed. Many politicians keep mistresses, so the public was not outraged by his infidelity. Instead, they were appalled by the small amount of money he gave her monthly, only 300,000 yen (Schlesinger 1997: 204).

9 Reed speculates that if there had been a double election for the Upper and Lower Houses in 1989, the Socialists would have been positioned well to perform strongly

in the Lower House election, perhaps capturing the majority and forcing a change in government (1996b: 66).

10 Voters would only be given a single vote under this plan (Reed and Thies 2001a: 164).

11 Shinoda points to four powers legally granted to prime ministers: (1) the power granted as cabinet head, (2) the power to appoint and dismiss cabinet members, (3) the power to dissolve the Diet, and (4) the capacity to use the Cabinet Secretariat staff (Shinoda 2000: 45). Informal powers come from the amount of support the prime minister has within the party, his influence over the bureaucracy, his popularity, and his experience (Shinoda 2000: 89–90).

12 The advisory council recommended a mixed system with 300 SMD seats and 200 PR seats. The PR seats would be contested in 11 regional districts. Kaifu's proposal called for 300 SMD seats and 171 PR seats with the PR seats being contested in one nation-wide district (Curtis 1999: 151–52).

13 The Recruit scandal was not the only incident that plagued the LDP at the time. The Uno sex scandal, an increase in the consumption tax, and a move to open the agricultural market to a certain degree, all acted along with the Recruit scandal to whittle away at LDP support (Allen 1991b: 165).

14 Vote share for these elections was calculated using election data provided by the Statistics Bureau and Statistical Training Institute (www.stat.go.jp/data/chouki/27. htm). Vote share is calculated by dividing a party's total number of votes by the total number of people who voted in the election.

4 Miyazawa Kiichi: an anti-reformer caught in "reform fever"

1 The party president was elected by 395 MPs and indirectly by the 1.75 million rank-and-file members who were given 101 votes ("Getting to Know Mr. Miyazawa": 33).

2 A group of pro-reform junior Diet members formed *Wakate Kaikaku Ha* (the Group of Young Diet Members Committed to Reform) six days prior to Miyazawa's public statement at Hasegawa's inauguration. On the same day as Miyazawa's statement, members from the economic, academic, and labor communities (*genronkai*) formed the Committee for the Promotion of Political Reform (Minkan Seiji Rincho 1993). These groups worked to counter the activity of Miyazawa and his supporters who wished to move away from radical reform (Taniguchi 1999: 102). Their junior/"outsider" status, however, made it difficult for them to influence the agenda.

3 The two-step plan involved putting the larger issue of electoral reform on the back burner and focusing on less comprehensive reform in the short-term (Taniguchi 1999: 104).

4 The Kōmeitō initially agreed to support the LDP in its efforts to pass the PKO bill. The Kōmeitō's increasingly close relations with the LDP after it lost its majority in the Upper House, however, drew criticism from the party faithful and caused the Kōmeitō to withdraw its support for the bill at some point ("Miyazawa Unravels": 33).

5 According to the Political Funds Control Law, contributions exceeding 1.5 million yen are illegal, and any donations over 1 million yen must be disclosed to the Home Ministry along with the contributor's name (T. Yamamoto 1975: 15–19).

6 Kanemaru would later resign from his Diet seat as well.

7 On 6 March 1993 Kanemaru and his administrative assistant were also indicted for violating the tax law. These indictments were followed by supplementary indictments for tax evasion on 27 March 1993 (Minkan Seiji Rincho 1993: 267).

8 For example, the money involved in Kyōwa was around 90 million yen, while it

was speculated that Sagawa involved hundreds of billion of yen ("Japan: Pass the Parcel": 28).

9 This window of opportunity would remain open for 15 months, closing with the passage of reform during the Hosokawa government in January 1994.

10 Percentages calculated from raw data in Taniguchi (1999: 142).

11 Given Kajiyama's opposition to reform, his earnest pursuit of this task is suspect. Kajiyama did not support reform because he equated a reform victory with an Ozawa victory (Curtis 1999: 93).

12 A string of construction scandals emerged in March 1993 following Sagawa, due in part to the thorough investigation of Kanemaru's affairs. These scandals ensured that the window of opportunity remained open throughout the duration of the Miyazawa administration. Collectively, this string of scandals was referred to as *Zenekon*. Ishii Toru, the mayor of Sendai, one the largest cities in Japan, was involved in two of these mini-scandals. First, he was accused of accepting money from the Hazama construction company in return for receiving government contracts. Ishii also reportedly accepted bribes from the Nishimatsu, Mitusi, and Shimizu construction companies. In fact, these four companies acted together under the leadership of Kagami Akira, the president of Hazama, in an attempt to displace the Kajima corporation, another construction company, from its dominant position in the Sendai region. Leaks from the prosecutor's office suggested that these companies set up a 1 billion yen slush fund to funnel "gifts" to politicians. In Mayor Ishii's case, he allegedly used these funds to support his 1992 re-election campaign, lining up several contracts in return for the donations (do Rosario 1993: 19).

5 Ozawa Ichirō: rebel with a cause

1 The final bill provided for an electoral system with 300 SMD seats and 200 PR seats. The PR representatives are selected from 11 regional blocs and the voters receive two votes, one for an SMD candidate and one for the PR list. The initial revisions to the Political Funds Control Law allowed each politician to maintain one fundraising organization with the maximum corporate contribution being 500,000 yen per company. The revisions to the Political Funds Control Law were set to be reviewed after five years with the aim of banning all corporate contributions. Finally, party subsidies were established at 250 yen per capita (Kawato 2000: 50).

2 Reed and Scheiner illustrate that the motivations for defection of the members of the Hata faction, which was led by Ozawa behind the scenes, were divided. Some members were motivated to leave the LDP out of loyalty to Ozawa; others were genuine reformers (2003: 474).

3 The *Ichi-Ichi* line represents a play on the first character of Ozawa's first name "Ichiro" and the first character of Ichikawa's last name (Curtis 1999: 121–22).

4 Reform Forum 21 was also referred as the Hata faction. This new entity briefly constituted a new faction within the LDP.

5 In the end the public supported the PKO bill, but their support was far from clear when the debate began during the Gulf War.

6 Sakamoto also provides polling evidence that supports the notion that the public did not connect electoral system reform with the abolition of corruption prior to the 1993 election (1999: 183, fn. 39).

7 Kabashima illustrates that a desire for an alternation in power was the greatest predictor for a vote for a new party in the 1993 Lower House election (1998: 44).

8 Due to different models and definitions of key variables such as electoral strength, analyses of the split of the LDP have come to varying conclusions. For example,

Kato concludes that "... the factors that reflect individual electoral conditions (political career and economic and political resources) were dominant influences on the choice of LDP members ... " (1998: 868). In contrast Cox and Rosenbluth contend "Individuals with lower seniority and thus lesser shares of the spoils of office; with less secure electoral futures within the LDP, as judged by electoral marginality in the most recent election; and with more experience contesting elections without the LDP label were more like to be among the defectors in 1976 (to the NLC), in June 1993 (mostly to the Shinseitō and Shintō Sakigake, a few to Nihon Shintō) and in November 1993 (to the cause of electoral reform)" (1995: 371). By analyzing those members who defected from the Takeshita faction to form the Hata faction prior to the LDP split separately, Reed and Scheiner uncover that electoral concerns motivated many, but not all of the remaining LDP defectors. Specifically, junior members with insecure seats were more likely to defect to increase their chances of re-election. In contrast, senior and urban politicians were increasingly likely to defect the more solid their electoral position (2003: 482).

9 The coalition and the LDP disagreed over the division of seats between single-member districts and proportional representation. Ozawa pushed the coalition to meet the LDP's demands halfway, resulting in a compromise bill that was submitted to the Diet in January 1994. This bill was rejected by the Upper House. As a result, the coalition set up a joint committee that formulated a bill acceptable to both sides with the majority of the negotiations going on behind the scenes. Sakamoto provides a detailed account of the negotiations over the content of the bill (1999: 119–24). Kawato also provides an excellent analysis of the options for political reform considered during the Hosokawa administration (2000: 31–36).

10 The Democratic Party of Japan, the largest opposition party in Japan at the time of this writing, selected Ozawa to be its new party head on 7 April 2006.

6 Junior politicians: ideas and actions without access

1 Three of the six members of the NLC were second-generation politicians. They had inherited support groups with ample financial resources and a large enough support base to provide them with the votes needed for re-election. Even though these politicians could secure their own re-election, raising the funds and popular support to build a viable opposition party was a formidable task (Pharr 1982: 38).

2 The NLC's ultimate goal remained contested throughout its existence. Some members hoped to attract a critical mass of new members to negotiate a return to the LDP on its own terms, others advocated forging an alliance with other centrist parties, and still others saw forming a second conservative party to challenge the LDP as the party's primary mission (Curtis 1988: 32).

3 In the informal promotion hierarchy within the LDP, most politicians are appointed to their first cabinet-level position as a sixth-term Diet member (Curtis 1988: 90).

7 Koizumi Junichirō: a new kind of leadership?

1 *Zoku* is most commonly translated as a "policy tribe." A *zoku* politician is a Diet member who has acquired expert knowledge in a particular policy area.

2 While Pempel points to several structural impediments to comprehensive economic reform throughout the 1990s, he does note that Koizumi has weakened some of these constraints with his decisive electoral victory in September 2005. This victory has increased the likelihood of significant structural reform in the future (2006: 57).

3 In "The Dynamics of Coalition Politics in Japan," Mulgan states that LDP

members continue to rely on interest groups for votes and pork barrel politics when backing up her assertion that voting remains more candidate centered than party centered (2003: 39).

4 Richard Samuels points to this reform cleavage as a legacy of the Nakasone administration (2003a: 27).

5 Krauss and Pekkanen claim that this cleavage is one directly tied to policy (2004: 32).

6 Despite its majority, the LDP joined in coalition with the New Kōmeitō. Together the two parties control two-thirds of the seats in the Lower House (Glosserman 2005).

7 Maclachlan cites *The Japan Times,* 7 and 12 March 2005 in reference to this public opinion survey (2006: 13).

8 Koizumi ran for the prime ministership again in 1998. He came in third following Obuchi and Kajiyama despite his top-ranking popularity with the public (Curtis 1999: 215).

9 Following the 11 September 2005 Lower House election, Koizumi reintroduced his second postal reform package to the Lower House. It passed the Lower House on 11 October 2005 by a vote of 338–138 (C. Watanabe 2005). The postal reform bill passed the Upper House on 14 October 2005 by a vote of 134–100 (Yoshida 2005b).

10 This chapter was completed in July 2006 when Prime Minister Koizumi was still in office.

8 Conclusion: political leadership in Japan

1 Scholars often assign actors involved in political reform different preferences. With electoral reform, the overriding preference is to win elections. What scholars argue a party needs to maximize in order to win elections varies, though. For example, in their analysis of the creation of the electoral system in South Korea in 1988, Brady and Mo (1992) assert that parties attempt to maximize their seat share in future elections. In contrast, conceiving preferences more broadly, Bawn (1993) argues that changes to Germany's electoral law in 1949 and 1953 can be seen as a bargaining process among parties that are trying to maximize their influence over policy outcomes. However, Bawn acknowledges that implicit in the notion of influencing policy is the need to increase a party's seat share in parliament (1993: 968). In the end, the interests of parties are complex. Parties might accept solutions which maximize their strength at the polls to a lesser degree if they also care about creating legitimate institutions that incorporate the opposition (Brady and Mo 1992: 425–26).

2 For a critique of rational choice, see Green and Shapiro (1994).

3 Aurelia George Mulgan makes a similar argument about the institutional constraints that limit the prime minister's policy-making effectiveness. She argues, "... a large part of the explanation for Japan's chronic leadership failure lies in Japanese adaptations of Westminster-style notions of Cabinet responsibility, entrenched bureaucratic prerogatives, the dominance of informal party subgroupings, faction-driven executive selection procedures, and inadequate Prime Ministerial and Cabinet support structures" (2000: 185).

4 Burns makes the distinction between transformational and transactional leadership. Transformational leadership occurs when leaders tap into the wants and needs of their followers and push for significant change which meets these needs. Transactional leadership is represented by an exchange between leaders and followers and is more consistent with the idea of policy change for votes (1978: 4).

5 The rigid seniority system has been showing signs of weakening during Koizumi's tenure as prime minister. Koizumi has appointed junior politicians to cabinet

posts, ignoring the previous norm of selecting politicians who had been elected five to six times. For example, two members in his cabinet in October 2005 were first-term Diet members: Takenaka Heizō, of the Upper House, serving as the minister of internal affairs and communications, and Inoguchi Kuniko, of the Lower House, acting as the minister of gender equality and social affairs. Both politicians had experience on relevant advisory councils prior to becoming Diet members.

Bibliography

Alexander, H.E. (1992) *Financing Politics: Money, Elections, and Political Reform*, 4th edn, Washington, DC: Congressional Quarterly.

Alexander, H.E. and Shiratori, R. (eds) (1994) *Comparative Political Finance Among the Democracies*, Boulder, CO: Westview Press.

Allen, L. (1991a) "Japan: Kakuei Tanaka/Lockheed Affair (1976–86)," in L. Allen *et al.* (eds) *Political Scandals and Causes Célèbres Since 1945: An International Reference Compendium*, Essex, UK: Longman Current Affairs.

—— (1991b) "Recruit Scandal Affair (1984–)," in L. Allen *et al.* (eds) *Political Scandals and Causes Célèbres Since 1945: An International Reference Compendium*, Essex, UK: Longman Current Affairs.

Altman, K.K. (1996) "Television and Political Turmoil: Japan's Summer of 1993," in S.J. Pharr and E.S. Krauss (eds) *Media and Politics in Japan*, Honolulu, HI: University of Hawaii Press.

Amyx, J. and Drysdale, P. (eds) (2003) *Japanese Governance: Beyond Japan Inc.*, New York: RoutledgeCurzon.

Asahi Shinbun (2005) "53% OK with Call for Snap Election," *Asahi.com*, 25 July. Online. Available: www.asahi.com/English/Heraldasahi/TKY200507250426.html (accessed 1 August 2005).

Asahi Shinbunsha (1977) *Asahi Nenkan 1977* (The Asahi Yearbook, 1977), Tokyo: Asahi Shinbunsha.

Baerwald, H.H. (1967) "Japan: 'Black Mist' and Pre-electioneering," *Asian Survey*, 7: 31–39.

Bawn, K. (1993) "The Logic of Institutional Preference: German Electoral Law as a Social Choice Outcome," *American Journal of Political Science*, 37, 4: 965–89.

Blechinger-Talcott, V. (2004) "Learning to Lead: Incentives and Disincentives for Leadership in Japanese Politics," *Japanese Political Reform: Progress and in Process*, Asia Program Special Report, January, Washington, DC: The Woodrow Wilson Center Asia Program. Online. Available: www.wilsoncenter.org/index.cfm?topic_id=1462&fuseaction=topics.publications&group_id=4985 (accessed 9 May 2006).

Brady, D. and Mo, J. (1992) "Electoral Systems and Institutional Choice: A Case Study of the 1988 Korean Elections," *Comparative Political Studies*, 24, 4: 405–29.

Breslauer, G.W. (2002) *Gorbachev and Yeltsin as Leaders*, New York: Cambridge University Press.

Burns, J.M. (1978) *Leadership*, New York: Harper & Row.

Calder, K.E. (1988) *Crisis and Compensation: Public Policy and Political Stability in Japan, 1949–1986*, Princeton, NJ: Princeton University Press.

Campbell, J.C. (1977) *Contemporary Japanese Budget Politics*, Berkeley, CA: University of California Press.

Carlyle, T. (n.d.) *Heroes, Hero Worship and the Heroic in History*, New York: A.L. Burt Company.

Christensen, R.V. (1994) "Electoral Reform in Japan: How It Was Enacted and Changes It May Bring," *Asian Survey*, 34: 589–605.

Corrado, A. (2005) "Money and Politics: A History of Federal Campaign Finance Law," in A. Corrado, T.E. Mann, D.R. Ortiz and T. Potter (eds) *The New Campaign Finance Reform Sourcebook*, Washington, DC: The Brookings Institution Press.

Cox, G.W. and Rosenbluth F. (1993) "The Electoral Fortunes of Legislative Factions in Japan," *The American Political Science Review*, 87, 3: 577–89.

——(1995) "Anatomy of a Split: the Liberal Democrats of Japan," *Electoral Studies*, 14, 4: 355–76.

Curtis, G.L. (1988) *The Japanese Way of Politics*, New York: Columbia University Press.

——(1999) *The Logic of Japanese Politics: Leaders, Institutions, and the Limits of Change*, New York: Columbia University Press.

Desmond, E.W. (1995) "Ichiro Ozawa: Reformer at Bay," *Foreign Affairs*, 74, 5: 117–31.

do Rosario, L. (1993) "The Rot Spreads: Sendai Mayor Arrested on Bribery Charges," *Far Eastern Economic Review*, 15 July: 19.

Doig, A. (1988) "The Dynamics of Scandals in British Politics," *Corruption and Reform*, 3: 241–46.

Doig, J.W. and Hargrove, E.C. (eds) (1987) *Leadership and Innovation: A Biographical Perspective on Entrepreneurs in Government*, Baltimore, MA: Johns Hopkins University Press.

"Down on the Farm" (1989) *The Economist*, 25 March: 40.

Dwyre, D. and Farrar-Myers, V.A. (2001) *Legislative Labyrinth: Congress and Campaign Finance Reform*, Washington, DC: Congressional Quarterly Press.

Edelman, M.J. (1964) *The Symbolic Uses of Politics*, Urbana, IL: University of Illinois Press.

Edström, B. (1996) "Prime Ministerial Leadership in Japanese Foreign Policy," in I. Neary (ed.) *Leaders and Leadership in Japan*, Richmond, Surrey: Japan Library.

Elgie, R. (1995) *Political Leadership in Liberal Democracies*, New York: St. Martin's Press.

Farley, M. (1996) "Japan's Press and the Politics of Scandal," in S.J. Pharr and E.S. Krauss (eds) *Media and Politics in Japan*, Honolulu, HI: University of Hawaii Press.

Feldman, O. (2000) *The Japanese Political Personality: Analyzing the Motivations and Culture of Freshman Diet Members*, New York: St. Martin's Press.

Feldman, O. and Valenty, L.O. (eds) (2001) *Profiling Political Leaders: Cross-cultural Studies of Personality and Behavior*, Westport, CT: Praeger.

Frohlich, N., Oppenheimer, J.E. and Young, O.R. (1971) *Political Leadership and Collective Goods*, Princeton, NJ: Princeton University Press.

Fujimoto K. (1992) *Kaifu Seiken to "Seiji Kaikaku"* (The Kaifu Administration and "Political Reform"), Tokyo: Ryūkei Shosha.

Fujita, H. (1980) *Nihon no Seiji to Kane* (Japanese Politics and Money), Tokyo: Keisō Shuppan Sābisu Sentā: Hatsubaisho Keiso Shōbō.

Gallagher, M. and Mitchell, P. (eds) (2005) *The Politics of Electoral Systems*, Oxford: Oxford University Press.

Gardner, J.W. (1990) *On Leadership*, New York: Free Press.

Gaunder, A. (1994) "Scandals and Their Varying Repercussions: A Case Study of the Lockheed and Douglas-Grumman Scandals in Japan," Master's Essay, University of California, Berkeley, CA, April.

——(2005) "Political Leadership and Campaign Finance Reform in Japan and the United States," paper presented at The Western Political Science Association, Oakland, CA., March.

Geddes, B. (1991) "A Game Theoretic Model of Reform in Latin American Democracies," *The American Political Science Review*, 85, 2: 371–92.

"Getting to Know Mr. Miyazawa" (1991) *The Economist*, 2 November: 33–34.

Glosserman, B. (2005) "Shades of Single-party Politics: Japan to go boldly backward for a while," *The Japan Times Online*, 18 September. Online. Available: www.japantimes.co.jp/cgi-bin/makeparfy.p15eo20050918bg.htm (accessed 13 October 2005).

Green, D.P. and Shapiro, I. (1994) *Pathologies of Rational Choice Theory: A Critique of Applications in Political Science*, New Haven, CT: Yale University Press.

Hanrei Roppō Henshū Iinkai (1997) *Mohan Roppō, 1997* (Exemplary Laws, 1997), Tokyo: Sanseidō.

Hayao, K. (1993) *The Japanese Prime Minister and Public Policy*, Pittsburgh, PA: University of Pittsburgh Press.

Hirano, S. (1996) *Ozawa Ichirō to no Nijūnen: "Seikai Saihen" Butaiura* (Twenty Years with Ozawa Ichirō: Behind the Scenes of "Reorganizing the Political World"), Tokyo: Purejidentosha.

Hirose, M. (1989) *Seiji to Kane* (Politics and Money), Tokyo: Iwanami Shoten.

Hiwatari, N. (2005) "Japan in 2004: 'Courageous' Koizumi Carries On," *Asian Survey*, 45: 41–53.

Hrebenar, R.J. (2000) *Japan's New Party System*, 3rd edn, Boulder, CO: Westview Press.

Iio, S. (1999) "Takeshita, Uno, Kaifu Naikaku" ("The Takeshita, Uno and Kaifu Cabinets"), in T. Sasaki (ed.) *Seiji Kaikaku 1800-Nichi no Shinjitsu* (The Truth Behind 1800 Days of Political Reform), Tokyo: Kōdansha.

Immergut, E.M. (1992) *Health Politics: Interest and Institutions in Western Europe*, Cambridge: Cambridge University Press.

Itoh, M. (2003) *The Hatoyama Dynasty: Japanese Political Leadership Through the Generations*, New York: Palgrave MacMillan.

Iwai, T. (1990) *"Seiji Shikin" no Kenkyū* (Research on Political Finance), Tokyo: Nihon Keizai Shinbunsha.

James, W. (1961) "Great Men and Their Environments," *Selected Papers on Philosophy*, London: J.M. Dent and Sons.

"Japan: Cavalry to the Rescue" (1992) *The Economist*, 9 May: 34–35.

"Japan: Dirty Dozen" (1992) *The Economist*, 5 September: 36, 38.

"Japan: Lockheed, Recruit and now …" (1992) *The Economist*, 18 January: 32–33.

"Japan: Pass the Parcel" (1992) *The Economist*, 22 February: 28–29.

"Japan: Young Turks" (1992) *The Economist*, 19 December: 37.

Japan Times (2001) "Koizumi vows no sanctuaries from reform," *The Japan Times*

Online, 8 May. Online. Available: www.japantimes.co.jp/cgi-bin/makeparfy.p15?
nn20010508al.htm (accessed 28 July 2005).

Johnson, C. (1976) "Japan 1975: Mr. Clean Muddles Through," *Asian Survey*, 16:
31–41.

——(1982) *MITI and the Japanese Miracle: The Growth of Industrial Policy, 1925–
1975*, Stanford, CA: Stanford University Press.

——(1986) "Tanaka Kakuei, Structural Corruption, and the Advent of Machine
Politics in Japan," *Journal of Japanese Studies*, 12: 1–28.

Jones, B.D. (ed.) (1989) *Leadership and Politics: New Perspectives in Political Science*,
Lawrence, KS: University Press of Kansas.

Kabashima, I. (1998) *Seiken Kōtai to Yūkensha no Taido Henyō* (Changing Voter
Attitudes and the Alternation of Power), Tokyo: Bokutakusha.

Kabashima, I. and Reed, S.R. (2001) "The Effect of the Choices Available on Voting
Behaviour: The Two Japanese Elections of 1993," *Electoral Studies*, 20: 627–40.

"Kaifu Loses his Minder" (1991) *The Economist*, 13 April: 33–34.

Kato, J. (1998) "When the Party Breaks Up: Exit and Voice among Japanese
Legislators," *The American Political Science Review*, 92, 4: 857–70.

Katz, R. (1998) *Japan: The System that Soured – The Rise and Fall of the Japanese
Economic Miracle*, Armonk, NY: M.E. Sharpe.

Katz, R.S. (2005) "Why Are There so Many (or so Few) Electoral Reforms?" in M.
Gallagher and P. Mitchell (eds) *The Politics of Electoral Systems*, Oxford: Oxford
University Press.

Katz, R.S. and Mair, P. (1995) "Changing Models of Party Organization and Party
Democracy: The Emergence of the Cartel Party," *Party Politics*, 1, 1: 5–28.

Kawato, S. (2000) "Strategic Contexts of the Vote on Political Reform Bills," *Japanese
Journal of Political Science*, 1, 1: 23–51.

Kearns, I. (1990) "The Recruit Scandal and Corruption in Japanese Political Life,"
Corruption and Reform, 5: 63–70.

Kellerman, B. (1984) *Leadership: Multidisciplinary Perspectives*, Englewood Cliffs,
NJ: Prentice-Hall.

Kernell, S. (1986) *Going Public: New Strategies of Presidential Leadership*,
Washington, DC: Congressional Quarterly Press.

Kingdon, J.W. (1984) *Agendas, Alternatives and Public Policies*, Boston, MA: Little
Brown and Company.

Kitaoka, S. (2004) "Japan's Dysfunctional Democracy," *Japanese Political Reform:
Progress and in Process*, Asia Program Special Report, January, Washington, DC:
The Woodrow Wilson Center Asia Program. Online. Available: www.wilsoncenter.
org/index.cfm?topic_id=1462&fuseaction=topics.publications&group_id=4985
(accessed 9 May 2006).

Kobayashi, Y. and Matsuaki T. (1992) "'Nihonshintō' wa Dai Ni no Shinjiku ka?"
("The Japan New Party: The Second New Liberal Club?") *Shokun*, 70 (July):
90–99.

Kohno, M. (1992) "Rational Foundations for the Organization of the Liberal Democratic Party in Japan," *World Politics*, 44, 3: 369–97.

——(1995) "'93-nendo no Seiji Hendō" ("The 1993 Political Upheaval"), *Rebaiasan*
(Leviathan), 17: 30–51.

——(1997) *Japan's Postwar Party Politics*, Princeton, NJ: Princeton University Press.

Koizumi, J. (2001) "Japan's Resolve for Reforms," *Presidents and Prime Ministers*,
10: 8-10, 27, 36.

——(2003) "General Policy Speech by Prime Minister Koizumi to the 157th Session of the Diet," *Shushō Kantei* (The Prime Minister and his Cabinet), 26 September. Online. Available: www.kantei.go.jp/foreign/koizumispeech/2003/09/26shoshin_e.html (accessed 14 October 2005).

Koizumi, J. and Kajiwara Kazuaki (eds) (1994) *Yūseishō Kaitairon* (A Discussion of the Dissolution of the Ministry of Postal Services), Tokyo: Kōbunsha.

Kōno, K. (1978) *Gichō Ichidai* (My Years as Speaker), Tokyo: Asahi Shinbunsha.

Krauss, E.S. (1982) "Japanese Parties and Parliament: Changing Leadership Roles and Role Conflict," in T.E. MacDougall (ed.) *Political Leadership in Contemporary Japan*, Ann Arbor, MI: Center for Japanese Studies, The University of Michigan.

Krauss, E.S. and Pekkanen, R. (2004) "Explaining Party Adaptation to Electoral Reform: The Discreet Charm of the LDP?" *Journal of Japanese Studies*, 30: 1–34.

Kujiraoka, H. (1993) *Miki "Seiji Kaikaku" Shian to wa nani ka* (What Is the Miki Plan for "Political Reform"), Tokyo: Iwanami Shoten.

Kunihiro, M. (2005) *Sōshu aru Hoshuseijika Miki Takeo* (An Honest Conservative Statesman: Miki Takeo), Tokyo: Tachibana Shuppan.

Kusunoki, S. (1997) "Shōsenkyokusei Hōan no Sassetsu" ("The Failure of the Small District System Bills"), in T. Nakamura and M. Miyazai (eds) *Kadoki toshite no 1950 Nendai* (The 1950s: Japan's Decade of Transition), Tokyo: Tōkyō Daigaku Shupankai.

Lam, Peng-Er (2002) "Structural Reforms in Japan: Promises and Perils," *Asian Affairs: An American Review*, 29, 2: 67–82.

Lamont-Brown, R. (1994) "Kakuei Tanaka – Man of Tangible Power," *Contemporary Review*, 265: 307–9.

MacDougall, T.E. (1988) "The Lockheed Scandal and the High Cost of Politics in Japan," in A.S. Markovits and M. Silverstein (eds) *The Politics of Scandal: Power and Process in Liberal Democracies*, New York: Holmes and Meier.

MacDougall, T.E. (ed.) (1982) *Political Leadership in Contemporary Japan*, Ann Arbor, MI: Center for Japanese Studies, The University of Michigan.

Maclachlan, P.L. (2004) "Post Office Politics in Modern Japan: The Postmasters, Iron Triangles, and the Limits of Reform," *Journal of Japanese Studies*, 30: 281–313.

——(2006) "Storming the Castle: The Battle for Postal Reform in Japan," *Social Science Japan Journal*, 9, 1: 1–18.

Machiavelli, N. (1985) *The Prince*, trans. H.C. Mansfield, Jr., Chicago, IL: The University of Chicago Press.

Mainichi Shinbunsha Seijibu (1975) *Seihen* (Political Change), Tokyo: Mainichi Shinbunsha.

Malbin, M.J. (ed.) (2003) *Life After Reform: When the Bipartisan Campaign Reform Act Meets Politics*, New York: Rowman and Littlefield Publishers.

Mann, T.E. and Sasaki T. (eds) (2002) *Governance for a New Century: Japanese Challenges, American Experience*, New York: Japan Center for International Exchange.

Markovits, A.S. and Silverstein, M. (eds) (1988) *The Politics of Scandal: Power and Process in Liberal Democracies*, New York: Holmes and Meier.

Masuda, T. (1976) *Miki Seiji Kenkyū* (Research on Miki's Politics), Tokyo: Hōchiki Shōji Shuppanbu.

Masumi, J. (1995) *Contemporary Politics in Japan*, trans. L.E. Carlile, Berkeley, CA: University of California Press.

Matsuura, M. and Ōtake, K. (1983) *Seiji Shikin* (Political Finance), Tokyo: Daiichi Hōki.

Mayhew, D.R. (1974) *Congress: The Electoral Connection*, New Haven, CT: Yale University Press.

Mazur, A.G. (1995) *Gender Bias and the State: Symbolic Reform at Work in Fifth Republic France*, Pittsburgh, PA: University of Pittsburgh Press.

Miki, M. (1989) *Shin Nakuba Tatazu: Otto Miki Takeo to no Gojūnen* (No Rising Without His Belief: Fifty Years with My Husband, Miki Takeo), Tokyo: Kōdansha.

Miki, T. (1984) *Gikai Seiji to tomo ni: Miki Takeo Enzetsu, Hatsugenshū* (In Conjunction with the Parliamentary Government: A Collection of Miki Takeo's Speeches and Proposals), Tokyo: Miki Takeo Shuppan Kinenkai.

Minkan Seiji Rincho (Committee for the Promotion of Political Reforms) (1993) *Nihon Henkaku no Vijon* (Grand Vision of Political Reforms), Tokyo: Kōdansha.

"Miyazawa's Moment" (1992) *The Economist*, 1 August: 29–30.

"Miyazawa Unravels" (1991) *The Economist*, 14 December: 33–34.

Moodie, G.C. (1988) "Studying Political Scandal," *Corruption and Reform*, 3: 241–46.

Moravcsik, A. (1999) "A New Statecraft? Supranational Entrepreneurs and International Cooperation," *International Organization*, 53: 267–306.

Mulgan, A.G. (2000) "Japan's Political Leadership Deficit," *Australian Journal of Political Science*, 35: 183–202.

—— (2002) *Japan's Failed Revolution: Koizumi and the Politics of Economic Reform*, Canberra: Asia Pacific Press.

—— (2003) "The Dynamics of Coalition Politics in Japan," in J. Amyx and P. Drysdale (eds) *Japanese Governance: Beyond Japan Inc.*, London: RoutledgeCurzon.

Murobushi, T. (1988) *Jitsuroku Nihon Oshokushi* (An Authentic Account of the History of Corruption in Japan), Tokyo: Chikuma Shobō.

Nakamura, K. (1981) *Miki Seiken 747-nichi* (The 747 days of the Miki Government), Tokyo: Gyōsei Mondai Kenkyūjo.

Narita, N. (1996) "Seiji kaikaku Hōan no Seiritsu Katei" ("The Legislative Process of Political Reform Bills"), *Hokudai Hōgaku Ronshū*, 46, 6: 405–87.

—— (1997) "Seiji Kaikaku Ron no Kokoromi" ("An Essay on the Process of Political Reform"), *Rebaiasan* (Leviathan), 20: 7–57.

Neary, I. (ed.) (1996) *Leaders and Leadership in Japan*, Richmond, Surrey: Japan Library.

Neustadt, R.E. (1990) *Presidential Power and the Modern Presidents: The Politics of Leadership from Roosevelt to Reagan*, New York: Free Press.

Nishikawa, Y. (2001) "'Miki Oroshi' to wa Chigau – Kaiku no Rinen, Yoron wa Mikata datta" ("The Ouster of Miki – the Idea of Reform, Public Opinion was on our Side"), *Tokyo Shinbun*, morning edition, 7 March: 2.

Noble, G.W. (1993) "Japan in 1992: Just Another Aging Superpower?" *Asian Survey*, 33: 1–11.

Nugent, M.L. and Johannes, J.R (eds) (1990) *Money, Elections, and Democracy: Reforming Congressional Campaign Finance*, Boulder, CO: Westview Press.

Ōshita, E. (2005) *Ozawa Ichirō no Seiken Dasshu Senryaku* (Ozawa Ichirō's Strategy for Capturing Power), Tokyo: Kawade Shobō Shinsha.

Ōtake, H. (1996) "Forces for Political Reform: The Liberal Democratic Party's Young Reformers and Ozawa Ichiro," *Journal of Japanese Studies*, 22: 269–94.

—— (1997) "Seiji Kaikaku o Mezashita Futatsu no Seiji Seiryoku: Jimintō Wakate Kaikakuha to Ozawa Gurūpu" ("Two Political Forces Working for Political

Reform: The LDP Group of Young Diet Members Committed to Reform and the Ozawa Group"), in H. Ōtake (ed.) *Seikai Saihen no Kenkyū: Shin Senkyo Seido ni yoru Sōsenkyo* (Research on the Reorganization of the Political World: General Elections Under the New Electoral System), Tokyo: Yūhikaku.

Ōtake, H. (ed.) (1997) *Seikai Saihen no Kenkyū: Shin Senkyo Seido ni yoru Sōsenkyo* (Research on the Reorganization of the Political World: General Elections Under the New Electoral System), Tokyo: Yūhikaku.

Ozawa, I. (1994) *Blueprint for a New Japan: The Rethinking of a Nation*, trans. Louisa Rubinfien, Tokyo: Kodansha International.

Paige, G.D. (1977) *The Scientific Study of Political Leadership*, New York: The Free Press.

Pempel, T.J. (2006) "A Decade of Political Torpor: When Political Logic Trumps Economic Rationality," in P.J. Katzenstein and T. Shiraishi (eds) *Beyond Japan: The Dynamics of East Asian Regionalism*, Ithaca, NY: Cornell University Press.

Pharr, S.J. (1982) "Liberal Democrats in Disarray: Intergenerational Conflict in the Conservative Camp," in T.E. MacDougall (ed.) *Political Leadership in Contemporary Japan*, Ann Arbor, MI: Center for Japanese Studies, The University of Michigan.

——(1990) *Losing Face, Status Politics in Japan*, Berkeley, CA: University of California Press.

Pharr, S.J. and Krauss, E.S. (eds) (1996) *Media and Politics in Japan*, Honolulu, HI: University of Hawaii Press.

Pitman, J. (1991) "Raw and Fishy: Japan's Sleazy New Prime Minister," *The New Republic*, 4 November: 16.

Reed, S.R. (1996a) "Political Corruption in Japan," *International Social Science Journal*, 48: 395–405.

——(1996b) "Bumu no Seiji: Shinjiyū Kurabu kara Hosokawa Renritsu Seiken e" ("The Politics of 'Booms': From the New Liberal Club to the Hosokawa Coalition Government"), *Rebaiasan* (Leviathan), 18: 61–70.

——(1997) "Providing Clear Cues: Voter Response to the Reform Issue in the 1993 Japanese General Election," *Party Politics*, 3, 2: 265–77.

——(1999a) "Political Reform in Japan: Combining Scientific and Historical Analysis," *Social Science Japan Journal*, 2, 2: 177–93.

——(1999b) "Punishing Corruption: The Response of the Japanese Electorate to Scandals," in O. Feldman (ed.) *Political Psychology in Japan: Behind the Nails that Sometimes Stick Out (and Get Hammered Down)*, Commack, NY: Nova Science Publishers.

——(2005) "Japan: Haltingly Toward a Two-Party System," in M. Gallagher and P. Mitchell (eds) *The Politics of Electoral Systems*, Oxford: Oxford University Press.

Reed, S.R. and Scheiner, E. (2003) "Electoral Incentives and Policy Preferences: Mixed Motives Behind Party Defections in Japan," *British Journal of Political Science*, 33: 469–90.

Reed, S.R. and Thies, M.F. (2001a) "The Causes of Electoral Reform in Japan," in M.S. Shugart and M.P. Wattenberg (eds) *Mixed-Member Electoral Systems: The Best of Both Worlds?* Oxford: Oxford University Press.

——(2001b) "The Consequences of Electoral Reform in Japan," in M.S. Shugart and M.P.Wattenberg (eds) *Mixed-Member Electoral Systems: The Best of Both Worlds?* Oxford: Oxford University Press.

Roosevelt, F.D. (4 March 1933) "Inaugural Address," *Inaugural Addresses of the Presidents of the United States from George Washington,1789, to Lyndon Baines Johnson, 1965*, compiled by the Legislative Reference Service, Library of Congress Washington, DC: US Government Printing Office, 1965.

Rose-Ackerman, S. (1999) *Corruption and Government: Causes, Consequences, and Reform*, Cambridge: Cambridge University Press.

Sakamoto, T. (1999) *Building Policy Legitimacy in Japan: Political Behavior beyond Rational Choice*, New York: St. Martin's Press.

Samuels, R.J. (2003a) "Leadership and Political Change in Japan: The Case of the Second Rincho," *Journal of Japanese Studies*, 29:1–31.

——(2003b) *Machiavelli's Children: Leaders and Their Legacies in Italy and Japan*, Ithaca, NY: Cornell University Press.

Sasaki T. (ed.) (1999) *Seiji Kaikaku 1800-Nichi no Shinjitsu* (The Truth Behind 1800 Days of Political Reform), Tokyo: Kōdansha.

Sasaki, T., Yoshida, S., Taniguchi, M. and Yamamoto S. (eds) (1999) *Daigishi to Kane: Seiji Shikin Zenkoku Chosa Hokoku* (Representatives and Money: Report on the National Political Funding Research), Tokyo: Asahi Shinbunsha.

Satō, S. and Matsuzaki, T. (1986) *Jimintō Seiken* (LDP Government), Tokyo: Chūo Kōronsha.

Satō, S., Kōyama, K. and Kumon, S. (1990) *Postwar Politician: The Life of Former Prime Minister Masayoshi Ohira*, trans. W.R. Carter, Tokyo: Kodansha International.

Scarrow, S.E. (1997) "Party Competition and Institutional Change: The Expansion of Direct Democracy in Germany," *Party Politics*, 3, 4: 451–72.

——(2004) "Explaining Political Finance Reforms: Competition and Context," *Party Politics*, 10, 6: 653–75.

Scheiner, E. (2006) *Democracy Without Competition in Japan: Opposition Failure in a One-Party Dominant State*, Cambridge: Cambridge University Press.

Schneider, M. and Teske, P. (1992) "Toward a Theory of the Political Entrepreneur: Evidence from Local Government," *American Political Science Review*, 86: 737–47.

Schlesinger, J.M. (1997) *Shadow Shoguns: The Rise and Fall of Japan's Postwar Political Machine*, New York: Simon and Schuster.

Schoppa, L.J. (2001) "Japan, the Reluctant Reformer," *Foreign Affairs*, 80: 76–90.

Selbin, E. (1999) *Modern Latin American Revolutions*, Boulder, CO: Westview Press.

Selznick, P. (1957) *Leadership in Administration: A Sociological Interpretation*, Evanston, IL: Row, Peterson.

Shinoda, T. (2000) *Leading Japan: The Role of the Prime Minister*, Westport, CT: Praeger.

——(2003) "Koizumi's Top-Down Leadership in the Anti-Terrorist Legislation: The Impact of Political Institutional Changes," *SAIS Review*, 23: 19–34.

Shugart, M.S. and Wattenberg, M.P. (2001) *Mixed-Member Electoral Systems: The Best of Both Worlds?* Oxford: Oxford University Press.

Silberman, B.S. and Harootunian, H.D. (eds) (1966) *Modern Japanese Leadership: Transition and Change*, Tucson, AZ: The University of Arizona Press.

Spencer, H. (1961) *The Study of Sociology*, Ann Arbor, MI: The University of Michigan Press.

Sorauf, F.J. (1988) *Money in American Elections*, Glenview, IL: Scott, Foresman/ Little, Brown College Division.

——(1992) *Inside Campaign Finance: Myths and Realities*, New Haven, CT: Yale University Press.

Sorifu Naikaku Sori Daijin Kanbo Kohoshitsu (1975) *Seron Chōsa Nenkan, 1975* (Public Opinion Research Yearbook, 1975), Tokyo: Ōkurashō Insatsukyoku.

——(1976) *Seron Chōsa Nenkan, 1976* (Public Opinion Research Yearbook, 1976), Tokyo: Ōkurashō Insatsukyoku.

——(1977) *Seron Chōsa Nenkan, 1977* (Public Opinion Research Yearbook, 1977), Tokyo: Ōkurashō Insatsukyoku.

——(1989) *Seron Chōsa Nenkan, 1989* (Public Opinion Research Yearbook, 1989), Tokyo: Ōkurashō Insatsukyoku.

——(1990) *Seron Chōsa Nenkan, 1990* (Public Opinion Research Yearbook, 1990), Tokyo: Ōkurashō Insatsukyoku.

——(1991) *Seron Chōsa Nenkan, 1991* (Public Opinion Research Yearbook, 1991), Tokyo: Ōkurashō Insatsukyoku.

——(1992) *Seron Chōsa Nenkan, 1992* (Public Opinion Research Yearbook, 1992), Tokyo: Ōkurashō Insatsukyoku.

——(1993) *Seron Chōsa Nenkan, 1993* (Public Opinion Research Yearbook, 1993), Tokyo: Ōkurashō Insatsukyoku.

——(1994) *Seron Chōsa Nenkan, 1994* (Public Opinion Research Yearbook, 1994), Tokyo: Ōkurashō Insatsukyoku.

Steinmo, S. (1993) *Taxation and Democracy: Swedish, British and American Approaches to Financing the Modern State*, New Haven, CT: Yale University Press.

Tachibana, T. (1974) "Tanaka Kakuei Kenkyū – Sono Kinmyaku to Jinmyaku" ("Tanaka Kakuei: His Money Connections and Personal Connections"), *Bungei Shunjū*, 52 (November): 92–131.

Takahashi, J. (2003) "Koizumi Renews Confrontational Posture," *The Japan Times Online*, 1 September. Online. Available: www.japantimes.co.jp/cgi-bin/makeparfy.p15?nn20030901a8.htm (accessed 28 July 2005).

"Takeshita Hears the Thud of the Axes" (1989) *The Economist*, 18 February: 29–30.

Tanaka, M. (1997) *Seiji Kaiku Roku Nen no Dotei* (The Six Year Path to Political Reform), Tokyo: Gyōsei.

Taniguchi, M. (1998) "Kiseiho 'Akuyo' no Susume" ("The Progressive Abuse of the Political Funds Control Law"), *Asashi Shinbun* 20 November.

——(1999) "Miyazawa Naikaku" (The Miyazawa Cabinet), in T. Sasaki (ed.) *Seiji Kaikaku 1800-Nichi no Shinjitsu* (The Truth Behind 1800 Days of Political Reform), Tokyo: Kōdansha.

——(2002) "Money and Politics in Japan," in T.E. Mann and T. Sasaki (eds) *Governance for a New Century*. New York: The Japan Center for International Exchange.

Toyoda K. (1983) *Kaifu Toshiki Zenjinzō* (Kaifu Toshiki: His Whole Profile), Tokyo: Gyōsei Mondai Kenkyūjo.

Tucker, R.C. (1977) "Personality and Political Leadership," *Political Science Quarterly*, 92: 383–93.

van Wolferen, K. (1989) *The Enigma of Japanese Power: People and Politics in a Stateless Nation*, New York: Alfred A. Knopf.

Watanabe, C. (2005) "Japan's Lower House OKs Postal Reform Plan," *WashingtonPost.com*, 11 October. Online. Available: www.washingtonpost.

com/wp-dyn/content/article/2005/10/10/AR20051010442.html (accessed 13 October 2005).

Watanabe, K. (1992) *Ano Hito: Hitotsu no Ozawa Ichirō Ron* (That Person: One Discussion of Ozawa Ichirō), Tokyo: Asuka Shinsa.

Watanabe, O. (1994) *Seiji Kaikaku to Kenpō Kaisei: Nakasone Yasuhiro kara Ozawa Ichirō e* (Political Reform and Constitutional Revision: From Nakasone Yasuhiro to Ozawa Ichirō), Tokyo: Aoki Shoten.

——(2005) *Kōzō Kaiku Seiji no Jidai: Koizumi Seikenron*, (The Era of the Politics of Structural Reform: A Discussion of the Koizumi Administration), Tokyo: Kadensha.

Weaver, R.K. and Rockman, B.A. (eds) (1993) *Do Institutions Matter?: Government Capabilities in the United States and Abroad*, Washington, DC: The Brookings Institution.

Weber, M. (1946) "Politics as Vocation," in H.H. Gerth and C.W. Mills (eds) *From Max Weber: Essays in Sociology*, trans. H.H. Gerth and C.W. Mills, New York: Oxford University Press.

——(1947) *The Theory of Social and Economic Organization*, trans. A. M. Henderson and T. Parsons, New York: Free Press.

Williams, D. (1996) "Ozawa Ichiro: The Making of a Japanese Kingmaker," in I. Neary (ed.) *Leaders and Leadership in Japan*, Richmond, Surrey: Japan Library.

Willner, A.R. (1984) *The Spellbinders: Charismatic Political Leadership*, New Haven, CT: Yale University Press.

Wolfe, E.L. (1995) "Japanese Electoral and Political Reform: Role of the Young Turks," *Asian Survey*, 35: 1059–74.

Yamaguchi, T. (1993) "Ozawa Ichirō no Kenkyū: Shoseiron to Shashin no Hakairyoku" ("Research on Ozawa Ichirō: The Destructive Power of Impractical Arguments and Self-Abandonment"), *Bungei Shunjū*, 71 (October): 142–77.

Yamamoto, K. (1992) *Seijika, Kōmuin no Hanzai to Jiken, 1945–1992* (Crimes and Incidents of Politicians and Government Officials, 1945–1992), Tokyo: Daisan Shokan.

Yamamoto, T. (1975) *Shōkai Seiji Shikin Kiseihō* (A Detailed Explanation of the Political Funds Control Law), Tokyo: Gyōsei.

Yayama, T. (1990) "The Recruit Scandal: Learning from the Causes of Corruption," *Journal of Japanese Studies*, 16: 93–114.

Yoshida, R. (2005a) "Politicians Begin Plotting Strategies for Sept. 11 Poll," *The Japan Times Online*, 10 August. Online. Available: www.japantimes.co.jp/cgi-bin/makeparfy.p15?nn20050810al.htm (accessed 10 August 2005).

——(2005b) "Postal Bills Become Law," *Japan Times Online*, 15 October. Online. Available: www.japantimes.co.jp/cgi-bin/makeprfy.p15?nn20051015a1.htm (accessed 1 November 2005).

Index

Note: numbers in **bold** refer to the location of tables and figures.